MID-CENTURY

AMERICAN

POETS

EDITED *by* JOHN CIARDI

Mid-Century
American
Poets

.

Twayne Publishers, Inc.   *New York 3*

MANUFACTURED BY

BOOKMAN ASSOCIATES

NEW YORK

ACKNOWLEDGMENTS

"Tywater," by Richard Wilbur, is from THE BEAUTIFUL CHANGES AND OTHER POEMS, copyright 1947, by Richard Wilbur. Used by permission of the author and the publishers, Harcourt, Brace and Company, Inc. Other poems by Richard Wilbur are reprinted by permission of the author.

"Blindman's Buff," *Vale* from Carthage," "A Walk on Snow," "Affirmations I, II, III," "From Ancient Fangs," "Poet," "For Two Girls Setting Out in Life," and "Crass Times Redeemed by Dignity of Souls," are reprinted from TERROR AND DECORUM, by Peter Viereck; copyright 1948 by Peter Viereck; used by permission of the publishers, Charles Scribner's Sons. "The Slacker Apologizes" is reprinted from the *University of Kansas City Review* and *Horizon* (London) by permission of the author. "Some Lines in Three Parts" is reprinted from *Harper's* (where it appeared as "The Birth of Song") by permission of the author. "Small Perfect Manhattan" is reprinted from *Commentary* by permission of the author. "My Kind of Poetry," originally written for this anthology, appeared with some changes in the *Saturday Review of Literature,* and is reprinted by permission of the author.

"The Minute," by Karl Shapiro, is reprinted from the *Nation* by permission of the author. "Buick," "Washington Cathedral," "The Fly," "Auto Wreck," "The Twins," are reprinted from PERSON PLACE AND THING, copyright 1942, by Karl Shapiro. Used by permission of the author and the publishers, Harcourt, Brace and Company, Inc. "Elegy for a Dead Soldier," "V-Letter," and "Full Moon: New Guinea," are reprinted from V-LETTER AND OTHER POEMS, copyright 1944, by Karl Shapiro, used by permission of the author and the publishers, Harcourt, Brace and Company, Inc. "The Dirty Word" arfd "Homecoming" are from TRIAL OF A POET, copyright 1947, by Karl Shapiro. Used by permission of the author and the publishers, Harcourt, Brace and Company, Inc.

"Bermuda Suite," by Winfield Townley Scott is reprinted from *Poetry* (Chicago) by permission of the author. Other poems by Mr. Scott appearing in this volume are copyrighted by the author and reprinted by permission of the author.

All poems in this volume by Delmore Schwartz are copyrighted by Delmore Schwartz and reprinted by permission of the author. "Two Problems in Writing of Poetry" appeared originally in *Partisan Review* as "Views of a Second Violinist" and is reprinted by permission of the author.

"Easter Eve, 1945," "Eyes of Night-Time," "The Place in the Ways," "The Motive of It All," "Tenth Elegy: Elegy in Joy," are from GREEN

FOREWORD

I

As THE mid-century comes upon us, it must be evident to all who care to look that America has achieved an important body of poetry. It must also be reasonably evident in retrospect that the nineteenth century in America failed to do so. There were beginnings in the nineteenth century—all of them achievements of historical interest, a small handful of them works that were poetry in their own right—but only the blindest partisan would argue that the American nineteenth century produced a body of poetry remotely comparable with that produced in England through the Romantic triumph and its Victorian sequel. Aside from the works of Walt Whitman and Emily Dickinson, it is not too gross an exaggeration to claim that the nineteenth-century American product amounted to a very slim volume of authentic poems, a library of English imitations, and a regrettably limited (or lost) body of folk balladry, mostly American Negro. And it must then immediately be added that the balladry—probably the most authentic poetry of the period —did not emerge into literary awareness until the twentieth century.

The golden periods of poetry have always been those in which the poets possessed a sense of being firmly rooted in a native tradition. But America in the nineteenth century was still largely a cultural colony of England. The American had yet to learn his own attitudes toward his continent, toward his new nation, and toward the rest of the cultural world. In prose, even as sophisticated a writer as Henry James made a career of his provincialism. In poetry, the American—even when he asserted his Americanism most strongly—usually betrayed that he was on the cultural defensive. The Genteel Tradition was a primary symptom of that cultural insecurity of which few literate Americans were wholly free. Now and then, as in the best of Longfellow and in such native idylls as Whittier's "Telling the Bees" (and certainly in parts of "Snowbound") the richness of a native feeling emerges whole and unselfconscious. More often, however, the American poets seemed to have it as their major business to prove their culture was as wide, their vocabulary as Latinate, their sensibility as nice, as that of, say, an Oxford don.

If you happen to have glanced at the *Oxford Book of Light Verse* edited by W. H. Auden, you may have noted that the refrain in "Frankie and Johnny" has been "corrected" from "He was her man but he done her wrong" to "He was her man but he *did* her wrong"—as ludicrously insensitive a piece of editorial nonsense as one could wish to embalm for a literary chamber of horrors. New Orleans, it seems, was to have the benefit of the English Public School System "whether it would or no," as Cooper was fond of saying in what he conceived to be the American tongue.

The instance is out of time, but not out of spirit with our earlier American poets, for throughout the nineteenth century, a dismaying proportion of what was native in the mind and tongue was still being processed through the literati's ideal of the Genteel Tradition.

I submit that this is no longer true, and in presenting this volume of poems from the latest generation of American poets—those poets reaching their maturity around the mid-century—it seems appropriate to consider the differences of cultural inheritance that permit them their sense of a self-indebted tradition. There are three properties contained in that inheritance that must come before all others:

1. *The barbaric yawp and its exhaustion.*

The "barbaric yawp" is Whitman's own phrase for the voice he raised in rebellion against the Genteel Tradition and its subservience to European culture. The cry is heard most characteristically in the "Song of the Exposition":

> Come, Muse, migrate from Greece and Ionia,
> Cross out please those immensely overpaid accounts . . .
> For know a better, fresher, busier sphere, a wide, untried
>   domain awaits, demands you. . . .

and ending:

> She's here, installed amid the kitchenware.

In later "yawpers"—in Masters, in Lindsay, in Sandburg—this apostrophe to the peculiar and overmuscled charm of the "better, fresher, busier" produced a school of poets whose principal char-

acteristic seemed to be a kind of shrill overinsistence. The ending
of Sandburg's "Chicago" is a fair example of the poetry of this
school:

> Laughing!
> Laughing the stormy, husky, brawling laughter of Youth,
> half-naked, sweating, proud to be Hog Butcher,
> Tool Maker, Stacker of Wheat, Player with
> Railroads and Freight Handler to the Nation.

And in another generation, as good a poet as Archibald Mac-
Leish (by now the "yawp" had become The American Dream)
could still feel poetically compelled to such dreary evocations as
(from "Burying Ground by The Ties"):

> AYEE! Ai! This is heavy earth on our shoulders:
> There were none of us born to be buried in this earth:
> Niggers we were Portuguese Magyars Polacks:

I know of no good poet writing today who feels compelled to
this sort of catalogue of the melting pot, or of the sweat-soaked
glories of barbaric America. The nineteenth-century faith in the
idea of progress is the basic oversimplification which informs such
poetry, and the death of that oversimplification among our poets is
one more symptom of our coming of age poetically. Further, the
poets no longer seem compelled to seek the American past as if
under some necessity to prove there *was* a past. It no longer needs
proof. Certainly present poets do explore American themes, and
future poets will again, but I doubt that they will ever again feel
it necessary to do so in the hortatory and oversimple manner that
characterizes the "yawp."

The "yawp" may best be seen in perspective as one of the ways
in which American poets explored their attitudes toward America
and the American continent. It died partly because of social and
philosophical changes in America itself, and partly because later
poets came to the conclusion that it was, if not an unreal, at least
an unrewarding attitude. The exploration, however, was certainly
inevitable: Americas cannot happen without noise. America had to
make loud poetry before it could make good poetry. The poets writ-
ing today are in a better position to write good poetry, in part be-
cause some of their ancestors showed them the perils of loud poetry.

2. *The capture of the American voice-box.*

One of the tasks facing every tradition of poetry, is the capture of the speaking rhythm, the inflection, and the idiom of its own tongue. This is not a question of reproducing common speech in such dialect-doggerel as is still put out by the cracker-barrel poets. It is rather a question of a poetic stylization of that speech that will allow expression of the widest variety of insights in a way that makes the expression seem inevitable. The difference between "creating" and "borrowing" such an instrument is the difference between a vigorous and a derivative poetry.

Certainly that process has not been wholly achieved in our time. It is doubtful, in fact, that it can ever be wholly achieved within a living language, for just as the great instrument created by the King James Bible formed the language of many generations of English poets and still continues to be richly available in the English family of tongues while it is constantly being modified by new tempi in the rhythms of life and speech, so every great tradition must pass through endless modification into a new tradition. But if that process is still in its forming stages in America, it must yet be apparent to the sensitive reader that American poets of the twentieth century have captured the essence of a real idiom. Just as surely as the poems of Robert Frost could only have been written by a man who grew up with New England in his mouth, so the poems of the poets here presented could only have been written by men who grew up with American suburb and metropolis and countryside in their speech, *and who had been prepared by their literary ancestors to detect the poetic possibilities of that speech.* I do not mean that the poems in this volume are self-consciously native. I simply know that the best of them could not have been written by, let us say, an Englishman, for their rhythm and inflection and idiom are unmistakably American. And for that reason they are the final evidence that America has found its own literature.

3. *The ferment of technique.*

The period of disillusionment that preceded and followed World War I, saw the shattering of many assurances. Many sensitive men with nothing else left to believe in, turned, in an ascetic or a Bohemian mood, to art for art's sake. With no obligation to any subject matter, they were accordingly free to exert all their ingenuities on form. And because their disillusionment had often taught them to despise old things, they were all the more likely to seek novelty for its own sake.

Ezra Pound was a born high priest for such a period. Acting as a transmitter of the continental *avant garde* experiments, and as an impetus in his own right, he became the leading figure in a series of movements in poetry all of which emphasized technique above subject matter. His slogan may well be taken from one of his own titles: *Make It New*. The manifestoes and petty dictatorships of these successive schools may easily appear a bit precious and a bit insane to the contemporary reader. And the succeeding decade may pass as the Glorious Twenties or the Mad Twenties, as you prefer. Still, the whole movement was marked by a venturesome excitement that despite all its excesses did produce poets of dignity and stature. And whatever its failings, it did leave succeeding poets with a stock of techniques richer and more varied than any that had earlier been available to American writers.

It is largely this triple inheritance that gives the present poets their sense of assurance. No one of them would begin to doubt that Americans can write poetry as capably as Englishmen. If anything, they are more likely to believe that the real future of English literature lies in the vigor and richness of the American tongue. Nor are they any longer concerned with technique for its own sake. In fact, it seems to be a familiar assumption among them that fidelity to the experience they are reporting is their proper concern, and that the poem can make its technique as it goes, working it out of the urgency of the poem's own experience.

Obviously it would not have been possible for these poets to be so calmly and self-assuredly American, had not earlier poets been naïvely and over-loudly American. Obviously, too, they could not have come so far in capturing the American voice-box had not earlier poets taught them to believe confidently in its possibilities. And certainly they could not have assumed such ready availability of techniques to subject matter had not earlier generations of poets ventured into every sort of experimentation, including some that may now seem quaintly mad.

With these assurances theirs by bequest, the poets here presented have been able to write a kind of poetry that will in time, I believe, be seen as both distinctive and accomplished. Unfortunately, readers of poetry have been slow to grasp the flavor of this poetry, and, in fact, many critics who should have known better have seen fit to condemn it on principles the poets themselves have rejected. And since a discriminating audience may be indispensable to the development of a valuable poetic tradition, it seems relevant to consider some of the failures of communication that result from poor reading rather than from poor poetry.

II

What does it take to read a poem?

I am thinking now of poetry not simply as a literary form but as a kind of human behaviour. By human behaviour I mean the reactions of a largely irrational nervous system under a sometimes dreadful and sometimes inspiring compulsion to rationalize itself. It may be argued that this is an undignified view of man, but I doubt that it is. I am not sure but what poetry may be postulated as the final dignity of that irrationality. In any case my premise is that the vital part of the poem begins in the unconscious mind of the poet. It follows that until the reader receives it with more than his conscious mind, the process of communication is not complete. The failure of that communication may be the result of poor writing and it may be the fault of poor reading, of a frog in the speaker's throat or of a buzzing in the listener's ear. At the present time one hears a great deal about the frog, but not much about the buzzing. If only out of didactic habit, therefore, I should like to discuss some of the specific ways in which I have observed readers to misbehave towards the poem.

Let us begin with a really difficult piece of symbolism:

> Hickory, dickory, dock,
> The mouse ran up the clock.
> The clock struck one,
> And down he run.
> Hickory, dickory, dock.

Not really complicated you say? Consider these questions: What does it mean? Why a clock? Why a mouse? Isn't it fairly unusual for mice to run up clocks? What is the point of inventing this esoteric incident? And since the mouse ran up it and down again, the chances are it's a grandfather clock: what does that signify? And isn't it a fairly obsolete notion? Why did the clock strike one? To rhyme with "run"? Why didn't the poem make the clock strike three and the mouse turn to flee? It didn't, but why? What is the origin and significance of all these unexplained symbols? (A symbol is something that stands for something else: what is the something else?) Or is this simply nonsense verse? (I find that hard to believe.) And even as nonsense, what is there in this particular combination of sounds and actions (symbolic actions?) that makes this jingle survive a long word-of-mouth transmission in the English voice-box? Why mightn't the poem as easily have read:

> Thickery, thackery, tea,
> An owl flew into the tree.
> The tree's down,
> The owl's flown.
> Thickery, thackery, tea.

I submit: (a) That my parody is a bad poem, that the original is a good one, and that a serious and learned series of lectures might be devoted to the reasons why each is so; (b) That none of the questions I have raised is meaningless and that in fact many critics have made a career of asking this sort of question; and (c) That neither you nor I know what the poem "means." I further submit that such considerations have frightened many readers away from good poems.

But—and this is the point—the child in whose babble the poem is immediate and alive has no critical theories and no troubles. He is too busy enjoying the pleasures of poetry. The moral is obvious: Do not demand that the poem be more rational than you are. The way to read a poem is with pleasure—with the child's pleasure in tasting the syllables on his tongue, with the marvel of the child's eye that can really see the mouse run up the clock, be panic-stricken, and run down again, with the child's hand-clapping rhythmic joy. In short, to read a poem, come prepared for delight.

But if a child can do it why can't you?

That question deserves attention, but before considering it, I should like to say one thing of which I am fairly certain: everyone writes poetry sometime in his life. Bad poetry is what we all have in common. Such poetry generally occurs in three categories: as invective, as obscenity, and as love-yelps.

The obscenity I assume everyone to be capable of documenting.

Here is an example of invective:

> Billy, Billy, dirty coat
> Stinks like a nanny goat.

and here is a fair example of the love-yelp:

> Have you ever been in love?
> I ask you: have you ever been in love?
> Have you?
> I have....................I know!

Billy, Billy, you will recognize of course as a kind of *Georgie Porgie puddin' and pie,* but if you think it peculiar to your childhood or to grandfather's, I urge you to look into the encyclopedia under Fescennine for an inkling of the antiquity of man's pleasure in jingling taunts at other men. Billy, Billy, as nearly as I know, was composed in our fourth-grade schoolyard by a former young poet now in the coal business, and was used to taunt our local sloven who has since washed up, cleaned up, grown up, and joined the police force. Almost inevitably, it earned its young author a punch in the nose—a fair example of the way criticism operates in our society to kill the poetic impulse. The love-yelp, a reasonably deplorable specimen of its class, was submitted for the Tufts College literary magazine when I was an undergraduate assistant editor. Anyone who will take the trouble to be reasonably honest can almost certainly summon from himself examples of at least one of these forms which he has attempted at one time or another, and enjoyed attempting.

If, then, the impulse to bad poetry is so widespread (though I insist that *Billy, Billy,* is not at all bad), why is it so few people enjoy reading what passes as good poetry? Why is it, for example, that in a nation of 146 million presumably literate people, the average sale for a book of poems is about 500 copies? Is it that the pleasures and outlets one finds in composing are purely private— that only one's own creation, good or bad, is interesting? Considering the variety of egos which have banded together to pass as the human race, that seems one reasonably good guess, but there is obviously more to it that is worth some speculation:

First, it seems fairly obvious that the process of growing up in a nuts-and-bolts world inhibits the poetry impulse in most people.

Somewhere along the line, they learn to say, "Let's face it; we must be practical." Dickens' School of Hard Facts is with us all, and poetry, like poor Sissy Jupe, is still required to blush because it can not define a horse as "Quadruped. Gramnivorous. Forty teeth, namely twenty-four grinders, four eye-teeth, and twelve incisive." So the literalist on his rostrum demands the rational: "What *does* hickory-dickory-dock *mean?* It *has to* mean *something."* It does indeed, but not anything you can paraphrase, not anything you can prove. It means only what every child knows—delight. And delight is not a function of the rational mind. As Archibald MacLeish has written, "A poem must not mean, but be." Whereby, of course, it does mean, but not nuts-and-bolts. To see what it does mean, you need only go and read Mother Goose to a child: you will then be observing a natural audience busy with the process of receiving poetry as it was intended to be received.

Point one, then, is delight: if you mean to enjoy the poem as a poem, stop cross-examining it, stop trying to force it to "make sense." The poem *is* sense. Or if you must cross-examine, remember at least that the third degree is not the poem. Most poems do reveal themselves most richly after close examination, but the examination is, at best, only a preparation for reading the poem. It is never the reading itself.

More precisely put, an understanding of the rational surfaces of the poem (the prose part of the poem) may, in some cases, point a direction toward the poem. The poem is never experienced, however, until it is felt in the same complex of mind and nerve from which it arose—the subconscious. That experience sometimes happens immediately, and is sometimes helped along by our conscious (rational) perceptions. But to substitute rational analysis for the larger contact of the subconscious is to reject the poem. The kind of communication that happens in a poem is infinitely closer to that of music than to that of prose.

Second, poetry must never be read as an exercise in "reading speed," that deplorable mental-mangle for increasing the rate of destruction of textbook English. The fastest reader is not the best reader any more than the best conductor of Beethoven is the man who gets the orchestra through the *Eroica* in the shortest elapsed time. Music declares its own pace. But so does good poetry. By rhyme, by rhythm, by the word-values of the poem, by the sequence of syllables, and by all these taken together, good poetry contains its own notation, and "We broke the brittle bright stubble like chaff" can no more be read at the same rate as "Bury the great duke with an Empire's lamentation" than *allegro vivace* can intelligently be played *adagio*.

Point two, then: Look for the notation within the poem. Every poem is in part an effort to reconstruct the poet's speaking voice. Listen for it. Listen to the poet on records and at public readings (but know the poems well before you do). You may discover more than you could have foreseen. In any case, when reading a book of poems you must be prepared to linger. That thin volume will take at least as much reading as a detective story.

Third (and of course related to our second consideration), read it aloud. Few poems will come whole at one hearing. Few piano pieces will. But once you have *learned* either, their pleasure is always ready to repeat and to augment itself. Even difficult poems are meant to go into the voice-box.

Fourth, there are still readers who must be specifically cautioned that twentieth-century poetry is not nineteenth-century poetry. That fact may seem rather obvious, but the point is not frivolously made. Your teachers and mine were products of nineteenth-century culture, and almost certainly the first poems you were given to read in school were nineteenth-century poems. I hasten to add that the nineteenth century was a great literary achievement, but it began with one dreadful flaw: it tended to take itself much too seriously. The mind of man seemed to suffer the illusion that it lived in a cathedral, and when man spoke he was not only too likely to pontificate, but he was pre-inclined to select from experience only the vast, the lofty, the divine-in-nature. The result was what Cleanth Brooks has called "the poetry of high-seriousness." Opposed to that tradition is the poetry of "wit," poetry in which the mind most definitely does not live in a cathedral but in the total world, open to the encounter of all sorts of diverse elements and prepared to take them as they come, fusing fleas and sunsets, love and charley-horses, beauty and trivia, into what is conceived to be a more inclusive range of human experience. Judge the poet of wit by the standards of high-seriousness, and he will likely appear crass and obnoxious; judge the poet of high-seriousness by the standards of wit, and he will likely appear a rather pompous and myopic ass.

The point, then, is quite simple: Judge the poet by his intent; if you tend to the illusion that you are on your way to church when you pick up a poem, stop off at the super-market and watch man against his background of groceries for a while. The church is still next door, and I am quite sure that one of the things "modern" poetry is trying to say, is that the cities of our life contain *both* church spires and wheaties, and that both of them, for better or worse, impinge upon man's consciousness, and are therefore the material of poetry.

A fifth consideration I can best present by asking a question: How do you, reader, distinguish between your responses to a very bad portrait of dear old Aunt Jane, and a very good one of Old Skinflint, the gentleman who holds your mortgage? The question is one that splits the reading audience straight down the middle. The tenacity with which the ladies of the poetry societies will hold on to Aunt Jane with a bluebird in her hair, and the persistence with which they reject all-that-is-not-bluebirds, reaches so far into the problem of a satisfactory approach to poetry (both reading and writing) that it has been necessary to evolve two terms: *poetry* for that which exists as an art form, *poesy* for that which exists as the sentimental bluebird in Aunt Jane's hair. Confusion is inevitable when these terms are not properly applied. The writers and readers of *poesy* always refer to their matter as *poetry* or *true poetry,* and defend it with as much violence as possible from "the ugly." Here is a fair example of *poesy*—a sonnet of course:

THRENODY

Truth is a golden sunset far away
Above the misty hills. Its burning eye
Lights all the fading world. A bird flies by
Alive and singing on the dying day.
Oh mystic world, what shall the proud heart say
When beauty flies on beauty beautifully
While blue-gold hills look down to watch it die
Into the falling miracle of clay?

Say: "I have seen the wing of sunset lift
Into the golden vision of the hills
And truth come flooding proud through the cloud rift,

And known that souls survive their mortal ills."
Say: "Having seen such beauty in the air
I have seen truth and will no more despair."

This is a specimen of what I will call "prop-room poesy." It fills the stage as a poem might, but it fills it with pieces discarded from other poems and left to gather dust in the prop-room of tradition. It makes a stage of the stage, and brings the stage's own dust on as the play, rather than bring on the life outside the theater.

The result may look like a poem, but is really no more than a collection of poetic junk. For example: "golden sunsets far away" (question: Have you ever seen a non-golden one near by?), "misty hills," "burning eye," "fading world," "a bird flies by alive and singing" (question: Have you ever seen a non-live one fly by?), "dying day," "the proud heart." . . .

I have tried many times to explain to the enthusiasts of this school that any reasonably competent craftsman could concoct such a poem in a matter of minutes, and with his tongue in his cheek. I said exactly that from a public platform once and claimed I could turn out such an illusion-of-the-sonnet in three minutes flat. I was challenged and given a first line to start with, but I failed: I discovered it is impossible, simply mechanically, to write off fourteen lines in three minutes. It took four minutes and eighteen seconds. The "sonnet" I have quoted above was the poem produced in answer to that challenge, and by way of further experimentation I sent it off to a magazine for "traditional poetry" and had it accepted for publication. In a moment of cowardice, I withdrew the poem for fear someone I respected might see my name attached to it. I was wrong, of course; no one whose poetic opinion I could respect would have been reading that magazine.

The fact remains beyond all persuasion, however, that the devotees of *poesy* are violent in their charges against Modern Poetry (their capitals) as ugly, coarse, immoral, and debased (their adjectives). My good friend Geraldine Udell, business manager of *Poetry, A Magazine of Verse,* the oldest magazine of good poetry in America, once showed me thirty-four letters received in one day's mail, accusing the magazine of debasing the pure tradition of English Poetry, and enclosing sample pages of *poesy* from a magazine for "traditional poetry" as specimens of what should be printed.

It is, you see, Aunt Jane and Old Skinflint with a vengeance. Poesy, which is always anti-poetry, wants it pretty. It wants well-worn props to which comfortable and vague reactions are already conditioned. Everyone understands the bluebird in Aunt Jane's hair; the response to it is by now so stereotyped that it will do for a birthday card. Poetry, on the contrary, insists on battering at life, and on making the poem capture the thing seen and felt in its own unique complex. It does not repeat; it creates. Therefore, some willingness to dismiss preconception from the reader's mind is necessary if one is to partake of that vital process. One is also required to get himself and his own loose-afflatus out of the way of the poem.

The fifth point then is simple: Poesy is not poetry.

A sixth and related consideration follows almost immediately. It concerns the preconception that demands moral affirmation of oneself from a poem, just as poesy demands a loose emotional affirmation of oneself. Consistently adhered to, this application of one's own morality as a test of the poem can lead to ridiculous ends. It would require, for example, the rejection of Milton by all who do not agree with his theology. It might reject beforehand all poems containing the word harlot, since harlots are immoral, and by that test we should have to reject such great lines as Blake's:

> The harlot's cry from street to street
> Shall weave Old England's winding sheet.

Or, shifted to political concern, it might require a new Communist Manifesto against any poem in which the lover is rich in his love, since it is bourgeois, decadent, and just plain indecent to be rich.

Similarly, I have known many present-day reviewers to reject a poem because it seems cheerful ("withdrawal from reality"), because it does not ("defeatist and negativist"), because it is immediately understandable ("facile and slight"), and because it requires re-reading ("obscurantist"). These are cartoons, of course, but they are cartoons of a real trend. The simple fact is that none of us can hope to be wholly free of preconceptions of one sort or another. I must confess, for example, that I still find Milton's theology a bit silly, and that my feeling prevents me from experiencing *Paradise Lost* as richly as I might. Even Milton's language creates blocks for me that he could not have intended and for which I am solely responsible. For whatever reason, I cannot read of Satan mounted on his "bad eminence" without an impulse to smile. I don't know why I want to smile at such a phrase, but I am sure the reason is within me and that it has nothing to do with the poem. I am being blocked in this case by a pre-set subjective response. I must, therefore, recognize the obstruction and try to allow for it. Unless I can do so, I am not permitting the poet his right to his own kind of vision and existence.

Point six then: the poem does not exist to confirm moral, political, or religious pre-judgments. The poem as a poem is in fact amoral. The poem, I say, not the poet. The poet may be the most moral of men, but when he writes poetry he is performing a ritual dance. He may even sermonize, but if the poem is to succeed as a poem, it must be a dancing sermon. What the poem says is always hickory-dickory-dock, that ineffable, wonderful, everlasting dance of joyous syllables that moves the mouse and winds the clock over and over again, and sends the child to sleep among the swinging nebulae. Or perhaps it is hickory-dickory-God, but still what the poem says is what the child dreams: "Look, Universe, I'm dancing." There is no immorality more wretched than the habit of mind which will insist on moralizing that dance.

The last necessity for good reading that I shall discuss here is tradition. If you will grant me the existence of an unintellectualized basis for poetry upon which the responses of all readers may meet, we can probably agree that a fair example of such a response may be found in, say, Juliet on her balcony swooning into moonlight at the sound of Romeo's song rising from the shrubbery. Hers is certainly a non-intellectualized response. It is certainly a living response. And a world-wide one: Black Jade in her moony garden in Peiping will respond in an almost identical way to Pao-yü's serenade from beyond the garden wall.

But wait: let us switch singers. Now Pao-yü is in Verona beneath Juliet's balcony, and Romeo is in Peiping outside Black Jade's garden. Both strike up a song. Why is it that each girl now hears not a swooning love-cry, but something more nearly a cat fight? The answer is—Tradition.

For the fact is, we are being educated when we know it least. We learn simply by living, and what we learn most automatically is the tradition in which we live. But the responses acquired effortlessly in one tradition will not serve us in another, any more than speaking pure Tuscan will help us in Peiping. Poetry, like all the great arts, exists in a tradition. Some of that tradition comes to us effortlessly, but the greater part of it must be consciously acquired by reading. Without it, you may find yourself in Black Jade's garden listening to Romeo and hearing a cat fight when what is being sung is love.

The final point, then, is that to read poetry you must read poetry. You must acquire by degrees and pleasurably (it's no good if there's no pleasure in it) the tradition of the English-American voice-box. You must come to the poem with the memory of great singing in your inner ear, for that memory haunts the second voice of all good poetry. This, you will recognize, is basically the critical theory that Matthew Arnold put forth as "the touchstone method." It says simply that all poetry is judged by great poetry. It requires, naturally, that you be acquainted with some great poetry.

On the other hand, I cannot lose the belief that it is more important to experience the poem than to judge it. Certainly there is real pleasure to be had from poems no one will ever consider great or near-great. Certainly, too, every mental action implies a kind of judgment. The question is one of emphasis, and generally it seems more desirable for the reader to conceive of himself as a participant in the action of the poem, rather than as a trial judge sitting in judgment upon its claim to immortality.

Time, of course, will hand down that verdict, and in a way from which there is no appeal. It may then happen that the verdict will be against modern poets, and against the principles on which they write. But until that verdict has been achieved it would be well to bear in mind that the reader is as liable to error as the poet, and that when the poem fails to communicate, the failure may as reasonably be charged against the one as against the other.

III

What is modern poetry?

The question is a familiar and often provoking one. The provocation, I think, lies in the word "modern," for in the only enduring sense, poetry is poetry in and of itself and beyond all adjectival classification. Nevertheless, a good deal of critical nonsense has raged about "modern" with the radical-silly generally ready to identify it with all-that-is-good, and the conservative-silly with all-that-is-bad. I suppose the strong emphasis that falls upon "modern" is partly a carry-over from its usage when applied to drugstores and television—something slick, plastic, and a bit overbearing in its own pretension to being the self-justified and final goal of evolution. It is this distortion of a good usable word that left me perhaps foolishly delighted when I found a publisher's list of "Modern Poetry" in an English periodical dated 1882. (Browning and, I think, Morris were the stars of the list.) It was so good to find the word so safely and antiseptically ensconced in time, that after shying away from its use for a number of years, I have decided to cling to it after all in its one right meaning—to denote poetry written too recently to have survived different generations of poetic taste.

In that sense there is certainly a "modern" poetry to be distinguished from other bodies of poetry, and the defining fact that it has not been time-tested certainly does create special conditions for its reception. There can be little doubt that one reads "To His Coy Mistress," for example, with a different orientation from that with which he reads a poem in this month's issue of *Poetry, A Magazine of Verse,* and the difference is a basic and simple one. The earlier poem is familiar and confirmed, the later is unfamiliar and tentative; when we read Marvell we are re-awakening an accomplished response, when we read a new poem we are seeking a new response. And even when we read an old poem for the first time, it comes to us more or less established by its survival.

In all times, I imagine, and certainly in our own, the very tentativeness of the "modern" has been an invitation to self-styled arbiters, for where there is no final judge, you may be certain every lawyer and clerk in town will race into court to grant himself a verdict. So it is that self-accredited critics in every stage of academic catalepsy, coterie psychosis, and journalistic idiocy have felt free to pronounce and define at will, until even the few well-balanced and sensitive critics have been partially obscured. Until, in fact, it is often difficult to decide who the good critics are. For criticism, too, is subject to the test by time, and historically fewer critics than poets have survived its condemnation of the silly and the pretentious.

I intend no offense to criticism as such. If I have found a great deal of what passes as criticism in our literary quarterlies to be unspeakably silly, and I have, the fact has taught me to value all the more highly the kind of criticism that seems to me to contain a valuable insight. Nevertheless, the fact that so many of the poets here represented have gone out of their way to decry the general criticism now abroad in the land (you will note that all of them reserve their admiration for "good" criticism, though none of them identify it) seems fairly conclusively to indicate one important fact: that the poets and the critics are considerably at odds in their view of modern poetry.

It follows that the resulting confusion (since the critics are generally more vocal than the poets) must have worked to distort the reader's understanding of what the poets are doing, or think they are doing. With this in mind, and considering that everyone else seems to have had his authoritative say about modern poetry, it occurred to me that it was high time someone asked the poets themselves. Out of that notion this volume was born, its simple principle being to gather together poems reasonably representative of the best work of a generation of poets, and to have each poet preface his poems with a guide to the reader's better understanding of his work and its intent.

It may well be asked whether there is any point in such exegesis. Isn't it apparent that good poetry is self-explanatory? And mightn't it reasonably be argued that should Chaucer or Shakespeare return to the living, neither could add much to our present understanding of his works? To be sure any number of textual questions, source matters, and disputed interpretations might be settled by such a spectral visit—though I am not at all sure that the ambiguous renderings in Shakespeare were any clearer to him than they are to us. But what could Chaucer-returned or Shakespeare-returned add to our awareness of the Wife of Bath or of Hamlet except by coaxing us back to a more careful reading? Nothing at all, I think. But though this is true of that poetry long established by time, it must yet be remembered that our concern is with modern poetry. In the case of the older poets, time has not only done its work of selection, but to a great extent of exegesis; the man who reads *Hamlet* today reads it with his responses pre-alerted by its long and distinguished history. *And with an equation for it in his mind to begin with;* he knows he will be puzzled by some of it, but all the puzzles have been guessed at. He may not be able to decide whether Hamlet was mad or sane, but he knows assuredly that this is one of the things that are supposed to puzzle him. He has been told that before he started. *He also knows what became of the poet and his times,* and this further prepares his attitude.

Just so, in years to come, in as few years as ten or twenty perhaps, the exegesis here offered by the poets will not be needed. What do you imagine has become of the excitement that attended publication of the *Spoon River Anthology?* And where are the great controversies about the "difficulty" of the early Auden? These over-emphases time smooths away, for poets and bodies of poetry are like any person we know: we understand his individual phrase or gesture or act better as we know him longer. Modern poets, in one sense, are the poets we know least about, and until time has made clear to us (and to them) their whole intent, until time has completed the circle whose arc they are now projecting, the poets themselves are likely to be their own best guides to themselves.

The poets presented in this book are all part of what will be recognized as a poetic "generation," roughly that generation that arrived within the last ten to fifteen years. Their impact upon American literature has had little time in which to be felt, but certainly it is all the more likely for that reason to influence, positively or negatively, the literature of the next twenty-five years or so. Already, in fact, there is a younger generation, no doubt influenced by some of these poets, but as distinct from them as these poets are from those of the twenties. The first arrivals of this newer generation point interestingly to somewhat vague shapes of things to come. Their poetry, if it remains at all consistent with its beginnings, is likely to be more decorative and less inclined to statement (Wallace Stevens and Dylan Thomas seem to be their most admired masters). It is already markedly more traditional in form, and (perhaps by way of compensation) more verbally excited within the stricter outline. It seems to be more volatile, more religio-romantic, and this may be a reaction to what I would call (variously qualified) the urbanity and sanity of the poetry of the present generation.

But it is too early for such glimpses as we have to give real substance to such speculation, and our concern is more properly with the poets here presented and with the generation whose spokesmen they are. For I do believe they are the best of their generation, and though it is obvious that in drawing up any such list of representatives, no two editors could be expected to agree wholly, I have taken the precaution of checking my own bent by requesting nominations from many readers and critics whose judgment I must respect and from the poets themselves. I must, of course, assume the final responsibility for the selection myself and I do so gladly, but I wish to thank all those who counseled me in this, and from whom I draw the substantial assurance that no name that incontestably belongs on such a list has been omitted.

Having arrived at a basic list beyond which the nominations and my own inclinations became indecisive, I then invited each poet to select a group of his own poems and to prepare a prose foreword for them in which he explained as best he could his personal writing principles or rejection of principle. Academically, I might have wished to impose more rigid limits on the form of their answers, but considering the variety of inclinations and temperaments to be anticipated in any such group, I abandoned all thought of requiring conformity. To provide a common point of departure, however, the following questionnaire was sent to each poet:

SUGGESTED QUESTIONS FOR THE STATEMENT OF WRITING PRINCIPLES

The anthology seeks to bring together the poets who have generally been recognized as having done their best work in the last 10 to 15 years, and who were not widely recognized before that time. They form, I suppose, a poetic generation. The most generally acknowledged leaders of this generation are being asked to record their attitudes toward the problems of writing. The specific suggestions made here are technical, BUT ANY STATEMENT YOU WISH TO MAKE ABOUT THE ETHICAL-PHILOSOPHICAL RELATION OF THE POET TO HIS WRITING WILL BE MOST WELCOME.

QUESTIONS: As nearly as you are able to systematize your own attitudes toward the technical problems of your own writing, what working principles (or rejection of principle) guide YOUR attitude toward:

1. The oral quality of the poem? (Is it meant to be read aloud?)
2. The audience of the poem? (To whom is it addressed? How "difficult" may a poem be? When is it "difficult"?).
3. The language of the poem? (Its idiom. Any special theories of diction?)
4. The function of overtone?
5. Levels of meaning?
6. Subject matter? (Any predilections? Restrictions?)
7. Imagery?

8. Symbolism?

9. Of rhyme and its function in the poem?

10. Of line length and of the function of the line-end (if any) in guiding the reading of the poem?

11. Of the structure of the total poem. (Formal? Free? What makes its unity?)

12. Of rhythm and meter?

These are suggestions only and may be considered in any order you choose, or in any groupings you choose.

The specific invitation accompanying the questionnaire was to answer it, abuse it, ignore it, or to do whatever else came to mind, within the limits of decency, but to put down on paper something that would help a reader to a more immediate response to the poems. Because it seemed more desirable to have answers true to the poet than to force a kind of consistency upon material that might be distorted by consistency, the questions were kept to a kind of shorthand that was intended to be as non-directive as possible. So you will note Miss Rukeyser writes of the genesis of a poem, Miss Bishop is honestly uncomfortable at this sort of thing, Mr. Jarrell has grudgingly consented to jot some answers, Mr. Roethke has written a breezy letter. And so on. Let me make it unmistakably clear that I think the breeziness, the discomfort, the grudging consent, and the avoidance of the mark, are all valuable and instructive responses, that all these attitudes are honest and probably inseparable from the drive that leads different persons differently to poetry, and that all of them do throw light on one central question: What do the poets of this generation feel about these matters?

Naturally I had foreseen some refusals to have anything to do with such a project, but though there was occasional reluctance, I was surprised and delighted to find that all the poets were amenable to the idea, that, in fact most of them were enthusiastic. My gratitude to them is all the greater when I consider how laborious it can be to put one's own half-sensed convictions into the glaring compromise of prose. Together, they have accumulated what I believe to be a valuable document of the American culture, and to their talent and its future this book is confidently dedicated.

I had at first intended to summarize and relate these prefaces in a detailed introductory analysis, but as the prefaces (and the poems) began to arrive, I saw more and more happily that they spoke for themselves in a way in which I must not meddle. The reader who will not take the time to find the richness of the originals is not likely to profit from the poverty of my skeletal approximations and their inevitable distortions.

Two facts, however, do seem central and will bear underlining as perhaps distinctive of the poets of this generation. The first is their very willingness, however qualified, to record their principles for the reader. Popular opinion and an endless array of magazine articles to the contrary, these poets *want* to be understood. That certainly does not mean that they write for Burma-Shave; every poet here who has touched upon the matter at all has made the point that a certain amount of difficulty may be inherent in the subject of the poem, and that in any case the poem must not seek as an end in itself to be understandable on a journalistic level. Valuable literature requires valuable concept, and the language most easily apprehended by subscribers to our popular magazines is not by definition the language that best captures insights into man's uncertain romance with the universe. What is here at issue, I think, is the difference between obscurity and unintelligibility. Obscurity is what is likely to happen when a poem undertakes a subject for which the reader is not sufficiently prepared; unintelligibility is what happens when the poem undertakes a subject for which the poet is not sufficiently prepared. What is obscure today may become quite reasonably clear tomorrow. (*The Wasteland* has certainly worked through this process.) But what is unintelligible today will be unintelligible forever, with the one temporal mercy that tomorrow the unintelligible will have disappeared into the sidereal trash-can.

At a time when the anti-poets have seized every occasion (most recently the dubious but still partly defensible Bollingen Award to Ezra Pound) to cry unintelligibility at every honest obscurity, accusing the poets of failings that more often than not lie in the reader, it is well to have the unmistakable evidence of the poets themselves on this point. For pre-eminently this is a generation not of Bohemian extravagance but of self-conscious sanity in an urbane and cultivated poetry that is the antithesis of the Bohemian spirit.

The second fact, and one that I find both impressive and hopeful, is the absence of authority. Though all of these poets have areas of agreement (that the poem is meant finally for the ear or the inner ear, that there are no restrictions upon subject matter or on diction or on imagery, that generally the poem should not be simple embroidery but should "say something") there is no evident grouping into programs and no hierarchy of arbiters in matters of taste. These poets are not imagists, nor vorticists, nor classicists, nor existentialists, and they bow to no Amy Lowell, or Ezra Pound, or Sam Johnson, or Jean Paul Sartre. They will *listen* to the authority of sense and talent, as it is, for instance, obvious that all of them have paid homage to Mr. Eliot's poetry and criticism, but once they have listened, they all insist on their own freedom to accept or reject according to their own view. It is never, then, a poetry of movements and manifestoes. It is more nearly a blend of the classical and the metaphysical, a poetry of individual appraisal, tentative, self-questioning, introspective, socially involved, and always reserving for itself the right to meet experience in its humanistic environment—the uncoerced awareness of the individual man, which in art must be subjected always to principles of craftsmanship. It is therefore a poetry of great variety, and of some difficulty, but a poetry capable of offering great rewards. It is my confident hope that the poems and the poet's talks that follow will display that variety, conquer a considerable amount of the difficulty, and make more evident the rewards.

JOHN CIARDI

Cambridge, Mass.
January, 1950

CONTENTS

Richard Wilbur

RICHARD WILBUR *was born in New York City in* 1921 *and was educated at Amherst and Harvard. He is at present at Harvard as a member of the Society of Fellows of Harvard University.* THE BEAUTIFUL CHANGES, *Wilbur's first book, appeared in* 1947.

THE GENIE IN THE BOTTLE

BEFORE ANSWERING the present questionnaire, I should like to say that I have certain reservations about it. For one thing, I think artists do well not to talk too much about art, their natural language being that of their media, and not that of abstract analysis. A writer who talks too much about writing runs the risk of becoming a Literary Figure. For another thing, I mistrust most "statements of principles" by artists, since they are necessarily in the nature of apologia. Works of art can almost never be truthfully described as applications of principles. They are not coerced into being by rational principles, but spring from imagination, a condition of spontaneous psychic unity. Asked to produce his "principles," the average artist (fearful of being thought frivolous if he declares that he has none) studies his best work of the past for whatever consistencies he can find. From this *post facto* enquiry, which another might have made as well as he, the artist derives a list of constants in his performance, which he then formulates as "principles." This self-codification may in some cases be harmless; but there is a danger in it, particularly for younger artists. The drawing up of an aesthetic Deuteronomy, the committing himself to a set of "working principles," is very likely to be a hindrance to a younger artist, if he has any taste for consistency. It may very well dissuade him from experiments he ought to make, and if so would prove a bad thing to have done.

These reservations of mine may serve to explain why some of my answers to the questionnaire below are a trifle short and oblique, why I have omitted several topics altogether, and why in certain cases I have re-phrased the questions to harmonize with my answers.

[1]

1. *Is the poem meant to be read aloud?*

Any poem written by a man or woman with an ear profits by being read aloud. But we are a long way now from the times of oral epic, scops, and ballad singers. Many modern poems take a bit more doing than one can manage in the course of a single hearing; the ear cannot gulp down in two minutes what the eye was meant to drink in at leisure. This is not to say that there is no pleasure to be got from partial comprehension: a good audience can respond to Yeats' "I saw a staring virgin stand" without a preparatory lecture on the *Vision*. But I find on the whole that I most enjoy hearing modern poems with which I am already familiar. In such cases there are no problems of discontinuous comprehension, and I can concentrate on how well the reader supplies the patterns of sound and emphasis, and the prevailing emotional tone.

It is said that there are more public poetry-readings these days than ever before, and that they are better than ever attended. If so, this is an opportunity for American poets to furnish the poetry public with a sharper awareness of that part of the meaning of a poem which is carried by the sound. Most poetry at present is not of course heard with the ear, but seen with the eye and heard, if at all, in the inner ear. The inner ear is that part of the memory which stores the sounds of words. The keenness of a reader's inner ear depends somewhat on his natural sensitivity to sound, but also on what kinds of sound he has heard. I strongly suspect that Americans in general are now suffering from degeneration of the inner ear, owing to the unpopularity or decline of many forms of heightened utterance (sermon, oration, declamation, recitation, soliloquy) and the taming and flattening of our daily speech.

Like all poets who value sound, I want the sounds in my poetry to be heard, and I am always grateful for the opportunity to read aloud. If, however, poets are to be of any use in regenerating the public's inner ear, they are going to have to study recitation. With several striking exceptions, our poets (myself included) read in such a way as to convince their audiences that "Heard melodies are sweet, but those unheard/Are sweeter."

2. *To whom is the poem addressed? How difficult may a poem be?*

A poem is addressed to the Muse. It is one function of the

Muse to cover up the fact that poems are not addressed to anybody in particular. During the act of writing, the poem is an effort to express a knowledge imperfectly felt, to articulate relationships not quite seen, to make or discover some pattern in the world. It is a conflict with disorder, not a message from one person to another. Once the poem is written and published, however, it belongs to anyone who will take it, and the more the better.

I am sure that in all poets there is a deep need to communicate. But a poet by his nature has to see and say things in his own way. Though the wish to communicate may be one desire which prompts the poet to write, the experience of writing cannot include any calculations as to the public intelligibility of what is written. While writing, the poet is singlemindedly pursuing a glimpsed perfection of utterance, and he is the only person to whom the poem *must* be clear. If the poet is something of a human being, and has talent, his poem's being clear to him is a near-guarantee that it will be clear to some, if not all, others.

The question of difficulty does not much interest me, really. I think there are many justifications for poetry's being difficult at present. On the other hand, I do not feel that all poetry *must* be difficult at present, or that the man who writes readily-understood poetry is criminally opposing the *Zeitgeist*. The League for Sanity in Poetry to the contrary, I think that among our good poets "wilful obscurity" is extremely uncommon. Those who attempt to arouse public opinion against difficulty in poetry are appealing, I think, to the laziness and uneasy pride of a half-educated and excessively comfortable middle class, whose intelligences have so long been flattered by all our great entertainment media that they cannot associate pleasure with effort, and therefore receive any demand for spiritual exertion as a calculated insult.

It seems to me that there are two ways of thinking about universality. A poem may be said to be universal when it is *for* everybody; it may also be said to be universal when it is *about* everybody. In these incoherent times, to try for the first kind of universality is generally to become a literary whore. Provisionally —that is, until the arrival of the millennium—I think we had better cling to the second criterion. A poem is not the less universal for being incomprehensible to some; so long as it deals humanly with some human experience, so that the imaginative order it contrives may enrich another, it may be said to be *about* everybody—and that is the only kind of universality we can sensibly desire. "To believe your own thought, to believe that what is true for you in your private heart is true for all men" seems to me no less possible now than in Emerson's time. The poetry of those who so believe, however difficult it may be, is never guilty of solipsism.

3. *What is your attitude toward the language of the poem?*

I have no special theory of diction, but I am strongly in favor of the greatest possible catholicity in the choice of words. Some of the poets of our older poetic generation accomplished, before and after the first world war, a necessary subversion of the poetic diction of their predecessors. Since then their imitators have been so slavish as to establish in current verse several recognizable *argots*. The Auden school of the 30's, which gave poetic language a refreshing infusion of slang and technical terminology, has also been aped quite enough now. In an age of separation and specialization, poets can serve the public sensibility by making continual recombinations of all our many modes of speech—by trying incessantly to counterfeit a general language. If this is to be done, we must hope that no particular combination will be allowed to harden into a poetic dialect.

The borrowing of words from other tongues should not be condemned as mere elegance. Self-confident cultures like the Elizabethan have always very cavalierly taken whatever they needed from foreign languages; and the Elizabethans pronounced their borrowings as they chose. Whenever a foreign tongue can supply us some word more exact or more suggestive than those at hand, I think we may profitably do the same.

4. *Do you have anything to say about allusion?*

I think the point should be made that one does not, merely by referring to the dying god or what not, evoke a legitimate emotional response. The value of the reference must in every case be proven. I think it possible that the basic aesthetic mistake in *Finnegan's Wake* is what one might call, in the language of the new critics, "the fallacy of mere reference." This is not of course to say that references must be *explained* in poetry. Artistic economy won't allow it. But it should be the use of the reference, and not its inherent prestige, which demands response.

5. *What is your attitude toward irony and paradox?*

There should be no flight from irony and paradox in writing poetry, rather an insistence on them. They are often the source, I think, of what richness and honesty we may sense in a poem. But "the corruption of the best is the worst," and it is unfortunately the case that these devices, which when honorably handled are the best means of telling the whole truth, can also be the slickest tools for saying nothing at all. Putting reverse English on one's words, uttering apparent contradictions and oxymorons —these can make for the stark, condensed presentation of divided feelings and irreconcilable facts. But when irony and paradox are employed as a compositional *tic,* when they are used as a means to simultaneous assertion and retraction, when they produce only a brilliant surface of mock-logic, then what one has is the current version of "pure poetry"—a highly camouflaged way of being *vox et praeterea nihil.*

In a poem which makes proper use of irony and paradox, the materials will be grandly polarized, and the contradictions made sharp. In a poem which makes cheating use of these devices, one will discover on analysis only a dispersion of flashy short-circuits, and one will end by feeling like poor Alice, when she and the Red Queen had flown so fast to get nowhere.

I dwell so much on this matter because I think that current critical enthusiasm for the ironic has led us to be somewhat uncritical of the perverse and the deviously aimless. For some time now, the ideal conception of the modern poet has been that of a deeply divided man—so much so that when Mr. Eliot turned to the writing of meditative-religious poetry, some complained of him as a lost leader who had "taken the easy way out." The complexity of the age still appears to demand a corresponding complexity in the poet: he is expected to refine our awareness of contradictions, rather than to resolve them, and whenever he approaches a synthesis of modern experience, through faith, politics, or what have you, we seem to prefer him at all costs to eschew serenity. I think it true that any simplicity of understanding is very likely, in 1950, to be fraudulent, and I imagine we may rightly persist in demanding that our ideal poet be as divided as honesty requires. But we need not extend our admiration from the divided man to the shattered man and the liquefied man. The poet ought not to be divided and re-divided to the point of disappearance, and our respect for irony should not betray us into a toleration of the "pure poetry" of intricate aboulia and evasion.

6. *What is your attitude toward subject-matter?*

Ideally, the "subject-matter" of poetry should be limitless. For the individual poet, however, limitation in subject-matter seems often to be a condition of power. The jack-of-all-subjects is likely to be master of none. As for bigness and smallness in subject-matter, I do not sympathize with the cultural historian who finds a poem "serious" and "significant" because it mentions the atomic bomb. Scope and assimilative power are highly to be respected, but there are other values in poetry, and Milton and Herrick have an equal loftiness in my private Pantheon.

It does not upset me to hear poetry paraphrased and its "subject-matter" stated. But I don't usually care for the sort of poem which too readily submits to paraphrase. A poem ought not to be fissionable. It ought to be impossible satisfactorily to separate "ideas" from their poetic "embodiment." When this can be done to a poem, it is a sign that the poem began with a prose "idea"—i.e., began wrongly—and that the writer was not a poet but a phrase-maker.

7. *Do you have anything to say about imagery?*

I think it a great vice to convey everything by imagery, particularly if the imagery is not interrelated. There ought to be areas of statement. But the statement should not equal and abolish the "objects" in the poem, as Arnold's does in *Rugby Chapel*. All those rocks and cataracts gone in a puff of piety! The statement should have obliquity, and congruence to the imagery, as Marianne Moore's does—not vitiating the objects, but rather finding in them another and ideal dimension.

8. *What about rhyme?*

Aside from its obvious value in the finished poem as a part of poetic form and as a heightener of language, rhyme seems to me an invaluable aid in composition. It creates difficulties which the utterance must surmount by increased resourcefulness. It also helps by liberally suggesting arbitrary connections of which the mind may take advantage if it likes. For example, if one has to rhyme with *tide,* a great number of rhyme-words at once come to mind (ride, bide, shied, confide, Akenside, etc.). Most of these, in combination with *tide,* will probably suggest nothing apropos, but one of them may reveal precisely what one wanted to say. If none of them does, *tide* must be dispensed with. Rhyme, austerely used, may be a stimulus to discovery and a stretcher of the attention.

9. *What is your attitude toward the structure of the total poem?*

As my friend Pierre Schneider has observed, some writers think of art as a window, and some think of it as a door. If art is a window, then the poem is something intermediate in character, limited, synecdochic, a partial vision of a part of the world. It is the means of a dynamic relation between the eye within and the world without. If art is conceived to be a door, then that dynamic relation is destroyed. The artist no longer perceives a wall between him and the world; the world becomes an extension of himself, and is deprived of its reality. The poet's words cease to be a means of liaison with the world; they take the place of the world. This is bad aesthetics—and incidentally, bad morals.

The use of strict poetic forms, traditional or invented, is like the use of framing and composition in painting: both serve to limit the work of art, and to declare its artificiality: they say, "This is not the world, but a pattern imposed upon the world or found in it; this is a partial and provisional attempt to establish relations between things."

There are other less metaphysical reasons for preferring strictness of form: the fact, for example, that subtle variation is unrecognizable without the pre-existence of a norm; or the fact that form, in slowing and complicating the writing-process, calls out the poet's full talents, and thereby insures a greater care and cleverness in the choice and disposition of words. In general, I would say that limitation makes for power: the strength of the genie comes of his being confined in a bottle.

CEREMONY

A striped blouse in a clearing by Bazille
Is, you may say, a patroness of boughs
Too queenly kind toward nature to be kin.
But ceremony never did conceal,
Save to the silly eye, which all allows,
How much we are the woods we wander in.

Let her be some Sabrina fresh from stream,
Lucent as shallows slowed by wading sun,
Bedded on fern, the flowers' cynosure:
Then nymph and wood must nod and strive to dream
That she is airy earth; the trees, undone,
Must ape her languor natural and pure.

Ho-hum. I am for wit and wakefulness,
And love this feigning lady by Bazille.
What's lightly hid is deepest understood,
And when with social smile and formal dress
She teaches leaves to curtsey and quadrille,
I think there are most tigers in the wood.

A SIMILE FOR HER SMILE

Your smiling, or the hope, the thought of it,
Makes in my mind such pause and abrupt ease
As when the highway bridgegates fall,
Balking the hasty traffic, which must sit
On each side massed and staring, while
Deliberately the drawbridge starts to rise:

Then horns are hushed, the oilsmoke rarefies,
Above the idling motors one can tell
The packet's smooth approach, the slip,
Slip of the silken river past the sides,
The ringing of clear bells, the dip
And slow cascading of the paddle wheel.

THEN WHEN THE AMPLE SEASON

Then when the ample season
Warmed us, waned, and went,
We gave to the leaves no graves,
To the robin gone no name,
Nor thought at the birds' return
Of their sourceless dim descent,
And we read no loss in the leaf,
But a freshness ever the same.

The leaf first learned of years
One not forgotten fall;
Of lineage now, and loss
These latter singers tell,
Of a year when birds now still
Were all one choiring call
Till the unreturning leaves
Imperishably fell.

STILL, CITIZEN SPARROW

Still, citizen sparrow, this vulture which you call
Unnatural, let him but lumber again to air
Over the rotten office, let him bear
The carrion ballast up, and at the tall

Tip of the sky lie cruising. Then you'll see
That no more beautiful bird is in heaven's height,
No wider more placid wings, no watchfuller flight;
He shoulders nature there, the frightfully free,

The naked-headed one. Pardon him, you
Who dart in the orchard aisles, for it is he
Devours death, mocks mutability,
Has heart to make an end, keeps nature new.

Thinking of Noah, childheart, try to forget
How for so many bedlam hours his saw
Soured the song of birds with its wheezy gnaw,
And the slam of his hammer all the day beset

The people's ears. Forget that he could bear
To see the towns like coral under the keel,
And the fields so dismal deep. Try rather to feel
How high and weary it was, on the waters where

He rocked his only world, and everyone's.
Forgive the hero, you who would have died
Gladly with all you knew; he rode that tide
To Ararat; all men are Noah's sons.

MUSEUM PIECE

The good grey guardians of art
Patrol the halls on spongy shoes,
Impartially protective, though
Perhaps suspicious of Toulouse.

Here dozes one against the wall,
Disposed upon a funeral chair.
A Degas dancer pirouettes
Upon the parting of his hair.

See how she spins! The grace is there,
But strain as well is plain to see.
Degas loved the two together:
Beauty joined to energy.

Edgar Degas purchased once
A fine El Greco, which he kept
Against the wall beside his bed
To hang his pants on while he slept.

AT YEAR'S END

Now winter downs the dying of the year,
And night is all a settlement of snow;
From the soft street the rooms of houses show
A gathered light, a shapen atmosphere,
Like frozen-over lakes whose ice is thin
And still allows some stirring down within.

I've known the wind by water banks to shake
The late leaves down, which frozen where they fell
And held in ice as dancers in a spell
Fluttered all winter long into a lake;
Graved on the dark in gestures of descent,
They seemed their own most perfect monument.

There was perfection in the death of ferns
Which laid their fragile cheeks against the stone
A million years. Great mammoths overthrown
Composedly have made their long sojourns,
Like palaces of patience, in the gray
And changeless lands of ice. And at Pompeii

The little dog lay curled and did not rise
But slept the deeper as the ashes rose
And found the people incomplete, and froze
The random hands, the loose unready eyes
Of men expecting yet another sun
To do the shapely thing they had not done.

These sudden ends of time must give us pause.
We fray into the future, rarely wrought
Save in the tapestries of afterthought.
More time, more time. Barrages of applause
Come muffled from a buried radio.
The New-year bells are wrangling with the snow.

LA ROSE DES VENTS

Poet: The hardest headlands
     Gravel down,
     The seas abrade
     What coasts we know,
     And all our maps
     In azure drown,
     Forewarning us
     To rise and go.

     And we shall dwell
     On the rose of the winds,
     Which is the isle
     Of every sea,
     Surviving there
     The tinted lands
     Which could not last
     Our constancy.

Lady: That roving wave
     Where Venus rose
     Glints in the floods
     Of farthest thought;
     What beauty there
     In image goes
     Dissolves in other
     And is not.

     There are some shores
     Still left to find
     Whose broken rocks
     Will last the hour;
     Forsake those roses
     Of the mind
     And tend the true,
     The mortal flower.

The French call the compass-rose the Rose of the Winds.

THE DEATH OF A TOAD

A toad the power mower caught,
Chewed and clipped of a leg, with a hobbling hop has got
 To the garden verge, and sanctuaried him
 Under the cineraria leaves, in the shade
  Of the ashen heartshaped leaves, in a dim,
   Low, and a final glade.

The rare original heartsblood goes,
Spends on the earthen hide, in the folds and wizenings, flows
 In the gutters of the banked and staring eyes. He lies
 As still as if he would return to stone,
  And soundlessly attending, dies
   Toward some deep monotone,

Toward misted and ebullient seas
And cooling shores, toward lost Amphibia's emperies.
 Day dwindles, drowning, and at length is gone
 In the wide and antique eyes, which still appear
  To watch, across the castrate lawn,
   The haggard daylight steer.

TYWATER

Death of Sir Nihil, book the *n*th,
Upon the charred and clotted sward;
Lacking the lily of our Lord,
Alases of the hyacinth.

Could flicker from behind his ear
A whistling silver throwing knife,
And with a holler punch the life
Out of a swallow in the air.

Behind the lariat's butterfly
Shuttled his white and gritted grin,

And cuts of sky would roll within
The noose-hole, when he spun it high.

The violent, neat, and practised skill
Was all he loved and all he learned.
When he was hit, his body turned
To clumsy dirt before it fell.

And what to say of him, God knows.
Such violence. And such repose.

THE TERRACE

We ate with steeps of sky about our shoulders,
High up a mountainside,
On a terrace like a raft roving
Seas of view.

The tablecloth was green, and blurred away
Toward verdure far and wide,
And all the country came to be
Our table too.

We drank in tilted glasses of rosé
From tinted peaks of snow,
Tasting the frothy mist, and freshest
Fathoms of air.

Women were washing linens in a stream
Deep down below,
The sound of water over their knuckles
A sauce rare.

Imminent towns whose weatherbeaten walls
Looked like the finest cheese
Bowled us enormous melons from their
Tolling towers.

Mixt into all the day we heard the spice
Of many tangy bees,
Eddying through the miles-deep
Salad of flowers.

When we were done we had our hunger still;
We dipped our cups in light;
We caught the fine-spun shade of clouds
In spoon and plate;

Drunk with imagined breathing, we inhaled
The dancing smell of height;
We fished for the bark of a dog, the squeak
Of a pasture gate.

But for all our benedictions and our gay
Readily said graces,
The evening stole our provender and
Left us there;

And darkness filled the specious space, and fell
Betwixt our silent faces,
Pressing against our eyes its absent,
Fathomless stare.

Out in the dark we felt the real mountains
Hulking in proper might,
And we felt the edge of the black wind's
Regardless cleave;

And we knew we had eaten not the manna of heaven
But our own reflected light,
And we were the only part of the night that we
Couldn't believe.

Peter Viereck

PETER VIERECK *was born in New York City in* 1916. *He has studied at Harvard and Oxford, and is at present Associate Professor of History at Mount Holyoke. He is the author of two works in political science*: METAPOLITICS: FROM THE ROMANTICS TO HITLER, *and* CONSERVATISM REVISITED. *His first book of poems,* TERROR AND DE-CORUM, *was awarded the Pulitzer Prize in Poetry for* 1948. *His second volume of verse,* POEMS, *will appear early in* 1950.

MY KIND OF POETRY

I

RIGHT FROM the start, I must disappoint many readers by the unexciting conservatism of my poetic techniques. After experimenting with more easy-going prosodies, I've found it more effective to adhere to the admittedly arbitrary laws of conventional rhyme and meter. In the history of English literature these have again and again been discarded as "outworn" but have returned to outwear the discarders. Irregular scansion can be useful onomatopoeia to bring out a jolt in the mood or the narrative. But as Amy Lowell's revolt illustrated, this is a habit-forming drug. Used once too often in poetry, irregularity becomes just another kind of regularity, that of prose.

Equally conservative is my passionate conviction that the time is now ripe for a frontal assault on obscurity as inartistic—*provided* the assault is not allowed to play into the hands of those who want a pretext for being lazy about poetry. The time is ripe for poets and readers, both making sincerer efforts at mutual understanding, to end the schism between them by restoring communication. The eighteenth-century motto "be thou clear!" expresses the timeliest need of American poetry in 1949.

It's not enough to say a poet must belong to none of the arty coteries. It's essential that he actively sin against their rituals. *My own sin is twofold.* (1) I've content—something to say about the profane world they scorn—and not only form; this makes me an "impure" poet. (2) I try to communicate to the qualified layman also, instead of only to fellow poets and critics; this makes me a philistine.

My style has been ironically summarized as "Manhattan classicism." In case labels are necessary at all, that's as accurate a label as any. Mine is not the arcadian escapism of an aloof anti-urban classicism but a classicism of the industrial age, with an ivory tower built where the subway rumbles loudest. Being classicist means that my poetry is equally interested in shaking off the vague sentimentalities of the pre-Eliot romanticism and the hermetic ingenuities of the post-Eliot version of neo-classicism. The latter contains (1) no fun and (2) no humanness, two "vulgar" qualities that are the lifeblood of art. What was new and imaginative in the master becomes a slot-machine stereotype in the disciples, who thereby create a new and more insidious type of Babbitt: the highbrow Babbitt-baiting Babbitt. Thus does an exciting literary movement age into a cocktail-party clique, a mutual admiration pact, a pressure group upon college English departments and Little Magazines. Think ye, because ye are virtuosos, there shall be no more cakes and ale?

In my book *Conservatism Revisited: The Revolt Against Revolt* (Scribner's, September, 1949) I've already defined my humanist and classical credo. Here I shall try instead to be more specific about concrete examples of my poetry. When they violate my conservative working principles, as they sometimes do, this is occasionally done on purpose, using disharmony to bring out the harmony by contrast. More often it may pretend to be on purpose but is really done out of insufficient competence, in which case: so much the worse for me and my writings rather than so much the worse for the principles.

Just as political liberty is not based on a radical smashing of traffic lights but on law and traditional established institutions, so poetry must be subjected to the challenge of form, the more rigorous and traditional and conservative the better, to bring out the response of beauty—if one may apply Toynbee's "challenge and response" to art. For my own poems, form—Toynbee's "challenge" —always means rhythm and usually means rhyme. I try to avoid those fraudulent rhymes that change the *consonants;* the rhyming of "thornbush" and "ambush" in my long poem "Crass Times" is an exception that I now regret. But for certain purposes, my rhymes use slightly different vowel sounds with the same consonants. An example is stanza two of "Crass Times." In his essay "Peter Viereck: the Poet and the Form" (*University of Kansas City Review,* summer, 1949) Professor John Ciardi of the Harvard English department analyzes my characteristic use of rhyme vowels more ably than I ever could. Therefore, I quote from him (in condensed form):

"Viereck has what Eliot has called 'the audio-imagination,' with a sure sense of how rhyme can function to punctuate, emphasize and resolve the flow of the poem. The reader who has thought of rhyme only as a regularly arranged ornamentation will do well to underscore this point in his mind. Skillfully used, rhyme is a rich device for controlling the reader's voice, teaching him to hear the poem as the poet heard it.

"For example, *Crass Times Redeemed By Dignity Of Souls.* This is an incantatory poem. The poet wants the poem read in a mechanical, litanized way. Such a reading requires a full voice stop at the end of each line. But normally, if the meaning does not pause, the voice continues on to the next line. You then have a run-on or *enjambement.* The first three lines in this passage do not provide a pause in meaning. Here, the poet makes rhyme function. The triple use of the strong 'oals' rhyme demands stress. Thus, despite the run-on, the rhyme produces the desired voice-stress. In the subsequent lines, this device is not needed since there is a meaning-pause at the end of each line with the exception of the next to the last. And there again you will note the rhyme of 'knives' becomes heavy, again requiring a stress. By 'heavy' I mean closely positioned as the second rhyme of a couplet, a strong 'ives' sound and a literal rhyme as opposed to the approximate rhyme of 'are' and 'hear' that precedes:

> " 'The weight that tortures diamonds out of coals
> Is lighter than the skimming hooves of foals
> Compared to one old heaviness our souls
> Hoist daily, each alone, and cannot share.
> To-be-awake, to sense, to-be-aware.
> Then even the dusty dreams that clog our skulls,
> The rant and thunder of the storm we are,
> The sunny silences our prophets hear,

> The rainbow of the oil upon the shoals,
> The crimes and Christmases of creature-lives,
> And all pride's barefoot tarantelle on knives
> Are but man's search for dignity of souls.' "

Rhyme and meter are the unchanging stage on which the changing actors stumble or dance. By keeping rhyme regular, I can provide a background which, by contrast, makes more effective the utmost variety, change, and imaginative flight. When rhyme and rhythm become too irregular, there is no contrast to spotlight the goings-on of the actors on the stage. This regularity demands that the vowels of full-voweled rhymes be the same. But in the case of rhymes whose vowels are short, quick, and inconspicuous (e.g., rhyming "heard" with "stirred"), I shall continue to use rhymes of slightly different vowels in order to increase the speed and to force the reader into *enjambement* (by not lingering over the rhyme) even when the line ends with a punctuation mark.

It would distract from a slow, strong, open-voweled rhyme to repeat the same vowel in the middle of the same or following line. So I usually avoid this. For example, if the rhyme-word is "mood," I should not in the same line or following line use any word with an "oo" sound. This would distract the ear of the reader from doing what I will it to do: namely, to remain in unconscious suspense waiting for the second half of the rhymed pair. If the end-word "viewed" is to rhyme with the earlier end word "mood," I don't want any intervening non-end-word like "cruel" or "blue." If I find that, for the sake of lilt or meaning, I must repeat the rhyme-vowel inside the line, then I try to repeat it twice. Thereby the two repetitions, by pairing with each other, cease to distract the ear from the third repetition in the rhyme-word at the end of that same line. I try to have strong, open vowel-sounds occur an odd number of times in a line (once, three times, five times), never an even number of times, except in unrhymed poems (Alcaic or Sapphic odes or blank verse), where I prefer even to odd. I make no fetish of this or any other rule, the total effect of a poem being more important than any single detail.

II

Free verse I write not at all: on principle. Unrhymed metrical verse only rarely. Almost all my poems are rhymed. For me the most difficult verse-form is the form that glib or sloppy craftsmen deem easiest: unrhymed iambic pentameter. I've begun many poems in this blank-verse form but not one have I been able to finish. The exception—"A Walk on Snow"—proves the rule: except for some 1947 interpolations about art, it was written so long ago (in 1932 in high school when I was 15) that I cannot even remember what sort of person or poet I then was. Since then, no luck.

I don't mean I've given up attempting blank verse. But I've destroyed all the attempts because they all bogged down into pale reflections of the blank verse style of either the Elizabethans or Milton or Swinburne. "A Walk on Snow" I included in my *Terror and Decorum* collection (against the advice of so fine a critic as I. A. Richards) because, no matter how redolent of juvenilia, it at least has a personal blank verse style: a poor thing perhaps but all my own. Even here I stuck to my typical pattern, later exemplified once in each stanza of "Poet" and "Kilroy" and in the final stanza of "For Two Girls," of breaking the pentameter monotony with an occasional tetrameter of emphatic meaning.

Alliteration as a working principle? For me, definitely yes. If done not too unobtrusively, a poet can use it triply instead of doubly; and triply is to my ear more effective. More than triply is too obvious. Doubly, by a mathematical paradox, sounds more crudely obvious than triply. Triply can or cannot be obvious, depending on how it's handled. It is only effective when the reader hears it unawares. Shakespeare was not afraid to use alliteration, not only doubly as in: "Ruin hath taught me thus to ruminate" but even in three successive words: "To leap large lengths of miles." In the nineteenth century, alliteration was overused and used too mechanically by Poe and Swinburne. It became discredited after such mechanical usage as Poe's "Came out of the lair of the lion/ With love in her luminous eyes." That fourth "l" ("luminous") is just too much of a good thing and becomes farce.

Wearing their heartlessness on their sleeve, modern poets go to the opposite extreme. Just as they are afraid to let themselves go emotionally and be wild, for fear of seeming ridiculous, with the result that their lyrics are unlyrical, so likewise are they afraid to let themselves go in alliteration, for fear of seeming crude, with the result that they lack lilt and music. They should take to heart the very wise words of a very vulgar song of the 1920's:

> "It don't mean a thing
> If it ain't got the swing."

My practice is to be both lyrically wild and musically alliterative when the meaning and mood of the poem are enhanced thereby, but never otherwise, never mechanically, never too frequently. Never alliteration for its own sake but only for the poem's total effect. In the following couplet, the purpose of the two triple-alliterations ("f" and "m") is not lilt or music, their usual purpose, but a heightened emotional emphasis to signalize the climax and turning-point of the whole poem:

> Then, with a final flutter, philomel—
> How mud-splashed, what a mangy miracle!—etc.
> (from "Some Lines In Three Parts")

It might be interesting to have each poet of the '40's name what poet influenced him most. Our answers might be wrong because we would not know of unconscious influences. Consciously, I'm most influenced by Yeats. In rhythmic technique his "Cold Heaven," published 1914, seems to me the greatest lyric in our language. Yeats is the poet whose rhythms I most imitate, especially his habit of a quick extra unaccented syllable amid an iambic or trochaic line. For example, the second syllable of "ignorant" when he speaks of "beauty's ignorant ear."

I've imitated this mannerism, though with a different purpose, in part III, line four of "Some Lines." The same type of quick extra unaccented syllable recurs in "cartilaginous": "A cártilá-ginous, móst rheumátic squéak." Were every alternating syllable in "cartilaginous" accented, as might normally be expected, then there would be no room for the word "most," and the line would read: "A cártiláginóus, rheumátic squéak." Contrasting the two readings, it will be noted that the latter is correct in iambics but pedestrian while the former gives the needed onomatopoeia of a rheumatic hobble and also the necessary ironic tone for describing owlish-pedantic wisdom in its painful effort to become the singing beauty of philomel, the nightingale.

Recently I heard an appeal for "liberating" poetry from the "tyranny of iambic pentameter"; but who will liberate poetry from such self-appointed liberators? My *typical* poem is a moderately long poem, often of several pages, in rhymed iambic pentameter, in which lyrical emotions and philosophical ideas are equally present and are fused into unity by expressing the ideas in sensuous metaphors. For variety or special emphasis, I periodically alternate the five-beat line with a shorter line, four-beat or three-beat. The shorter line occurs several times per stanza in "Kilroy" but, more typically, once only per stanza in "Poet," "Some Lines," "A Walk on Snow," etc. When long, this "typical" poem of mine is divided into stanzas of varying length, coinciding with changes of mood. "Crass Times," otherwise typical, omits the shorter line from all stanzas because, when a sound of steady incantation is desired, then monotony becomes for once desirable and variety undesirable.

Stanza two of "Poet" expresses my insistence on making intellectual concepts sensuous. In a prose essay, rhymes are rhymes, exclamation marks are exclamation marks, nouns are nouns. This being poetry, they become three-dimensional physical creatures with lives of their own. The passage describes the revolt of the outworn romantic claptrap against the dead classical poet who has hitherto tamed them:

> "Words that begged favor at his court in vain—
> Lush adverbs, senile rhymes in tattered gowns—
> Send notes to certain exiled nouns
> And mutter openly against his reign.
> While rouged clichés hang out red lights again,
> Hoarse refugees report from far-flung towns
> That exclamation marks are running wild
> And prowling half-truths carried off a child."

Mine is a poetry of ideas. Above all, ideas connected with ethics or with the search for ethical values. Often my poems use history as grist for their mill, not only history of the past but of the future (chapter five of *Terror and Decorum* is called "News From the 60th century"). Ideas are the heroes, villains, and agonisants of an unusually large number of my poems. Unlike the arid didacticism of some eighteenth-century poetry of ideas, my ideas are presented not abstractly but sensuously: lyrical and philosophical at the same instant. Lyricism teaches ideas to dance rather than to plod along like a Ph. D. thesis:

> "Here abstractions have contours; here flesh is wraith;
> On these cold and warming stones, only solidity throws no shadow.
> Listen, when the high bells ripple the half-light:
> Ideas, ideas, the tall ideas dancing."
> (from "Incantation.")

III

Poets pretend to ignore their critics with lordly dandyism. In truth, I've constantly learnt from hostile critics and am grateful to them for my most valuable revisions and deletions. Intelligent hostile criticism is all the more important to me, indeed indispensable, in view of my inability to discriminate between my worse and better poems. I agree with Professor D. C. Allen's strictures (*Contemporary Poetry*, Baltimore, Spring, 1949):

> "This deliberate effort to ruin a poem by what seems a consciously chosen unpoetic word or phrase is Viereck's main weakness as a poet. As there are scars that disfigure individual poems, so there are poems that disfigure the collection. I wish they had never been written or, having been written, destroyed. One can hope that the next collection will be smaller and more selective."

In turn, some of my non-hostile critics have succeeded in explicitly and consciously summarizing those of my working principles which I follow only implicitly and semiconsciously and am unable to summarize competently. An example of such summarizing is Louis Fuller in the *Antioch Review* (Spring, 1949): "What has not been sufficiently noted by those who have a corner on modern poetry is that this book may be read and enjoyed *without any special key,* and without serving any *special novitiate.* Mr. Viereck doesn't write down, or up; he simply writes as person to person. If there is any misunderstanding of meaning or intention, it is not because he has tried to create it." Another example is Selden Rodman writing in the *Saturday Review* (October 9, 1948):

> "He is never trying to bait and hence is never deliberately elusive. Indeed, one of the qualities that make *Terror and Decorum* more of a *break with the Eliot-dominated past* than any recent book is this very passion to communicate. The soldiering has contributed to his verse as a whole its racy colloquialism and its sense of identity with ordinary people. Academic training has given him a working knowledge of the styles of a half dozen literatures and a familiarity with cross-reference almost Joycean in scope. . . . Out of extreme complexity, simplicity. From sophistication beyond cleverness, innocence. In Shakespeare, Donne, Blake, Hopkins, the later Yeats, perhaps in all of the greatest poetry, it is the 'formula' toward which Viereck, more than any contemporary poet, seems to be moving."

The above "formula" of a difficult simplicity, though unattainable for my practice, is the truest summary of the ideal behind all my "working principles."

Several critics of *Terror and Decorum* beamed upon what they called "its wit"; others frowned upon "its frivolous clowning around." Both were referring to the same element; both misconstrued its aim. The element of so-called wit or buffoonery is a means, not an end. Usually it is found concerning things that are "no laughing matter." It is my means of expressing the tragedy inseparable from living and the terror inseparable from the shock of beauty. Tragedy is brought out better by wit—through incongruity and grotesque understatement—than by the lurid overstatement of poems like Poe's "Ulalume" that are forever saying "Boo!" to the reader.

This double-talk use of frivolity is the basis of section II of *Terror and Decorum* entitled "Six Theological Cradle Songs." Their motto might have been. "Six cradles make six coffins." These songs are to be read simultaneously on two levels: (1) humorous nursery rhymes for children; (2) sinister allegories for adults. The same sinister-naïve, double-level technique recurs in many of my other poems, such as the concluding dialogue between man and a sadistic reality ("sky," nature, God) in "From Ancient Fangs." This method is no newfangled affectation but inherent in nursery rhymes, fairy tales, myths, and the language of childhood; for example, the *frisson* of so familiar a Mother Goose couplet as: "Here comes a candle to light you to bed,/ And here comes a chopper to chop off your head." In this connection David Daiches wrote of *Terror and Decorum* (New York Herald-Tribune book section, November 21, 1948):

> "When the wit is wholly absorbed in the form, we get something quite distinctive in modern poetry—witty, but not with the wit of the early Auden; subtle, but not with the subtlety of the neo-Yeatsians; speculative, but still and essentially lyrical. . . . 'Better Come Quietly' and 'Exorcism' have an admirable sardonic humor which is positively terrifying."

"Better Come Quietly," the example cited by Mr. Daiches, is the first of the "Six Theological Cradle Songs." It is meant to be chanted with a childishly over-obvious stress on the accented words, just as a child jumping rhythmically on the springs of its crib might chant. The overstress is indicated here and in other poems of mine by capital letters. As used by me, this typographical device does not mean "more important" (though capital letters often are used to mean this) but means: "read this at a raucous shout." The same voice function of capitals occurs in "Exorcism" in the Athos And Assisi chapter. On the allegorical level of its double-talk, "Better Come Quietly" is a medieval morality play of the four ages of man from embryo into afterlife. In each age, the questioning demand for consolation receives the same answer from the triple chorus that haunts us all:

Baby John: O kinsfolk and gentlefolk, PLEASE be forgiving,
     But nothing can lure me to living, to living.
     I'm snug where I am; I don't WISH to burst through.
Chorus of Nurses, Furies, and Muses: That's what YOU think.
     If only you KNEW!
Baby John: Well then YES, I'll be BORN, but my EARTH will
     be heaven;
     My dice will throw nothing but seven-eleven;
     Life is tall lilacs, all giddy with dew.
Chorus of Nurses, Furies, and Muses: That's what YOU think.
     If only you KNEW!
Baby John: Well then YES, there'll be sorrows, be sorrows that
     best me;

But these are mere teasings to test me, to test me.
We'll ZOOM from our graves when God orders us to.
Chorus of Nurses, Furies, and Muses: That's what YOU think.
If only you KNEW!
Baby John: Well then YES, I'll belie my belief in survival.
But IF there's no God, then at least there's no devil:
If at LAST I must die—well, at LEAST when I do,
It's clear I won't sizzle.
Chorus of Nurses, Furies, and Muses: If only you KNEW!

IV

There's an essential element I haven't discussed so far and am unable to define. Yet I am dedicated to it side by side with my classicism in a synthesis of antitheses. The title *Terror and Decorum* and lines like "What terror crowns the sweetness of all song?" formulate this dualism of what Nietzsche called the Dionysian and the Appolonian; also the dualism of the primordial "dark gods" of the unconscious and the more rational, civilized conscious mind. The creative tension of these antitheses is in the shiver of holy dread, the tragic exaltation which makes the hair stand on end and is the difference between poetry and verse.

My nearest approach to catching this element is in "Some Lines In Three Parts." The poem describes the attempt of the ego, trapped in its vulnerable mortal skull, to burst free by means of song. Completed after *Terror and Decorum* and appearing in *Harper's* magazine this poem is (I believe) my best so far. Part III of the poem photographs the ego in the fleeting moment of metamorphosis from owl, the bird of wisdom, into philomel, the bird of song. This moment of "holy dread," being as unbearably ugly as birth and creativity always are, is the moment of the birth of beauty:

"What hubbub rocks the nest? What panic-freighted
Invasion—when he tried to sing—dilated
The big eyes of my blinking, hooting fowl?
A cartilaginous, most rheumatic squeak
Portends (half mocks) the change; the wrenched bones creak;
Unself descends, invoked or uninvited;
Self ousts itself, consumed and consummated;
An inward-facing mask is what must break.

The magic feverish fun of chirping, all
That professorial squints and squawks indicted,
Is here—descends, descends—till wisdom, hoarse
From bawling beauty out, at last adores,
Possessed by metamorphosis so strong.
Then, with a final flutter, philomel—
How mud-splashed, what a mangy miracle!—
Writhes out of owl and stands with drooping wing.
Just stands there. Moulted, naked, two-thirds dead.
From shock and pain (and dread of holy dread)
   Suddenly vomiting.
Look away quick; you are watching the birth of song."

Yet even here, I can only grope. I am unable to say more or to
see deeper because I don't understand enough about the all-impor-
tant night-side of art, its magic. I can only repeat falteringly that
its magic contains "more things between heaven and earth, Horatio,
than are dreamt of" in the day-side of "your philosophy." Who
does understand it? Perhaps Robert Graves in *The White Goddess*
or the Yeats of "Ego Dominus Tuus"? Perhaps Lowes in *The Road
To Xanadu,* Frazer in *The Golden Bough,* or Jessie Weston in
From Ritual To Romance? Or is the answer in Schopenhauer,
Freud, Orpheus, Icarus, Kilroy? I don't know. I wish I did.

Different poets take such different attitudes towards poetic magic
that it is helpful for each to clarify his attitude for the reader. In
Terror and Decorum the "Author's Note on Marabouts and
Planted Poets" and the poems "The Killer and the Dove," "Poet,"
"A Walk on Snow," "Africa and My New York," and my mock-
archaic "Ballad of the Jollie Gleeman" together give a composite
picture of the artist as culture-hero, the showman as shaman, the
clown as priest. Uneasy lies the clown that wears a head, according
to "A Walk on Snow":

Not priest but clown, the shuddering sorcerer
Is more astounded than his rapt applauders:
"Then all those props and Easters of my stage
Came true? But I was joking all the time!"
Art, being bartender, is never drunk;
And magic that believes itself, must die. . . .
Unfrocked magicians freeze the whole night long;

> Holy iambic cannot thaw the snow
> They walk on when obsessive crystals bloom.

A key word is "obsessive." This is true in the lines above. It is true in "Dolce Ossessione," where the beauty left by the artist (is it lies? is it truth?) remains to be picked up not by the lean-ribbed scavenger cats (just who are *they?*) but by the child, the future:

> "I'll urge Obsession on: an eel, I'll swim
> To every far Sargasso of my whim. . . .
> A flame-scaled trout, I'll shimmer through your nets—
> Like lies?, like truth?—and gasp on fatal sands.
> Trailed fawning by lascivious hungry cats,
> What child will scoop me up, what pudgy hands?"

V

Many poets wince automatically whenever any critic paraphrases their poems, as if an elephant were trampling on butterfly wings. The "heresy of paraphrase" it is called. To be sure paraphrase is helpful only in conjunction with the other tools of criticism. By itself, paraphrase is inadequate because it gives only the What of a poem, not the How. Nevertheless, a lucid rendering of the What can usually throw a little more light on the How, form and content being inseparable. Even a little light helps inasmuch as our new credo must be that communication is artistic, obscurity inartistic, and a deep simplicity the first virtue.

The use of words like "heresy" in current criticism is typical. It is a hierarchical word, deriding the non-élite reader. It helps show how pontifical discussions of poetry have become since the triumph of the Eliotizing epigones. Such ruling trends (penny-wise but Pound-foolish in the case of the 1949 Bollingen Prize) explain the awe of the fancier critics for the 98 per cent incoherent, 2 per cent lovely, and persistently fascist and anti-semitic *Pisan Cantos* of the man who has done so much to establish the Eliot movement. Does this imply fascist sympathies (as has been overhastily alleged) in either the New Critics or in Eliot? Emphatically not! Rather, their attitude toward Pound implies an untenable doctrinaire attempt to separate form from content and to separate poetry from its inextricable moral and historical context. One should feel a deep pity for those poor reviewers who struggled so painfully to praise the *Pisan Cantos* because they dared not, for reasons of *avant-garde* prestige, admit they couldn't make head or tail out of them.

Eliot is a great poet, who happens also to be a brilliantly self-contradictory critic. Not he so much as his ungreat imitators are to blame for the fact that their cult of his criticism and their accompanying cult of studied obscurity are stifling the growth of poetry today. Charming and velvet-gloved, this dictatorship is based not on coercion but on an ambiguous mixture of snobbism and real excellence.

Fresh air? No hope for that yet. Not until a new generation of poets and critics—honest enough not to crave praise from the precious, courageous enough not to fear the sarcasm of the pretentious—throws open the windows in the hermetic house.

With their tone of "we the mandarins," the "heresy"-scorning exquisites forbid anybody except crossword-puzzle decoders to get fun out of poetry, not to mention beauty. The poetry-murdering vocabulary to which this has ultimately led is the "Glossary of the New Criticism" published in *Poetry* magazine (Chicago, November-January, 1948-49). Originally the New Criticism was a needed liberating revolution. It produced such masterpieces as Ransom's "Painted Head" and Tate's "Mediterranean." It freed our metrics from the sloppy, smug clichés of the nineteenth century. Today, the New Criticism, already a very old criticism, has become a bar to further esthetic progress, producing nimble imitative pedants and enslaving our metrics with its own twentieth-century clichés. Read a fresh and joyous poem like Ransom's "Armageddon"; then contemplate the "Glossary of the New Criticism." So doing, you will feel like an enthusiast of the early idealistic phase of the French Revolution contemplating the intolerant "Committee of Public Safety"—or, to draw a more accurate parallel, contemplating the dictatorship of the stale and unimaginative Directorate.

Every poet should read that unbelievably humorless "Glossary" to learn why twenty years of brilliant nonsense have helped alienate the general public from poetry and its critics. No wonder all modern poetry is dismissed (unjustly) as a snore and an allusion by that audience of intelligent non-experts who are neither professional poets nor professional critics. It is precisely this lost audience to whom my own poetry is directed, which is why these remarks are not irrelevant to a discussion of my working principles.

Such an audience can be seduced only temporarily by snob appeal or by acrobatics. It can be intimidated only temporarily by being told to admire—or else be damned as philistine—the poetic reputations created synthetically with an almost convincing air of authority by the too-clever-to-be-true jargon of coteries. Critics and poets will not win back the intelligent general reader until they speak to him humanly and clearly—in the truly classic sense —instead of more royally than the king, more classically than the Greeks, and more pontifically than any pope. This is the assumption on which all my poetry and criticism are written: *"En ceste foy"* (to recall the Villon refrain) *"je vueil vivre et mourir."*

BLINDMAN'S BUFF

Night-watchmen think of dawn and things auroral.
Clerks wistful for Bermudas think of coral.
The poet in New York still thinks of laurel.
(But lovers think of death and touch each other
As if to prove that love is still alive.)

The Martian space-crew, in an Earthward dive,
Think of their sweet unearthly earth Up There,
Where darling monsters romp in airless air.
(Two lovers think of death and touch each other,
Fearing that day when only one's alive.)

We think of cash, but cash does not arrive.
We think of fun, but fate will not connive.
We never mention death. Do we survive?
(The lovers think of death and touch each other
To live their love while love is yet alive.)

Prize-winners are so avid when they strive;
They race so far; they pile their toys so high
Only a cad would trip them. Yet they die.
(The lovers think of death and touch each other;
Of all who live, these are the most alive.)

When all the lemming-realists contrive
To swim—where to?—in life's enticing tide,
Only a fool would stop and wait outside.
(The lovers stop and wait and touch each other.
Who twinly think of death are twice alive.)

Plump creatures smack their lips and think they thrive;
The hibernating bear, but half alive,
Dreams of free honey in a stingless hive.
He thinks of life at every lifeless breath.
(The lovers think of death.)

A WALK ON SNOW

1

Pine-trail; and all the hours are white, are long.
But after miles—a clearing: snow and roundness.
Such circle seemed a rite, an atavism,
A ripple of the deep-plunged stone of Myth.
I crossed that ring to loiter, not to conjure.
Stood in the center as in melodrama.
Wondered: if this center were a gate?
A gate from earth to non-earth? Gate where fingers,
Where rays perhaps, are fumbling signals through?
       Or are stars cold for all their brightness,
Deaf to our urgencies as snowflakes are?
Then magic blazed: a star spoke through the gate:
"I am not cold; I am all warm inside."

2

At once new longing charged and shook the air
Like spreading tremors of a storm's spilt moan.
Star-tunes lured old tellurian lonelinesses.
Like chord-joined notes of one sky-spanning octave,
Orbs blent in universal tremolo.
       "Star, star, reachable star!
Truly," I called, "you are all warm inside."
Shy through the gate came answer, frail in space:
"Good luck, brother. It's not so far across."

3

Being absurd as well as beautiful,
Magic—like art—is hoax redeemed by awe.
(Not priest but clown, the shuddering sorcerer
Is more astounded than his rapt applauders:
"Then all those props and Easters of my stage
Came true? But I was joking all the time!")
Art, being bartender, is never drunk;

And magic that believes itself, must die.
My star was rocket of my unbelief,
Launched heavenward as all doubt's longings are;
    It burst when, drunk with self-belief,
I tried to be its priest and shouted upward:
"Answers at last! If you'll but hint the answers
For which earth aches, that famous Whence and Whither;
Assuage our howling Why with final fact."

4

At once the gate slammed shut, the circle snapped,
The sky was usual and broad and silent.
A snowflake of impenetrable cold
Fell out of sight incalculably far.
Ring all you like, the lines are disconnected.
Knock all you like, no one is ever home.
(Unfrocked magicians freeze the whole night long;
Holy iambic can not thaw the snow
They walk on when obsessive crystals bloom.)
Shivering I stood there, straining for some frail
Or thunderous message that the heights glow down.
    I waited long; the answer was
The only one earth ever got from sky.

VALE FROM CARTHAGE

(*Spring,* 1944)

I, now at Carthage. He, shot dead at Rome.
Shipmates last May. "And what if one of us,"
I asked last May, in fun, in gentleness,
"Wears doom, like dungarees, and doesn't know?"
He laughed, *"Not see Times Square again?"* The foam,
Feathering across that deck a year ago,
Swept those five words—like seeds—beyond the seas

Into his future. There they grew like trees;
And as he passed them there next spring, they laid
Upon his road of fire their sudden shade.
Though he had always scraped his mess-kit pure
And scrubbed redeemingly his barracks floor,
Though all his buttons glowed their ritual-hymn
Like cloudless moons to intercede for him,
No furlough fluttered from the sky. He will
Not see Times Square—he will not see—he will
Not see Times
                    change; at Carthage (while my friend,
Living those words at Rome, screamed in the end)
I saw an ancient Roman's tomb and read
"Vale" in stone. Here two wars mix their dead:
  Roman, my shipmate's dream walks hand in hand
  With yours tonight ("New York again" and "Rome"),
  Like widowed sisters bearing water home
  On tired heads through hot Tunisian sand
  In good cool urns, and says, "I understand."
Roman, you'll see your Forum Square no more;
What's left but this to say of any war?

AFFIRMATIONS

(I, II, III)

I. GLADNESS ODE

Because you made me glad, I was the net.
"Why do you haunt me?" asked the midnight lake.
  "To fish," I said, "that rounded fire.
    Am not afraid to fall."

No, though that halo moved and moved and moved,
It could not hide from me for all its slyness.
  (Beneath the waters warningly
    Moon's Icaruses sprawl.)

High watchers glowed their pity on the lake:
"To wear a mirrored circle like a crown,
  Is it for this the young men drown?"
    But I, being net, must haul.

Before you made me glad, I feared such splashing;
Futile invoker then: "Dive me-ward, moon."
  But now it's I who dive defiant
    Cold curves like a ball.

The lake sang out in grace-notes scrawled by stars.
I was the net, and all my strands were glad.
  I pulled the moon out of the water;
    It wasn't heavy at all.

II. IN DEFENCE OF GLADNESS

  Not enough: the moonward
Arms of "I want, I want." Our least futile
Gesture, bold and debonair, is it not to
Touch, to clutch? But life we catch only

  In reflection, in reflected blazing,
And if for this we need an ally, then—
Not art after all? Love? Possibly love?
"Infirm of purpose, O Muse, poor cat i' the adage,"
  Says love, "give *me* the daggers!"

III. THE KILLER AND THE DOVE

This poacher, for an old obsession's sake,
Still stalks dove-whiteness, mirrored in his lake.
True wings shine overhead, too high to capture,
Moon of his blood and feather of his rapture.

"Help, holy dove; I'm masked in earthbound meshes;
Fly down, You vowel of God, You first-born Word.
(Then I'll fly up, yes I, less white a bird.)
Free me; I sink as if my feet were fishes.

"I sink; am I unwelcome in your welkin?
Reach down from sky and rip at my disguising:
Be knot, but first be knife.
                    . . . Beware up there; I'm rising
To You—to You!—
                to pounce:
                        my name is falcon."

THE SLACKER APOLOGIZES

"An artist is a philistine despite himself, a patriotic moralist with a bad conscience. When his art shouts 'beauty,' his conscience shouts 'duty.' Solution unsatisfactory."
                    —THE MANNDELBAUM CHRONICLES

We trees were chopping down the monsters in the
        Street to count their rings.
WHO BLESSED OUR WAR? The oak invoked: "Within **Thee**
Crush, Mother, quakingly these red-sapped things
        Whose burrowings
Wrong Thy good dirt. Kill, kill all alien kings."

Crowned by black moss or by obscener yellow
        The flowerless monsters stood
On soil-blaspheming asphalt. How they'd bellow
Each time we hacked them—just as if their crude
        Numb root pairs could
Feel feeling. O Goddess, the glory of being wood!

Then games of peace. WHO WAS THE POET? I!
        I was the willow lyre.
Even the oak was silent; melody
Maddened whole meadows like a forest-fire
        To hear my choir
Of leaves beat, beat, and beat upon each wire

Of winds I tamed and tuned so artfully
      It seemed an artless game.
You!, weed back there!, don't think I didn't see
You yawning. Bored? Well, try to do the same!
         What? Suddenly lame?
Come, come, step up and sing—or wither in shame.

Then crooned the crass young weed: *"Last night my stamen*
      Could hear her pistil sigh.
Though far the gardens that her petals flame in,
We touched in dreams the hour that bee flew by.
      My pollen's shy
Deep nuzzling tells her: weeds must love or die."

Fools. How they cheered. But wait, I set them right:
      "Verse, verse, not poetry.
Jingles for jungles: grosser groves delight
In honey, but educated tastes decree
      Austerity.
True art is bitter, but true art sets free.

"True art—how can I serve thee half enough?
      Had I a thousand sprays
And every spray a thousand sprigs, they'd sough
For beauty, beauty, beauty all their days—
      And still not praise
Not half the whirlwind-wonder of thy ways."

At this the oak, our captain, roared me down;
      "Mere beauty wilts the will.
Why are we here? To sing and play the clown?"
The forest answered: "We are here to kill."
      . . . While monsters still
Defile Thy loam, while trees know right from wrong,

Forgive me, Mother, for the guilt of song.

FROM ANCIENT FANGS

(the time of this poem is in the far future,
shortly after peace and love return to earth.)

i

Like lamp of intricate stained-glass which hangs
    From curved blue ceiling,
A fat bright-bellied insect hangs up there.
    At night, on traveler,
It drops like rich and heavy poison welling
    From ancient fangs.

ii

That insect's not the only thing which falls.
So many things must fall in their short day.
Careers and wine-cups; bombs and tennis-balls.
Even the sun. But sky? The sky must stay.

But now the sky itself is caving in.
O good old sky, O lid that keeps us snug,
Dear blue in which we always used to trust
As in the nurse our childhood bullied so,
When comfort was to see her loyal grin,
Ugly and safe, beam down on us below:
Dear sky, we pray to you, hold on, you must!
Hold tighter, sky. Be roof to us, not rug.

iii

"It seems I'm being prayed to; I
    Am sky,
Older than hours and than miles more far,
    Your spectator.
When worlds grow honest, noble, clean or clever,
    I fall and smother them forever.
To keep your high roof high, stop being good.
    All sights bore Me now but blood.

The main thing is to kill. And kill. And kill.
First with your Springfield. Then with steel.

"And when steel breaks, with hands and stumps of hands.
And when you've killed all strangers, kill your friends.
And if you've used up humans, stone a rat.
Call it a whim—I like My world like that.
It's your world, too. The only world you'll get."

iv

"At school they never used to talk like You."
    "No, not like Me."
"People back home don't want such things to do."
    "Perhaps. We'll see."
"Men won't splash harmless blood just for Your thirst."
    "No, not at first."

P O E T

"Toute forme créée, même par l'homme, est immortelle. Car la forme est indépendante de la matière, et ce ne sont pas les molécules qui constituent la forme."

(Baudelaire, MON COEUR MIS A NU)

1

The night he died, earth's images all came
To gloat in liberation round his tomb.
Now vengeful colors, stones, and faces dare
    To argue with his metaphor;
And stars his fancy painted on the skies
Drop down like swords
                        to pierce his too wide eyes.

2

Words that begged favor at his court in vain—
Lush adverbs, senile rhymes in tattered gowns—

Send notes to certain exiled nouns
And mutter openly against his reign.
While rouged clichés hang out red lights again,
Hoarse refugees report from far flung towns
That exclamation-marks are running wild
And prowling half-truths carried off a child.

3

But he lives on in Form, and Form shall shatter
   This tuneless mutiny of Matter.
His bones are dead; his voice is horribly strong.
Those famed vibrations of life's dancing dust,
Whose thrice-named pangs are "birth" and "death" and "lust,"
Are but the split iambics of his song.
Scansion of flesh in endless ebb and flow,
The drums of duty and renown's great gong—
Mere grace-notes of that living thousand-year
Tyrannic metronome whose every gear
Is some shy craftsman buried long ago.
What terror crowns the sweetness of all song?

4

What hardness leaps at us from each soft tune,
And hammers us to shapes we never planned?
This was a different dying from our own.
   Call every wizard in the land—
Bell, book, and test tube; let the dark be rife
With every exorcism we command.
In vain. This death is stronger than our life.

5

In vain we drive our stakes through such a haunter
Or woo with spiced applaudings such a heart.
His news of April do but mock our Winter
Like maps of heaven breathed on window-frost
By cruel clowns in codes whose key is lost.

Yet some sereneness in our rage has guessed
That we are being blessed and blessed and blessed
When least we know it and when coldest art
  Seems hostile,

                useless,

                              or apart.

6

Not worms, not worms in such a skull
But rhythms, rhythms writhe and sting and crawl.
He sings the seasons round, from bud to snow.
And all things are because he willed them so.

FOR TWO GIRLS
SETTING OUT IN LIFE

(a morality play)

*"The two young ladies separated. Juliette, who wanted to be-
come a grand lady, how could she consent to be accompanied by
a girl whose virtuous and plebeian inclinations might dishonor her
social prestige? And Justine, for her part, how could she expose
her good name to the companionship of a perverse creature who
was looking forward to a life of vile lewdness and public debauch-
ery? They bade each other an eternal adieu, and next morning
they both left the convent."—Marquis de Sade,* JUSTINE *Or* THE
MISFORTUNES OF VIRTUE, 1791.

i

The sick man, though, had wit who thought you up.
Who can not picture you that fatal morning?
Homeless, not even knowing where you'll sup,
You sigh, "Adieu!" and ask yourselves, "What next?"
I sound like old Polonius—don't be vexed
If I give too avuncular a warning;
But having scanned your futures in a text,
I gasp at all the ways you'll be misled
(Your nuns behind you and your males ahead)

And want to save you from your author's plot.
When he says, "Follow me," you'd better not!

ii

Justine, by all means do be virtuous
But not in so provocative a fashion.
I'm being frank; please listen: solely thus
Can you elude that lamentable passion
For which your author lends his name to us.
The night he ties you down in Bondy Wood,
You'll learn what happens to the gauchely good.

iii

Yet, you'll endure, Justine. Most stubbornly!
To love mankind, to preach tranquillity
To Etna or reverse a spinning planet
By bleating trustfully your Pauline tracts—
Such supernatural smugness is sheer granite:
No, not eroded by whole cataracts
Of fondlers groping through—beyond—your body
To sate in flesh the spirit's old distress
And plunge their seekings in some final sea.
Meanwhile, far off, a certain chic Grand Lady
Half-hears a voice each night (too kind for spleen)
That weeps for all her daytime wilfulness:
*"Juliette! Juliette! What have you done to me?
It's I—your other self—your poor Justine."*

iv

And you Juliette: have fun while doing ill.
Be un-immaculate *while yet you may*
(I drop this hint to give the plot away).
But when you dance with sweating stable-lads
Or tired Dukes who giggle at your skill,
Don't think it's you who dance; the ghosts of gods
Who died before our oldest gods were young,
Twirl savagely in your polite salon:

That sofa where reclining comes so easy,
Is far more haunted than you'll ever guess.
Your lips raise shrines as mystic as Assisi
From whiteness they so piously caress.
O you are very wise (your playful nights,
That seem so casual, are primordial rites)
And very silly (promise me you'll stay
A pretty little girl who'll never spell
"Chthonic" nor learn her Freud too sadly well).
Last week I think I met you on Broadway.

v

Two truths, two sisters. An obsessive pair:
Serene in their unalterable rôles
Whether their frantic author flog or kiss them.
And either truth rebukes our limbo where
Girls are not Bad but merely Indiscreet,
Girls are not Good but merely Very Sweet,
And men are filed in their own filing-system
With frayed manila-folders for their souls—
Once labeled GOD'S OWN IMAGE: USE WITH CARE
But now reclassified as OBSOLETE.

vi

Justine! Juliette! We need you, both of you,
"Girls of mild silver or of furious gold."
Revoke your spat; it is our own feud, too.
You smile? Yet you can bless us if you will.
And then—and then—identities unveiled,
Tall tales rehearsed and poutings reconciled—
    Two opposites will find each other
    And sob for half a day together;
For heaven and hell are childhood playmates still.

CRASS TIMES REDEEMED BY
DIGNITY OF SOULS

*(For Ted Spencer. Lines in memory of the humanistic
ideals of my brother, Corporal George S. Viereck, Jr.,
killed in action by the Nazis in 1944)*

i

The music of the dignity of souls
Molds every note I hum and hope to write.
I long to tell the Prince of aureoles—
Groper-in-clay and breather-into-dolls,
Kindler of suns, and chord that spans our poles—
What goading reverence His tunes incite.
Then lips whose only sacrament is speech,
Sing Him the way the old unbaptized night
Dreads and
                 needs and
                        lacks and
                               loves the light.
May yet when slick with poise I overreach,
When that high ripening slowness I impeach,
Awe of that music jolt me home contrite:
O harshness of the dignity of souls.

ii

The tenderness of dignity of souls
Sweetens our cheated gusto and consoles.
It shades love's lidless eyes like parasols
And tames the earthquake licking at our soles.
Re-tunes the tensions of the flesh we wear.
Forgives the dissonance our triumphs blare.
And maps the burrows of heart's buried lair
Where furtive furry Wishes hide like moles.
O hear the kind voice, hear it everywhere
(It sings, it sings, it conjures and cajoles)
Prompting us shyly in our half-learnt rôles.

It sprouts the great chromatic vine that lolls
In small black petals on our music scrolls
(It flares, it flowers—it quickens yet controls).
It teaches dance-steps to this uncouth bear
Who hops and stumbles in our skin and howls.

The weight that tortures diamonds out of coals
Is lighter than the skimming hooves of foals
Compared to one old heaviness our souls
Hoist daily, each alone, and cannot share:
To-be-awake, to sense, to-be-aware.
Then even the dusty dreams that clog our skulls,
The rant and thunder of the storm we are,
The sunny silences our prophets hear,
The rainbow of the oil upon the shoals,
The crimes and Christmases of creature-lives,
And all pride's barefoot tarantelle on knives
Are but man's search for dignity of souls.

iii

The searcher for the market price of souls,
Seth the Accuser with the donkey head,
Negation's oldest god, still duns the dead
For these same feathery Egyptian tolls—
But now, bland haggler, deprecates his quest
(The devil proving devils can't exist).
His boutonnière is a chic asphodel;
He makes Id's whirlpool seem a wishing-well,
Reflecting crowns to outstretched beggar-bowls.
No horns, no claws; that cheap exotic phase
Belonged to his first, gauche, bohemian days.
The nice, the wholesome, and the commonplace
Are Trilbys he manipulates in jest
Till their dear wheedlings subtly swerve our goals:—

MASK ONE: an honest, cleancut, sporting face
Such as will cheer for wrong with righteous grace,

Hiking in shorts through tyranny's Tyrols.
MASK TWO: a round and basking babyface
Distracts our souls, so archly does it beg,
Upblinking like a peevish pink poached-egg.
THIRD MASK: his hide-out is that ageing face
Which waits for youth in mirrors like an ambush
And lives our ardent "when"s as yawning "if"s
And, puffing corncobs, drawls between two whiffs,
"Why stick your neck out? Nonsense never pays!"
And rips our aspirations like a thornbush.
Unmasked on tombs by shrieking hieroglyphs,
Seth was his true—his hungry—donkey face,
Nibbling our souls as if their groans were grass,
This grazer on the dignity of souls.

iv

He, the huge bridegroom of all servile souls,
Swaps little jokes with little envious trolls
To snuff the radiance of tragedy
And vend us Pleasure, which turns out to be
An optimistic mechanized despair.
O hear the glib voice, hear it everywhere
(It shouts, it shouts, it cadges and cajoles).
It feeds the earthquake fawning at our soles.
It hands out free omnipotence as doles.
Replaces tall towns with still deeper holes.
To make us God, needs just one hair's-breadth more.

The Agents said, "All ungregarious souls
Are priggish outlaws, stubborn Seminoles."
In Confidential Chats and Friendly Strolls,
They warned us each:
                       "You are alone, you are
The last, you are the lost—O flee—you are
The straggling warrior of the lost last war
To vindicate the dignity of souls."

V

We answered: *"Tell the Prince who brays at souls,*
Your long-eared Lord with thornless crowns to sell,
That all his halos have a sulphur smell;
And though they flash like flying orioles
Or lure like bonfires on mountain knolls,
These gaudy girandoles are
                              blackness still."

Torn out of blackness, soon to choke on black,
Leaning on nothingness before and back,
Tight-lashed to lies by veins and nerves and Will,
My life is darkness. Yet I live to tell
How shimmering, how gaily freedom prowls
In flesh that guards its consciousness of souls.
Then love that gives and gives and loves the more,
Free us the way the good the daily light
Heals and
          shreds and
                      liberates the night.
Though blinking—burning—shivering in the white
Blaze that each dust-heap blest with speech extols,
May every dark and kindled "I" revere
In every "you" that self-same fire-core,
In every soul the soul of all our souls.

SOME LINES IN THREE PARTS

I

One tawny paw is all it takes to squash
This owl who nests in brows his grounded stare.
What ailed me from the arsenals of shape
To rent so armorless a pilgrim's cape?
And who am "I"? Were I all soul, I'd smash
Through this poor pelt—through, out, no matter where,

Just to wrench free one instant. Or else I'd hoot
With hideous ululations—*"let me out!"*—
    Straight up at Such as cooped me here:
"How did you get me into such a scrape?"

II

But "I" being less than soul, of dustier plume,—
If I escape, it is myself I lose.
Great hooting flapping ruffled ego, close
Your hopeless wings again and bless aloud—
Seeing only song flits through—this slandered home,
This sweet snug roost built from such stinking trash.
Sing out its theme (there never was but one),
Throw back your head and sing it all again,
Sing the bewildered honor of the flesh.
I say the honor of our flesh is love.
I say no soul, no god could love as we—
A forepaw stalking us from every cloud—
Who loved while sentenced to mortality.
    Never to be won by shields, love fell
Oh only to the wholly vulnerable.

III

What hubbub rocks the nest? What panic-freighted
Invasion—when he tried to sing—dilated
The big eyes of my blinking, hooting fowl?
A cartilaginous, most rheumatic squeak
Portends (half mocks) the change; the wrenched bones creak;
Unself descends, invoked or uninvited;
Self ousts itself, consumed and consummated;
An inward-facing mask is what must break.
The magic feverish fun of chirping, all
That professorial squints and squawks indicted,
Is here—descends, descends—till wisdom, hoarse
From bawling beauty out, at last adores,
Possessed by metamorphosis so strong.
Then, with a final flutter, philomel—

How mud-splashed, what a mangy miracle!—
Writhes out of owl and stands with drooping wing.
Just stands there. Moulted, naked, two-thirds dead.
From shock and pain (and dread of holy dread)
     Suddenly vomiting.
Look away quick; you are watching the birth of song.

SMALL PERFECT MANHATTAN

Unable to breathe, I inhaled the classic Aegean.
Losing my northern shadow, I sheared the noon
     Of an almond grove. The tears of marble
          Thanked me for laughter.

Shapes! And "Release, release" rustled the quarries;
"One touch will free the serenity locked in our stones."
     But archipelagos of olives
          Distracted me shorewards,

Where sails were ripening toward an African sleep.
This south wind was no friend of the wind of harps.
     Not destiny but destination
          Incited the grain-ships.

"Nevertheless be of cheer," said a jolly skipper;
"I sell sick goats that once were deft at flutes.
     The lizard who now is proconsul of Carthage
          Will bury you sweetly."

Then No to sweet Charon. Then home—then not to Sahara,
The elephants'-graveyard of classics—ascended the singing
     Green I wove just the size of the brow of
          Small perfect Manhattan.

Muriel Rukeyser

MURIEL RUKEYSER *was born in New York City in 1913, and was educated at Vassar, Columbia, and the Harvard Summer School. Miss Rukeyser is widely known as a campaigner for civil liberties, and as a newspaper editor. Her biography of Willard Gibbs won critical acclaim as a scholarly interpretation. At present Miss Rukeyser lives in San Francisco. Her published volumes of poetry are:* THEORY OF FLIGHT, U.S. I, A TURNING WIND, THE SOUL AND BODY OF JOHN BROWN, BEAST IN VIEW, THE GREEN WAVE, *and* ORPHEUS.

THE GENESIS OF *ORPHEUS*

THE LAWS of exchange of consciousness are only suspected. Einstein writes, "Now I believe that events in nature are controlled by a much stricter and more closely binding law than we recognize today, when we speak of one event being the *cause* of another. We are like a child who judges a poem by the rhyme and knows nothing of the rhythmic pattern. Or we are like a juvenile learner at the piano, *just* relating one note to that which immediately precedes or follows. To an extent this may be very well when one is dealing with very simple and primitive compositions; but it will not do for an interpretation of a Bach fugue."

I believe that one suggestion of such law is to be found in the process of poetry.

Essentials are here, as in mathematical or musical creation—we need no longer distinguish, for we are speaking of the process itself, except for our illustrations. Only the essential is true: Joseph Conrad, in a letter of advice, drives this home by recommending deletions, explaining that these words are "not essential and therefore not true to the fact."

The process has very much unconscious work in it. The conscious process varies: my own experience is that the work on a poem "surfaces" several times, with new submergence after each rising. The "idea" for the poem, which may come as an image thrown against memory, as a sound of words that sets off a travel-

ing of sound and meaning, as a curve of emotion (a form)
plotted by certain crises of events or image or sound, or as a
title which evokes a sense of inner relations; this is the first
"surfacing" of the poem. Then a period of stillness may follow.
The second surfacing may find the poem filled in, its voices dis-
tinct, its identity apparent, and another deep dive to its own
depth of sleep and waiting. A last surfacing may find you ready
to write. You may have jotted down a course of images, or a first
line, or a whole verse, by now. This last conscious period finds
you with all the work on yourself done—at least this is typical
of the way I write a fairly sustained poem—and ready for the
last step of all, the writing of the poem. Then the experience is
followed, you reach its conclusion with the last word of your
poem. One role is accomplished. At this point, you change into
the witness. You remember what you may, and much or little
critical work—re-writing—may be done.

I know most clearly the process of writing a recent, fairly
extended poem, *Orpheus.** The beginnings go far back, to child-
hood and a wish for identity, as rebirth, as co-ordination, as form.
My interests here are double: a desire for form, and perhaps a
stronger desire to understand the wish for form. The figure of
Orpheus stands for loss and triumph over loss, among other
things: the godhead of music and poetry, yes, in a mythology I
was always familiar with at a distance at which it could be better
dealt with than the mythology, say, of the Old Testament. In a
poem written when I was nineteen, after a long hospitalization
for typhoid fever contracted in an Alabama station-house during
the second Scottsboro trial—a poem called "In Hades, Orpheus,"
I focussed the poem on Eurydice, the ill woman who yearns back-
ward from the burning green of the world to the paleness and
rest—and death—of the hospital. Then the interest in Orpheus
himself took precedence: I was at the brilliant performance of
Gluck's *Orpheus* which Tchelitchew designed for the Metropoli-
tan Opera, and was moved by that play of loss and the dragging
loves and the music and thorny volcanic Hell; so moved and dis-
turbed that, years later, I wished to go on from there, not to re-
visit those scenes of Hell.

Orpheus, Centaur Press, San Francisco, 1949.

On Forty-Second Street, late one night, I saw the nightwalkers
go past the fifth-run movie houses, the Marine Bar, the Flea
Circus, not as whole people, but as a leg, part of a shoulder, an
eye askew. Pieces of people. This went into notes for a poem
that never was written. They say, "MARINE BAR, portraits of
an eye and the mouth, blue leg and half a face." This was eight
years before the poem was written. Then there was a period of
writing other poems and prose, of being away from New York and
returning, and then a time of great scattering, a year later, when
I wrote what became the beginning of "The Antagonists":

> Pieces of animals, pieces of all my friends
> prepare assassinations while I sleep. . . .

This was a poem that began with the tearing of the "I" and moved
on to a reconciliation in love and intensity. Near the phrases, in
my notebook, I wrote "bringing the dead back to life."

Four years later, reading Thomson and Geddes' *Life,* I be-
came interested again in morphology and specifically in the fact
that no part of the body lives or dies to itself. I read what I could
about the memory and lack of memory of fragments, of ampu-
tees, and of dislocated nerve centers. And at the same time I was
writing as part of another poem,

> Orpheus in hell remembered rivers
> and a music rose
> full of all human voices;
> All words you wish are in that living sound.
> And even torn to pieces
> one piece sang
>> Come all ye torn and wounded here
>> together
>> and one sang to its brother
>> remembering.

There, in Carmel, the course of the poem suddenly became clear.
It did not concern Eurydice—not directly—it was of a later time.
The murder of Orpheus began it; that early unsolved murder.
Why did the women kill him? Reinach has written a paper about
the murder. Was it because he loved Eurydice and would not

approach them? Was it because he was homosexual, and they were losing their lovers to him? Was it because he had seen their orgies without taking part? All these theories had been advanced. But my poem started a moment later. I had it now! *Pieces of Orpheus,* I wrote: that would be the title. The scene is the mountain top, just after the murder. The hacked pieces lie in their blood, the women are running down the slope, there is only the mountain, the moon, the river, the cloud. He was able to make all things sing. Now they begin: "the voice of the Cloud to the killers of Orpheus," I wrote. I knew what would follow. The pieces of the body would begin to talk, each according to its own nature, but they would be lost, they would be nothing, being no longer together. Like those in love, apart, I thought. No, not like anything. Like pieces of the body, knowing there had been pain, but not able to remember what pain—knowing they had loved, but not remembering whom. They know there must be some surpassing effort, some risk. The hand moves, finds the lyre, and throws it upward with a fierce gesture. The lyre flies upward in night, whistling through the black air to become the constellation; as it goes up, hard, the four strings sing *Eurydice.* And *then* the pieces begin to remember; they begin to come together; he turns into the god. He is music and poetry; he is Orpheus.

I was not able to write the poem. I went back to Chicago and to New York that winter, and, among a hundred crucial pressures, looked up some of the Orphic hymns in the New York Public Library. I wrote "The mountaintop, in silence, after the murder" and "lions and towers of the sky" and "The pieces of the body begin to remember" and "He has died the death of the god." Now there begin to be notes. This is the middle of winter, six years after the night on Forty-Second Street.

Again in California, in a year of intense physical crisis, threat, renewal, loss, and beginning. Now the notes begin to be very full. He did not look at Eurydice. He looked past her, at Hell. Now the wounds are the chorus: Touch me! Love me! Speak to me! This goes back to the yearning and self-pity of early love-poems, and a way must be found to end the self-pity.

Months later, the phrases begin to appear in fuller relationship. "The body as a circus, these freaks of Orpheus." Body Sonnets is one rejected notion. "Air-trees, nerve-trees, bloodmaze"; Pindar said of him "Father of Songs."

"Sing in me, days and voices," I write; and a form takes shape. I will solve a problem that has been moving toward solution. My longer poems, like the "Elegies" and "The Soul and Body of John Brown," contained songs. This poem will move toward its song: its own song and Orpheus' song. A poem that leads to a song! The pieces that come together, become a self, and sing.

Now I was ready to write. There were pages of notes and false starts, but there was no poem. There were whole lines, bits of drawing, telephone messages in the margin. Now something was ready; the poem began, and the first section was written.

It was slower to come to the second and third sections; as they were finished, the song too was ready; but now I turned into reader. The resurrection itself needed sharpening. These symbols must not be finished; the witness himself wants to finish. But this friend is right, the women must be part of his song, the god must include his murderers if murder is part of his life. And this correspondent is right, pain is not *forgotten*. All of this re-writing is conscious throughout, as distinct from the writing of the poem, in which suggestions, relations, images, phrases, sailed in from everywhere. For days of reminder and revery, everything became Orpheus. Until it was time to go back to the title. The working title was "Pieces of Orpheus." But that was for myself. No longer the pieces, but the rebirth, stands clear. The name alone should head the poem. So: two words are crossed out: it is ready.

EASTER EVE 1945

War of time O it seizes the soul tonight
I wait for the great morning of the west
confessing with every breath mortality.
Moon of this wild sky struggles to stay whole
and on the water silvers the ships of war.
I go alone in the black-yellow light
all night waiting for day, while everywhere the sure
death of light, the leaf's sure return to the root
is repeated in million, death of all man to share.
Whatever world I know shines ritual death,
wide under this moon they stand gathering fire,
fighting with flame, stand fighting in their graves.
All shining with life as the leaf, as the wing shines,
the stone deep in the mountain, the drop in the green wave.
Lit by their energies, secretly, all things shine.
Nothing can black that glow of life; although
                              each part go crumbling down
                              itself shall rise up whole.

Now I say there are new meanings; now I name
death our black honor and feast of possibility
to celebrate casting of life on life. This earth-long day
between blood and resurrection where we wait
remembering sun, seed, fire; remembering
that fierce Judaean Innocent who risked
every immortal meaning on one life.
Given to our year as sun and spirit are,
as seed we are blessed only in needing freedom.
Now I say that the peace the spirit needs is peace,
not lack of war, but fierce continual flame.
For all men: effort is freedom, effort's peace,
it fights. And along these truths the soul goes home,
                              flies in its blazing to a place
                              more safe and round than Paradise.

Night of the soul, our dreams in the arms of dreams
dissolving into eyes that look upon us.
Dreams the sources of action, the meeting and the end,
a resting-place among the flight of things.
And love which contains all human spirit, all wish,
the eyes and hands, sex, mouth, hair, the whole woman—
fierce peace I say at last, and the sense of the world.
In the time of conviction of mortality
whatever survive, I remember what I am.—
The nets of this night are on fire with sun and moon
pouring both lights into the open tomb.
Whatever arise, it comes in the shape of peace,
fierce peace which is love, in which moves all the stars,
and the breathing of universes, filling, falling away,
and death on earth cast into the human dream.
                    What fire survive forever
                    myself is for my time.

THE MOTIVE OF ALL OF IT

The motive of all of it was loneliness,
All the panic encounters and despair
Were bred in fear of the lost night, apart,
Outlined by pain, alone. Promiscuous
As mercy. Fear-led and led again to fear
At evening toward the cave where part fire, part
Pity lived in that voluptuousness
To end one and begin another loneliness.

This is the most intolerable motive: this
Must be given back to life again,
Made superhuman, made human, out of pain
Turned to the personal, the pure release:
The rings of Plato and Homer's golden chain
Or Lenin with his cry of Dare We Win.

EYES OF NIGHT-TIME

On the roads at night I saw the glitter of eyes:
my dark around me let shine one ray; that black
allowed their eyes: spangles in the cat's, air in the
    moth's eye shine,
mosaic of the fly, ruby-eyed beetle, the eyes that never weep,
the horned toad sitting and its tear of blood,
fighters and prisoners in the forest, people
aware in this almost total dark, with the difference,
the one broad fact of light.

Eyes on the road at night, sides of a road like rhyme;
the floor of the illumined shadow sea
and shallows with their assembling flash and show
of sight, root, holdfast, eyes of the brittle stars.
And your eyes in the shadowy red room,
scent of the forest entering, various time
calling and the light of wood along the ceiling
and over us birds calling and their circuit eyes.
And in our bodies the eyes of the dead and the living
giving us gifts at hand, the glitter of all their eyes.

THIS PLACE IN THE WAYS

Having come to this place
I set out once again
on the dark and marvelous way
from where I began:
belief in the love of the world,
woman, spirit, and man.

Having failed in all things
I enter a new age
seeing the old ways as toys,
the houses of a stage

painted and long forgot;
and I find love and rage.

Rage for the world as it is
but for what it may be
more love now than last year
and always less self-pity
since I know in a clearer light
the strength of the mystery.

And at this place in the ways
I wait for song.
My poem-hand still, on the paper,
all night long.
Poems in throat and hand, asleep,
and my storm beating strong!

AJANTA

I. THE JOURNEY

Came in my full youth to the midnight cave
Nerves ringing; and this thing I did alone.
Wanting my fulness and not a field of war,
For the world considered annihilation, a star
Called Wormwood rose and flickered, shattering
Bent light over the dead biling up in the ground,
The biting yellow of their corrupted lives
Streaming to war, denying all our words.
Nothing was left among the tainted weather
But world-walking and shadowless Ajanta.
Hallucination and the metal laugh
In clouds, and the mountain-spectre riding storm.
Nothing was certain but a moment of peace,
A hollow behind the unbreakable waterfall.
All the way to the cave, the teeming forms of death,
And death, the price of the body, cheap as air,

I blessed my heart on the expiation journey
For it had never been unable to suffer:
When I met the man whose face looked like the future,
When I met the whore with the dying red hair,
The child myself who is my murderer.
So came I between heaven and my grave
Past the serene smile of the *voyeur*, to
This cave where the myth enters the heart again.

II. THE CAVE

Space to the mind, the painted cave of dream.
This is not a womb, nothing but good emerges:
This is a stage, neither unreal nor real,
Where the walls are the world, the rocks and palaces
Stand on a borderland of blossoming ground.
If you stretch your hand, you touch the slope of the world
Reaching in interlaced gods, animals, and men.
There is no background. The figures hold their peace
In a web of movement. There is no frustration,
Every gesture is taken, everything yields connections.
The heavy sensual shoulders, the thighs, the blood-born flesh
And earth turning into color, rocks into their crystals,
Water to sound, fire to form; life flickers
Uncounted into the supple arms of love.
The space of these walls is the body's living space;
Tear open your ribs and breathe the color of time
Where nothing leads away, the world comes forward
In flaming sequences. Pillars and prisms. Riders
And horses and the figures of consciousness,
Red cow grows long, goes running through the world.
Flung into movement in carnal purity,
These bodies are sealed—warm lip and crystal hand
In a jungle of light. Color-sheeted, seductive
Foreboding eyelid lowered on the long eye,
Fluid and vulnerable. The spaces of the body
Are suddenly limitless, and riding flesh
Shapes constellations over the golden breast,

Confusion of scents and illuminated touch—
Monster touch, the throat printed with brightness,
Wide outlined gesture where the bodies ride.
Bells, and the spirit flashing. The religious bells,
Bronze under the sunlight like breasts ringing,
Bronze in the closed air, the memory of walls,
Great sensual shoulders in the web of time.

III. LES TENDRESSES BESTIALES

A procession of caresses alters the ancient sky
Until new constellations are the body shining:
There's the hand to steer by, there the horizon Breast,
And the Great Stars kindling the fluid hill.
All the rooms open into magical boxes,
Nothing is tilted, everything flickers
Sexual and exquisite.
The panther with its throat along my arm
Turns black and flows away.
Deep in all streets passes a faceless whore
And the checkered men are whispering one word.
The face I know becomes the night-black rose.
The sharp face is now an electric fan
And says one word to me.
The dice and the alcohol and the destruction
Have drunk themselves and cast.
Broken bottle of loss, and the glass
Turned bloody into the face.
Now the scene comes forward, very clear.
Dream-singing, airborne, surrenders the recalled,
The gesture arrives riding over the breast,
Singing, singing, tender atrocity,
The silver derelict wearing fur and claws.
O love, I stood under the apple branch,
I saw the whipped bay and the small dark islands,
And night sailing the river and the foghorn's word.
My life said to you: I want to love you well.

The wheel goes back and I shall live again,
But the wave turns, my birth arrives and spills
Over my breast the world bearing my grave,
And your eyes open in earth. You touched my life.
My life reaches the skin, moves under your smile,
And your throat and your shoulders and your face and your thighs
Flash.
     I am haunted by interrupted acts,
Introspective as a leper, enchanted
By a repulsive clew,
A gross and fugitive movement of the limbs.
Is this the love that shook the lights to flame?
Sheeted avenues thrash in the wind,
Torn sheets, the savage parks.
I am plunged deep. Must find the midnight cave.

IV. BLACK BLOOD

A habit leading to murder, smoky laughter
Hated at first, but necessary later.
Alteration of motives. To stamp in terror
Around the deserted harbor, down the hill
Until the woman laced into a harp
Screams and screams and the great clock strikes,
Swinging its giant figures past the face.
The Floating Man rides on the ragged sunset
Asking and asking. Do not say, Which loved?
Which was beloved? Only, Who most enjoyed?
Armored ghost of rage, screaming and powerless.
Only find me and touch my blood again.
Find me. A girl runs down the street
Singing Take me, yelling Take me Take
Hang me from the clapper of a bell
And you as hangman ring it sweet tonight,
For nothing clean in me is more than cloud
Unless you call it.—As I ran I heard
A black voice beating among all that blood:
"Try to live as if there were a God."

V. THE BROKEN WORLD

Came to Ajanta cave, the painted space of the breast,
The real world where everything is complete,
There are no shadows, the forms of incompleteness.
The great cloak blows in the light, rider and horse arrive,
The shoulders turn and every gift is made.
No shadows fall. There is no source of distortion.
In our world, a tree casts the shadow of a woman,
A man the shadow of a phallus, a hand raised
The shadow of the whip.
Here everything is itself,
Here all may stand
On summer earth.
Brightness has overtaken every light,
And every myth netted itself in flesh.
New origins, and peace given entire
And the spirit alive.
In the shadowless cave
The naked arm is raised.
Animals arrive,
Interlaced, and gods
Interlaced, and men
Flame-woven.
I stand and am complete.
Crawls from the door,
Black at my two feet
The shadow of the world.

World, not yet one,
Enters the heart again.
The naked world, and the old noise of tears,
The fear, the expiation and the love,
A world of the shadowed and alone.

The journey, and the struggles of the moon.

TENTH ELEGY. ELEGY IN JOY

Now green, now burning, I make a way for peace.
After the green and long beyond my lake,
among those fields of people, on these illuminated
hills, gold, burnt gold, spilled gold and shadowed blue,
the light of enormous flame, the flowing light of the sea,
where all the lights and nights are reconciled.
The sea at last, where all the waters lead.
And all the wars to this peace.

For the sea does not lie like the death you imagine;
this sea is the real sea, here it is.
This is the living. This peace is the face of the world,
a fierce angel who in one lifetime lives
fighting a lifetime, dying as we all die,
becoming forever, the continual god.

Years of our time, this heart! The binding of the alone,
bells of all loneliness, binding our lands and our music,
branches full of motion each opening its own flower,
lands of all song, each speaking in his own voice.
Praise in every grace
among the old same war.

Years of betrayal, million death breeding its weaknesses
and hope, buried more deep more black than dream.
Every elegy is the present: freedom eating our hearts,
death and explosion, and the world unbegun.
Now burning and unbegun, I sing earth with its war,
and God the future, and the wish of man.
Though you die, your war lives: the years fought it,
fusing a dead world straight.

The living will be giving you your meanings,
widening to love because of the love of man.
All the wounds crying
I feare, and hope: I burne, and frese like yse . . .
saying to the beloved

For your sake I love cities,
on your love I love the many,
saying to the people,
for your sake I love the world.
The old wounds crying
I find no peace, and all my warres are done.
     Out of our life the living eyes
     See peace in our own image made,
     Able to give only what we can give:
     Bearing two days like midnight. "Live,"
     The moment offers; the night requires
     Promise effort love and praise.

Now there are no maps and no magicians.
No prophets but the young prophet, the sense of the world.
The gift of our time, the world to be discovered.
All the continents giving off their several lights,
the one sea, and the air. And all things glow.

Move as this sea moves, as water, as force.
Peace shines from its life, its war can become
at any moment the fierce shining of peace,
and all the life-night long many voices are saying
The name of all things is Glowing.

A beginning, a moment of rest that imagines.
And again I go wandering far and alone,
I rise at night, I start up in the silence—
lovely and silver-black the night remembers.
In the cities of America I make my peace;
among the bombs and commands,
the sound that war makes
NO   NO
We see their weeping and their lifetime dreams.

All this, they say to us, because of you.
Much to begin. Now be your green, your burning,
bear also our joy, come to our meeting-place

and in the triumph of the reconceived
lie down at last together face to face.

We tell beginnings: for the flesh and answer,
for the look, the lake in the eye that knows,
for the despair that flows down in widest rivers,
cloud of home; and also the green tree of grace,
all in the leaf, in the love that gives us ourselves.

The word of nourishment passes through the women,
soldiers and orchards rooted in constellations,
white towers, eyes of children:
saying in time of war What shall we feed?
I cannot say the end.

Nourish beginnings, let us nourish beginnings.
Not all things are blest, but the
seeds of all things are blest.
The blessing is in the seed.

This moment, this seed, this wave of the sea, this look, this instant
        of love.
Years over wars and an imagining of peace. Or the expiation
        journey
toward peace which is many wishes flaming together,
fierce pure life, the many-living home.
Love that gives us ourselves, in the world known to all
new techniques for the healing of a wound,
and the unknown world. One life, or the faring stars.

SONG

The world is full of loss; bring, wind, my love,
   My home is where we make our meeting-place,
   And love whatever I shall touch and read
   Within that face.

Lift, wind, my exile from my eyes;
   Peace to look, life to listen and confess,
   Freedom to find to find to find
   That nakedness.

NIGHT FEEDING

Deeper than sleep but not so deep as death
I lay there dreaming and my magic head
Remembered and forgot. On first cry I
Remembered and forgot and did believe.
I knew love and I knew evil:
Woke to the burning song and the tree burning blind,
Despair of our days and the calm milk-giver who
Knows sleep, knows growth, the sex of fire and grass,
Renewal of all waters and the time of the stars
And the black snake with gold bones.

Black sleeps, gold burns; on second cry I woke
Fully and gave to feed and fed on feeding.
Gold seed, green pain, my wizards in the earth
Walked through the house, black in the morning dark
Shadows grew in my veins, my bright belief,
My head of dreams deeper than night and sleep.
Voices of all black animals crying to drink,
Cries of all birth arise, simple as we,
Found in the leaves, in clouds and dark, in dream,
Deep as this hour, ready again to sleep.

Theodore Roethke

THEODORE ROETHKE *was born in Saginaw, Michigan, in 1908. H* *was educated at the University of Michigan and Harvard, and has taught at Lafayette College, Penn State, and Bennington. He is at present Associate Professor of English at the University of Washington. He has published two volumes of poetry:* OPEN HOUSE, *and* THE LOST SON.

OPEN LETTER

Dear——,

YOU MUST realize that only a most high regard for you as a person induces me to say anything. For don't most statements or credos degenerate into elaborate defenses of one's own sort of thing: into the sales talk, the odious pimping for oneself? And how vulgar to be solemn about miseries and agitations which one has been permitted to escape by the act of creation itself! Furthermore, these particular poems—and I say this detachedly and humbly—are not, in any final sense, mine at all: they are a piece of luck (good or bad, as you choose to judge). For once, in other words, I am an instrument.

But I can hear you saying, That's all very well, old fellow. An instrument, yes. But remember: a conscious instrument. It's no good your trying to play the blubbering boy or implying that you're some kind of over-size aeolian harp upon which strange winds play uncouth tunes. Or, you may continue, changing the metaphor, let's say you fish, patiently, in that dark pond, the unconscious, or dive in, with or without pants on, to come up festooned with dead cats, weeds, tin cans, and other fascinating debris—I still insist that my little request for a few more clues isn't the same as asking you to say hello mom on the television. There need be no undue exposure; you won't have to pontificate. Remember: some noble spirits in the past—Blake, Yeats, Rilke, and others—have been willing to hold forth on their own work. . . .

You see, dear——, I know your attitude so well that I find my-

self being caught up in it! But believe me: you will have no
trouble if you approach these poems as a child would, naïvely, with
your whole being awake, your faculties loose and alert. (A large
order, I daresay!) *Listen* to them, for they are written to be heard,
with the themes often coming alternately, as in music, and usually
a partial resolution at the end. Each poem—there are now eight
in all and there probably will be at least one more—is complete
in itself; yet each in a sense is a stage in a kind of struggle out
of the slime; part of a slow spiritual progress; an effort to be
born, and later, to become something more. As an example, look
at the development of one of the earliest of these, "The Lost
Son":

It is the "easiest" of the longer ones, I think, because it
follows a narrative line indicated by the titles of the first four
sections: "The Flight," "The Pit," "The Gibber," "The Return."
"The Flight" is just what it says it is: a terrified running away—
with alternate periods of hallucinatory waiting (the voices, etc.);
the protagonist so geared-up, so over-alive that he is hunting, like
a primitive, for some animistic suggestion, some clue to existence
from the sub-human. These he sees and yet does not see: they are
almost tail-flicks, from another world, seen out of the corner of
the eye. In a sense he goes in and out of rationality; he hangs in
the balance between the human and the animal.

"The Pit" is a slowed-down section; a period of physical and
psychic exhaustion. And other obsessions begin to appear (sym-
bolized by mole, nest, fish). In "The Gibber" these obsessions
begin to take hold; again there is a frenetic activity, then a
lapsing back into almost a crooning serenity ("What a small
song," etc.). The line, "Hath the rain a father?" is from Job—
the only quotation in the piece. (A third of a line, notice—not a
third of a poem). The next rising agitation is rendered in terms
of balked sexual experience, with an accompanying "rant," al-
most in the manner of the Elizabethans, and a subsequent near-
blackout.

Section IV is a return, a return to a memory of childhood that
comes back almost as in a dream, after the agitation and exhaus-
tion of the earlier actions. The experience, again, is at once literal
and symbolical. The "roses" are still breathing in the dark; and

the fireman can pull them out, even from the fire. After the dark night, the morning brings with it the suggestion of a renewing light: a coming of "Papa." Buried in the text are many little ambiguities, not all of which are absolutely essential to the central meaning of the poem. For instance, the "pipe-knock." With the coming of steam, the pipes begin knocking violently, in a greenhouse. But "Papa," or the florist, as he approached, often would knock the pipe he was smoking on the sides of the benches, or on the pipes. Then, with the coming of steam and "papa"—the papa on earth and heaven are blended—there is the sense of motion in the greenhouse, my symbol for the whole of life, a womb, a heaven-on-earth.

In the final untitled section, the illumination, the coming of light suggested at the end of the last passage occurs again, this time to the nearly-grown man. But the illumination is still only partly apprehended; he is still "waiting." The beginning of the next poem, "The Long Alley," is a relapse into sinuous river-imagery: an ambivalent brooding by the edge of the city. And then a new phase begins swiftly.

This crude account tells very little about what actually happens in the poem; but at least you can see that the method is cyclic. I believe that to go forward as a spiritual man it is necessary first to go back. Any history of the psyche (or allegorical journey) is bound to be a succession of experiences, similar yet dissimilar. There is a perpetual slipping-back, then a going-forward; but there is *some* "progress." Are not some experiences so powerful and so profound (I am not speaking of the merely compulsive) that they repeat themselves, thrust themselves upon us, again and again, with variation and change, each time bringing us closer to our own most particular (and thus most universal) reality? We go, as Yeats said, from exhaustion to exhaustion. To begin from the depths and come out—that is difficult; for few know where the depths are or can recognize them; or, if they do, are afraid.

Some of these pieces, then, begin in the mire; as if man is no more than a shape writhing from the old rock. This may be due, in part, to the Michigan from which I come. Sometimes one gets the feeling that not even the animals have been there before; but the marsh, the mire, the Void, is always there, immediate and terrifying. It is a splendid place for schooling the spirit. It is America.

None the less, in spite of all the muck and welter, the dark, the *dreck* of these poems, I count myself among the happy poets. "I proclaim, once more, a condition of joy!" says the very last piece. All cats and agitations are not the same in the dark; likewise, each ecstasy has, I think, its special character. For instance in a later piece, "Praise to the End!" a particular (erotic) act occurs, then is accounted for by nonsense songs out of the past. There are laments for lost powers and then a euphoric passage, a sublimation of the original impulse in an ecstasy; but—and this is the point—in this passage the protagonist, for all his joy, is still "alone," and only one line mentions anything human:

"I've crawled from the mire, alert as a saint or a dog." Except for the saint, everything else is dog, fish, minnow, bird, etc., and the euphoric ride resolves itself into a death-wish. Equationally, the poem can be represented: onanism equals death, and even the early testament moralists can march out happily. (Is the protagonist "happy" in his death-wish? Is he a mindless euphoric jigger who goes blithering into oblivion? No. In terms of the whole sequence, he survives: this is a dead-end explored. His self-consciousness, his very will to live saves him from the *annihilation* of the ecstasy).

Each of these poems presented its own series of problems. The earliest piece of all (in terms of the age of the protagonist) is written entirely from the viewpoint of a very small child: all interior drama; no comment; no interpretation. To keep the rhythms, the language "right," i.e. consistent with what a child would say or at least to create the "as if" of the child's world, was very difficult technically. I don't believe anyone else has been foolish enough to attempt a tragedy in this particular way. The rhythms are very slow; there is no cutesy prattle; it is not a suite in goo-goo.

A word or two about habits of mind or technical effects peculiar to this sequence. ("Peculiar" is not used in the sense of odd, for they are traditional poems. Their ancestors: German and English folk literature, particularly Mother Goose; Elizabethan and Jacobean drama, especially the songs and rants; the Bible;

Blake and Traherne; Dürer.) Much of the action is implied or, particularly in the case of erotic experience, rendered obliquely. The revelation of the identity of the speaker may itself be a part of the drama; or, in some instances, in a dream sequence, his identity may merge with someone else's, or be deliberately blurred. This struggle for spiritual identity is, of course, one of the perpetual recurrences. (This is not the same as the fight of the adolescent personality for recognition in the "real" world). Disassociation often precedes a new state of clarity.

Rhythmically, it's the spring and rush of the child I'm after—and Gammer Gurton's concision: *mütterkin's* wisdom. Most of the time the material seems to demand a varied short line. I believe that, in this kind of poem, the poet, in order to be true to what is most universal in himself, should not rely on allusion; should not comment or employ many judgment words; should not meditate (or maunder). He must scorn being "mysterious" or loosely oracular, but be willing to face up to genuine mystery. His language must be compelling and immediate: he must create an actuality. He must be able to telescope image and symbol, if necessary, without relying on the obvious connectives: to speak in a kind of psychic shorthand when his protagonist is under great stress. He must be able to shift his rhythms rapidly, the "tension." He works intuitively, and the final form of his poem must be imaginatively right. If intensity has compressed the language so it seems, on early reading, obscure, this obscurity should break open suddenly for the serious reader who can hear the language: the "meaning" itself should come as a dramatic revelation, an excitement. The clues will be scattered richly—as life scatters them; the symbols will mean what they usually mean—and sometimes something more.

Perhaps I have made these remarks sound like strictures; if so, the phrase "in this kind of poem" should precede each one. I don't mean to imply that these poems fulfill such rigorous requirements or that their substance or their technique represents an answer to anything, a "direction." It is a dark world in which to work and the demands, other than technical, made upon the writer are savage. Even these words come painfully—and I doubt that they have much value. I remember a statement from Jung that turned up in a student's notebook. "The truth is that poets are human beings, and that what a poet has to say about his work is far from being the most illuminating word on the subject."

So, *kind*, throw all this away and read them aloud!

Love,

T.

The next phase? Something much longer: dramatic and *playable*. Pray for me.

THE LOST SON

1. THE FLIGHT

At Woodlawn I heard the dead cry:
I was lulled by the slamming of iron,
A slow drip over stones,
Toads brooding in wells.
All the leaves stuck out their tongues;
I shook the softening chalk of my bones,
Saying,
Snail, snail, glister me forward,
Bird, soft-sigh me home,
Worm, be with me.
This is my hard time.

Fished in an old wound,
The soft pond of repose;
Nothing nibbled my line,
Not even the minnows came.

Sat in an empty house
Watching shadows crawl,
Scratching.
There was one fly.

Voice, come out of the silence.
Say something.
Appear in the form of a spider
Or a moth beating the curtain.

Tell me:
Which is the way I take;
Out of what door do I go,
Where and to whom?

Dark hollows said, lee to the wind,
The moon said, back of an eel,
The salt said, look by the sea,

Your tears are not enough praise,
You will find no comfort here,
In the kingdom of bang and blab.

Running lightly over spongy ground,
Past the pasture of flat stones,
The three elms,
The sheep strewn on a field,
Over a rickety bridge
Toward the quick-water, wrinkling and rippling.

Hunting along the rivers,
Down among the rubbish, the bug-riddled foliage,
By the muddy pond-edge, by the bog-holes,
By the shrunken lake, hunting, in the heat of summer.

The shape of a rat?
        It's bigger than that.
        It's less than a leg
        And more than a nose,
        Just under the water
        It usually goes.

Is it soft like a mouse?
Can it wrinkle its nose?
Could it come in the house
On the tips of its toes?

        Take the skin of a cat
        And the back of an eel,
        Then roll them in grease,—
        That's the way it would feel.

        It's sleek as an otter
        With wide webby toes
        Just under the water
        It usually goes.

2. THE PIT

Where do the roots go?
    Look down under the leaves.
Who put the moss there?
    These stones have been here too long.
Who stunned the dirt into noise?
    Ask the mole, he knows.
I feel the slime of a wet nest.
    Beware Mother Mildew.
Nibble again, fish nerves.

3. THE GIBBER

At the wind's mouth,
By the cave's door,
I listened to something
I had heard before.

Dogs of the groin
Barked and howled
The sun was against me
The moon would not have me.

The weeds whined,
The snakes cried,
The cows and briars
Said to me: Die.

What a small song. What slow clouds. What dark water.
Hath the raine a father? All the caves are ice. Only the snow's here.
I'm cold. I'm cold all over. Rub me in father and mother.
Fear was my father, Father Fear.
His look drained the stones.

    What gliding shape
    Beckoning through halls,
    Stood poised on the stair,
    Fell dreamily down?

From the mouths of jugs
Perched on many shelves,
I saw substance flowing
That cold morning.

Like a slither of eels
That watery cheek
As my own tongue kissed
My lips awake.

Is this the storm's heart? The ground is unstilling itself.
My veins are running nowhere. Do the bones cast out their fire?
Is the seed leaving the old bed? These buds are live as birds.
Where, where are the tears of the world?
Let the kisses resound, flat like a butcher's palm;
Let the gestures freeze; our doom is already decided.
All the windows are burning! What's left of my life?
I want the old rage, the lash of primordial milk!
Goodbye, goodbye, old stones, the time-order is going.
I have married my hands to perpetual agitation,
I run, I run to the whistle of money.

Money money money
Water water water

How cool the grass is.
Has the bird left?
The stalk still sways.
Has the worm a shadow?
What do the clouds say?

These sweeps of light undo me.
Look, look, the ditch is running white!
I've more veins than a tree!
Kiss me, ashes, I'm falling through a dark swirl.

4. THE RETURN

The way to the boiler was dark,
Dark all the way,
Over slippery cinders
Through the long greenhouse.

The roses kept breathing in the dark.
They had many mouths to breathe with.
My knees made little winds underneath
Where the weeds slept.

There was always a single light
Swinging by the fire-pit,
Where the fireman pulled out roses,
The big roses, the big bloody clinkers.

Once I stayed all night.
The light in the morning came slowly over the white
Snow.
There were many kinds of cool
Air.
Then came steam.

Pipe-knock.

Scurry of warm over small plants.
Ordnung! Ordnung!
Papa is coming!

A fine haze moved off the leaves;
Frost melted on far panes;
The rose, the chrysanthemum turned toward the light.
Even the hushed forms, the bent yellowy weeds
Moved in a slow up-sway.

5

It was beginning winter,
An in-between time,
The landscape still partly brown:

The bones of weeds kept swinging in the wind,
Above the blue snow.

It was beginning winter
The light moved slowly over the frozen field,
Over the dry seed-crowns,
The beautiful surviving bones
Swinging in the wind.

Light traveled over the wide field;
Stayed.
The weeds stopped swinging.
The mind moved, not alone,
Through the clear air, in the silence.

    Was it light?
    Was it light within?
    Was it light within light?
    Stillness becoming alive,
    Yet still?

A lively understandable spirit
Once entertained you.
It will come again.
Be still.
Wait.

THE SHAPE OF THE FIRE

1

What's this? A dish for fat lips.
Who says? A nameless stranger.
Is he a bird or a tree? Not everyone can tell.

Water recedes to the crying of spiders.
An old scow bumps over black rocks.
A cracked pod calls.

Mother me out of here. What more will the bones allow?
Will the sea give the wind suck? A toad folds into a stone.
These flowers are all fangs. Comfort me, fury.
Wake me, witch, we'll do the dance of rotten sticks.

Shale loosens. Marl reached into the field. Small birds pass over
    water.
Spirit, come near. This is only the edge of whiteness.
I can't laugh at a procession of dogs.

    In the hour of ripeness the tree is barren,
    The she-bear mopes under the hill.
    Mother, mother, stir from your cave of sorrow.

A low mouth laps water. Weeds, weeds, how I love you.
The arbor is cooler. Farewell, farewell, fond worm.
The warm comes without sound.

2

Where's the eye?
The eye's in the sty
The car's not here
Beneath the hair.
When I took off my clothes
To find a nose,
There was only one shoe
For the waltz of To,
The pinch of Where.

Time for the flat-headed man. I recognize that listener,
Him with the platitudes and rubbery doughnuts,
Melting at the knees, a varicose horror.
Hello, hello. My nerves knew you, dear boy.
Have you come to unhinge my shadow?
Last night I slept in the pits of a tongue.
The silver fish ran in and out of my special bindings;
I grew tired of the ritual of names and the assistant keeper of
    the molluscs:

Up over a viaduct I came, to the snakes and sticks of another
          winter,
A two-legged dog hunting a new horizon of howls.
The wind sharpened itself on a rock;
A voice sang:

> Pleasure on ground
> Has no sound,
> Easily maddens
> The uneasy man.
>
> Who, careless, slips
> In coiling coze
> Is trapped to the lips,
> Leaves more than shoes;
>
> Must pull off clothes
> To jerk like a frog
> On belly and nose
> From the sucking bog.

My meat eats me. Who waits at the gate?
Mother of quartz, your words writhe into my ear.
Renew the light, lewd whisper.

3

The wasp waits.
          The edge cannot eat the centre.
The grape glistens.
          The path tells little to the serpent.
An eye comes out of the wave.
          The journey from flesh is longest.
A rose sways least.
          The redeemer comes a dark way.

4

Morning-fair, follow me further back
Into that minnowy world of weeds and ditches,
When the herons floated high over tne white houses,
And the little crabs slipped into silvery craters,
When the sun for me glinted the sides of a sand grain
And my intent stretched over the buds at their first trembling.

That air and shine: and the flicker's loud summer call:
The bearded boards in the stream and the all of apples;
The glad hen on the hill; and the trellis humming.
Death was not. I lived in a simple drowse:
Hands and hair moved through a dream of wakening blossoms.
Rain sweetened the cave and the dove still called;
The flowers leaned on themselves, the flowers in hollows;
And love, love sang toward.

5

To have the whole air!—
The light, the full sun
Coming down on the flowerheads,
The tendrils turning slowly,
A slow snail-lifting, liquescent;
To be by the rose
Rising slowly out of its bed,
Still as a child in its first loneliness;
To see cyclamen veins become clearer in early sunlight
And mist lifting, drifting out of the brown cat-tails;
To stare into the after-light, the glitter left on the lake's surface
When the sun has fallen behind a wooded island;
To follow the drops sliding from a lifted oar,
Held up, while the rower breathes, and the small boat drifts quiet-
        ly shoreward;
To know that light falls and fills, often without our knowing,
As an opaque vase fills to the brim from a quick pouring,
Fills and trembles at the edge yet does not flow over,
Still holding and feeding the stem of the contained flower.

CHILD ON TOP OF A GREENHOUSE

The wind billowing out the seat of my britches,
My feet crackling splinters of glass and dried putty,
The half-grown chrysanthemums staring up like accusers,
Up through the streaked glass, flashing with sunlight,
A few white clouds all rushing eastward,
A line of elms plunging and tossing like horses,
And everyone, everyone, pointing up and shouting!

VERNAL SENTIMENT

Though the crocuses poke up their heads in the usual places,
The frog scum appear on the pond with the same froth of green,
And boys moon at girls with last year's fatuous faces,
I never am bored, however familiar the scene.

When from under the barn the cat brings a similar litter—
Two yellow and black, and one that looks in between—
Though it all happened before, I cannot grow bitter:
I rejoice in the spring, as though no spring had been.

ACADEMIC

The stethoscope tells what everyone fears:
You're likely to go on living for years,
With a nurse-maid waddle and shop-girl simper,
And the style of your prose growing limper and limper.

MY PAPA'S WALTZ

The whiskey on your breath
Could make a small boy dizzy;
But I hung on like death:
Such waltzing was not easy.

We romped until the pans
Slid from the kitchen shelf;
My mother's countenance
Could not unfrown itself.

The hand that held my wrist
Was battered on one knuckle;
At every step you missed
My right ear scraped a buckle.

You beat time on my head
With a palm caked hard by dirt,
Then waltzed me off to bed
Still clinging to your shirt.

THE HERON

The heron stands in water where the swamp
Has deepened to the blackness of a pool,
Or balances with one leg on a hump
Of marsh grass heaped above a muskrat hole.

He walks the shallow with an antic grace.
The great feet break the ridges of the sand,
The long eye notes the minnow's hiding place.
His beak is quicker than a human hand.

He jerks a frog across his bony lip.
Then points his heavy bill above the wood.
The wide wings flap but once to lift him up.
A single ripple starts from where he stood.

INTERLUDE

The element of air was out of hand.
The rush of wind ripped off the tender leaves
And flung them in confusion on the land.
We waited for the first rain in the eaves.

The chaos grew as hour by hour the light
Decreased beneath an undivided sky.
Our pupils widened with unnatural night,
But still the road and dusty field kept dry.

The rain stayed in its cloud; full dark came near:
The wind lay motionless in the long grass.
The veins within our hands betrayed our fear.
What we had hoped for had not come to pass.

Karl Shapiro

KARL SHAPIRO *was born in Baltimore in* 1913 *and attended the University of Virginia, Johns Hopkins, and the Enoch Pratt Library School. He is at present Associate Professor of English at Johns Hopkins and a member of the American Academy of Arts and Letters. His volumes of poetry are:* POEMS (*privately printed in* 1935), PERSON PLACE AND THING, V-LETTER (*Pulitzer Prize* 1944), ESSAY ON RIME, *and* TRIAL OF A POET. *He was one of the authors of* POETS AT WORK, *a critical study sponsored by the Lockwood Memorial Library of the University of Buffalo. While serving as Consultant in Poetry to the Library of Congress, he prepared a bibliography of works on prosody.*

THE CASE HISTORY OF *THE MINUTE*

EDITOR'S ·NOTE: Enumerated below are the successive drafts of "The Minute" as Mr. Shapiro rescued them from the writing process. The final poem is reprinted at the end. It is significant that Mr. Shapiro has rejected all prose commentary on the process on the grounds that the commentary would probably result in rationalization. Without commentary then, this is what came onto the page from its source in the poet's mind, this is what he rejected, what he altered, and what he kept. The writing principles of the poem must be implicit in that process, and by observing the process itself, the reader will be able to trace the principles with a minimum of distortion. The drafts are numbered in order, stanza by stanza.

THE MINUTE

FIRST STANZA

1

Round little timekeeps set with crystal eye.
The crooked rays of tricky sidereal day.

Sometimes it gave forth music or a wooden bird leaped from a
         lock. Sometimes it was a dancing ship.
Each watch has its exploding point, each tick stabs at an angel.
A chime is a false note struck by a mistake.
Our real timekeeper is the stars.
Sundial and hour glass lose us in shadow
We drink and love to lose time
Under the fatherly dome of the universe and the town
Beside the golden and maternal dial

2

So say the watchmen: time is a tremulous egg
Laid in the city at midnight under the dome
Of zero, and beside the golden maternal dial.

3

So say the watchmen. Time is a tremulous (or perilous or delicate)
         egg
Laid (or hatched) in the city at midnight under the dome
Beside the golden dial
On a million bureaus of the home
Under the dome, beside the golden dial.

4

What shall we say of time, the tremulous egg
Laid in the city at midnight, under the dome
Of sidereal dark, beside the golden dial,
The man's face with the maternal smile.
The earliest minute protrudes a leg
Upon a million bureaus of the home.
O time, O tremulous egg
Hatched in the town at midnight, under the dome
Of sidereal dark, beneath the golden dial.

5

At zero of sidereal night
Now while the towers pace the sidereal corridors

Pace the gloomy corridors of night
Pace in the corridors of sidereal dark.

6

So say the watchmen. Time is a tremulous egg
Laid in the city at midnight under the dome
Of sidereal dark, beside the golden dial.
The town creaks into a maternal smile
As time puts forth a whir, a hair-like leg
On all the million bureau-tops of town.

7

When the office building paces
The gloomy sidereal halls of night
The suffering clock with golden dial
Births

8

The office building paces the corridors of cloud
While all the clocks with wide and golden dials
Suffer and glow.
The office buildings pace the marble aisles

9

While the chief clock with dark and golden dial
Suffers and glows
Now through the marble halls of night

10

The office buildings pace the marble dark
While all the clocks with dark and golden dials
Suffer and glow

11

The office building paces the marble dark

Final draft of stanza one.

12

The office building treads the marble dark,
The mother clock with wide and golden dial
Suffers and glows. Now is the hour of birth
Of the tremulous egg. Now is the time of correction.
O midnight, zero of eternity,
Soon on a million bureaus of the city
Will lie the new born minute.

STANZAS TWO, THREE, AND FOUR

1

Then far off in the distant bed I turn
Titanically, expelling from my lungs
The bitter gas of life
Meanwhile all about the atmosphere
Range the clean angels, stabbed by the ticking
Somewhere in ether, somewhere in atmosphere.
Clean angels ranging round the atmosphere
Are studying that noise like a strange dirt
But will not pick it up
Nor carry it gingerly out of harm's way
Thousands had gathered at a jewel to hear
The crude beat, yet admiring the balance
While the loathsome minute grows in length and strength.

2

The new born minute on the bureau lies
Scratching the glass with happy kick, cutting (etching)
With diamond foot, with diamond cry the crystal gaze
With evil frost of timelessness, etching with evil frost.

Final draft of stanzas two, three, and four.

3

The new born minute on the bureau lies,
Scratching the glass with infant kick, cutting

With diamond cry the crystal and expanse
Of timelessness. This pretty trick of death
Etches its name upon the air. I turn
Titanically in distant sleep, expelling
From my lungs the bitter gas of life.

The loathsome minute grows in length and strength,
Bending its spring to forge an iron hour
That rusts from link to link, the last one bright,
The late one dead. Between the shining works
Range the clean angels studying the tick
Like a strange dirt, but will not pick it up.
Nor move it gingerly out of harm's way.

An angel is stabbed and is carried aloft howling,
For devils have gathered on a ruby jewel
Like red mites on a berry; others arrive
To tend the points with oil and smooth the heat.
See how the vicious faces, lit with sweat,
Worship the train of wheels; see how they pull
The tape-worm Time from nothing into thing.

STANZA FIVE

1

I with my hot heart lie awake, away,
Smiling at that Swiss perfect engine room
Driven by tiny evils. The crashing gong of clocks
The crashing gongs of mammoth clocks in towers
Even of metal hands the size of masts
And gongs that crash around in towers
And hands as high as iron masts. I sleep
While the departing angels in one covey
Rise and sweep past my ear with frightening farewells
Sweep
Shrill
Which at a sign the angels in a flock
Sweep past my hearing with melodious fear

At which sad sign the angels in a flock
Rise and sweep past me with melodious fear.

Final draft of stanza five.

2

I with my distant heart lie wide awake
Smiling at that Swiss-perfect engine room
Driven by tiny evils. Knowing no harm
Even of gongs that loom and move in towers,
And hands as high as iron masts, I sleep,
At which sad sign the angels in a flock
Rise and sweep past me, querulous with fear.

FINAL FORM

(NOTE: With a few final changes and a variation in the last line, the poem
appeared in "The Nation" in the following form. When the poem appears in
book form, however, Mr. Shapiro intends to change the last phrase from
"spinning threads of fear" back to "querulous with fear.")

THE MINUTE

The office building treads the marble dark,
The mother-clock with wide and golden dial
Suffers and glows. Now is the hour of birth
Of the tremulous egg. Now is the time of correction.
O midnight, zero of eternity,
Soon on a million bureaus of the city
Will lie the new-born minute.

The new born minute on the bureau lies,
Scratching the glass with infant kick, cutting
With diamond cry the crystal and expanse
Of timelessness. This pretty trick of death
Etches its name upon the air. I turn
Titanically in distant sleep, expelling
From my lungs the bitter gas of life.

The loathsome minute grows in length and strength,
Bending its spring to forge an iron hour
That rusts from link to link, the last one bright,
The late one dead. Between the shining works
Range the clean angels, studying that tick
Like a strange dirt, but will not pick it up.
Nor move it gingerly out of harm's way.

An angel is stabbed and is carried aloft howling,
For devils have gathered on a ruby jewel
Like red mites on a berry; others arrive
To tend the points with oil and smooth the heat.
See how their vicious faces, lit with sweat,
Worship the train of wheels; see how they pull
The tape-worm Time from nothing into thing.

I with my distant heart lie wide awake
Smiling at that Swiss-perfect engine room
Driven by tiny evils. Knowing no harm
Even of gongs that loom and move in towers,
And hands as high as iron masts, I sleep,
At which sad sign the angels in a flock
Rise and sweep past me, spinning threads of fear.

HOMECOMING

Lost in the vastness of the void Pacific
My thousand days of exile, pain,
Bid me farewell. Gone is the Southern Cross
To her own sky, fallen a continent
Under the wave, dissolved the bitterest isles
In their salt element,
And here upon the deck the mist encloses
My smile that would light up all darkness
And ask forgiveness of the things that thrust
Shame and all death on millions and on me.

We bring no raw materials from the East
But green-skinned men in blue-lit holds
And lunatics impounded between-decks;
The mighty ghoul-ship that we ride exhales
The sickly-sweet stench of humiliation,
And even the majority, untouched by steel
Or psychoneurosis, stare with eyes in rut,
Their hands a rabble to snatch the riches
Of glittering shops and girls.

Because I am angry at this kindness which
Is both habitual and contradictory
To the life of armies, now I stand alone
And hate the swarms of khaki men that crawl
Like lice upon the wrinkled hide of earth,
Infesting ships as well. Not otherwise
Could I lean outward piercing fog to find
Our sacred bridge of exile and return.
My tears are psychological, not poems
To the United States; my smile is prayer.

Gnawing the thin slops of anxiety,
Escorted by the ground swell and by gulls,
In silence and with mystery we enter
The territorial waters. Not till then

Does that convulsive terrible joy, more sudden
And brilliant than the explosion of a ship,
Shatter the tensions of the heaven and sea
To crash a hundred thousand skulls
And liberate in that high burst of love
The imprisoned souls of soldiers and of me.

ELEGY FOR A DEAD SOLDIER

I

A white sheet on the tail-gate of a truck
Becomes an altar; two small candlesticks
Sputter at each side of the crucifix
Laid round with flowers brighter than the blood,
Red as the red of our apocalypse,
Hibiscus that a marching man will pluck
To stick into his rifle or his hat,
And great blue morning-glories pale as lips
That shall no longer taste or kiss or swear.
The wind begins a low magnificat,
The chaplain chats, the palmtrees swirl their hair
The columns come together through the mud.

II

We too are ashes as we watch and hear
The psalm, the sorrow, and the simple praise
Of one whose promised thoughts of other days
Were such as ours, but now wholly destroyed,
The service record of his youth wiped out,
His dream dispersed by shot, must disappear.
What can we feel but wonder at a loss
That seems to point at nothing but the doubt
Which flirts our sense of luck into the ditch?
Reader of Paul who prays beside this fosse,
Shall we believe our eyes or legends rich
With glory and rebirth beyond the void?

III

For this comrade is dead, dead in the war,
A young man out of millions yet to live,
One cut away from all that war can give,
Freedom of self and peace to wander free.
Who mourns in all this sober multitude
Who did not feel the bite of it before
The bullet found its aim? This worthy flesh,
This boy laid in a coffin and reviewed —
Who has not wrapped himself in this same flag,
Heard the light fall of dirt, his wound still fresh,
Felt his eyes closed, and heard the distant brag
Of the last volley of humanity?

IV

By chance I saw him die, stretched on the ground,
A tattooed arm lifted to take the blood
Of someone else sealed in a tin. I stood
During the last delirium that stays
The intelligence a tiny moment more,
And then the strangulation, the last sound.
The end was sudden, like a foolish play,
A stupid fool slamming a foolish door,
The absurd catastrophe, half-prearranged,
And all the decisive things still left to say.
So we disbanded, angrier and unchanged,
Sick with the utter silence of dispraise.

V

We ask for no statistics of the killed,
For nothing political impinges on
This single casualty, or all those gone,
Missing or healing, sinking or dispersed,
Hundreds of thousands counted, millions lost.
More than an accident and less than willed
Is every fall, and this one like the rest.
However others calculate the cost,

To us the final aggregate is *one*,
One with a name, one transferred to the blest;
And though another stoops and takes the gun,
We cannot add the second to the first.

VI

I would not speak for him who could not speak
Unless my fear were true: he was not wronged,
He knew to which decision he belonged
But let it choose itself. Ripe in instinct,
Neither the victim nor the volunteer,
He followed, and the leaders could not seek
Beyond the followers. Much of this he knew;
The journey was a detour that would steer
Into the Lincoln Highway of a land
Remorselessly improved, excited, new,
And that was what he wanted. He had planned
To earn and drive. He and the world had winked.

VII

No history deceived him, for he knew
Little of times and armies not his own;
He never felt that peace was but a loan,
Had never questioned the idea of gain.
Beyond the headlines once or twice he saw
The gathering of a power by the few
But could not tell their names; he cast his vote,
Distrusting all the elected but not the law.
He laughed at socialism; *on mourrait
Pour les industriels?* He shed his coat
And not for brotherhood, but for his pay.
To him the red flag marked the sewer main.

VIII

Above all else he loathed the homily,
The slogan and the ad. He paid his bill
But not for Congressmen at Bunker Hill.

Ideals were few and those there were not made
For conversation. He belonged to church
But never spoke of God. The Christmas tree,
The Easter egg, baptism, he observed,
Never denied the preacher on his perch,
And would not sign Resolved That or Whereas.
Softness he had and hours and nights reserved
For thinking, dressing, dancing to the jazz.
His laugh was real, his manners were home made.

IX

Of all men poverty pursued him least;
He was ashamed of all the down and out,
Spurned the panhandler like an uneasy doubt,
And saw the unemployed as a vague mass
Incapable of hunger or revolt.
He hated other races, south or east,
And shoved them to the margin of his mind.
He could recall the justice of the Colt,
Take interest in a gang-war like a game.
His ancestry was somewhere far behind
And left him only his peculiar name.
Doors opened, and he recognized no class.

X

His children would have known a heritage,
Just or unjust, the richest in the world,
The quantum of all art and science curled
In the horn of plenty, bursting from the horn,
A people bathed in honey, Paris come,
Vienna transferred with the highest wage,
A World's Fair spread to Phoenix, Jacksonville,
Earth's capitol, the new Byzantium,
Kingdom of man — who knows? Hollow or firm,
No man can ever prophesy until
Out of our death some undiscovered germ,
Whole toleration or pure peace is born.

XI

The time to mourn is short that best becomes
The military dead. We lift and fold the flag,
Lay bare the coffin with its written tag,
And march away. Behind, four others wait
To lift the box, the heaviest of loads.
The anesthetic afternoon benumbs,
Sickens our senses, forces back our talk.
We know that others on tomorrow's roads
Will fall, ourselves perhaps, the man beside,
Over the world the threatened, all who walk:
And could we mark the grave of him who died
We would write this beneath his name and date:

EPITAPH

Underneath this wooden cross there lies
A Christian killed in battle. You who read,
Remember that this stranger died in pain;
And passing here, if you can lift your eyes
Upon a peace kept by a human creed,
Know that one soldier has not died in vain.

V—LETTER

I love you first because your face is fair,
    Because your eyes Jewish and blue,
Set sweetly with the touch of foreignness
Above the cheekbones, stare rather than dream.
Often your countenance recalls a boy
    Blue-eyed and small, whose silent mischief
Tortured his parents and compelled my hate
    To wish his ugly death.
Because of this reminder, my soul's trouble,
And for your face, so often beautiful,
    I love you, wish you life.

I love you first because you wait, because
        For your own sake, I cannot write
Beyond these words. I love you for these words
That sting and creep like insects and leave filth.
I love you for the poverty you cry
        And I bend down with tears of steel
That melt your hand like wax, not for this war
        The droplets shattering
Those candle-glowing fingers of my joy,
But for your name of agony, my love,
        That cakes my mouth with salt.

And all your imperfections and perfections
        And all your magnitude of grace
And all this love explained and unexplained
Is just a breath. I see you woman-size
And this looms larger and more goddess-like
        Than silver goddesses on screens.
I see you in the ugliness of light,
        Yet you are beautiful,
And in the dark of absence your full length
Is such as meets my body to the full
        Though I am starved and huge.

You turn me from these days as from a scene
        Out of an open window far
Where lies the foreign city and the war.
You are my home and in your spacious love
I dream to march as under flaring flags
        Until the door is gently shut.
Give me the tearless lesson of your pride,
        Teach me to live and die
As one deserving anonymity,
The mere devotion of a house to keep
        A woman and a man.

Give me the free and poor inheritance,
        Of our own kind, not furniture

Of education, nor the prophet's pose,
The general cause of words, the hero's stance,
The ambitions incommensurable with flesh,
     But the drab makings of a room
Where sometimes in the afternoon of thought
     The brief and blinding flash
May light the enormous chambers of your will
And show the gracious Parthenon that time
     Is ever measured by.

As groceries in a pantry gleam and smile
     Because they are important weights
Bought with the metal minutes of your pay,
So do these hours stand in solid rows,
The dowry for a use in common life.
     I love you first because your years
Lead to my matter-of-fact and simple death
     Or to our open marriage,
And I pray nothing for my safety back,
Not even luck, because our love is whole
     Whether I live or fail.

THE DIRTY WORD

The dirty word hops in the cage of the mind like the Pondicherry vulture, stomping with its heavy left claw on the sweet meat of the brain and tearing it with its vicious beak, ripping and chopping the flesh. Terrified, the small boy bears the big bird of the dirty word into the house, and grunting, puffing, carries it up the stairs to his own room in the skull. Bits of black feather cling to his clothes and his hair as he locks the staring creature in the dark closet.

All day the small boy returns to the closet to examine and feed the bird, to caress and kick the bird, that now snaps and flaps its wings savagely whenever the door is opened. How the boy trembles and delights at the sight of the white excrement of the bird! How

385·25

the bird leaps and rushes against the walls of the skull, trying to escape from the zoo of the vocabulary! How wildly snaps the sweet meat of the brain in its rage.

And the bird outlives the man, being freed at the man's death-funeral by a word from the rabbi.

(But I one morning went upstairs and opened the door and entered the closet and found in the cage of my mind the great bird dead. Softly I wept it and softly removed it and softly buried the body of the bird in the hollyhock garden of the house I lived in twenty years before. And out of the worn black feathers of the wing have I made these pens to write these elegies, for I have outlived the bird, and I have murdered it in my early manhood.)

BUICK

As a sloop with a sweep of immaculate wing on her delicate spine
And a keel as steel as a root that holds in the sea as she leans,
Leaning and laughing, my warm-hearted beauty, you ride, you ride,
You tack on the curves with parabola speed and a kiss of goodbye,
Like a thoroughbred sloop, my new high-spirited spirit, my kiss.

As my foot suggests that you leap in the air with your hips of a
        girl,
My finger that praises your wheel and announces your voices of
        song,
Flouncing your skirts, you blueness of joy, you flirt of politeness,
You leap, you intelligence, essence of wheelness with silvery nose,
And your platinum clocks of excitement stir like the hairs of a fern.

But now with your eyes that enter the future of roads you forget;
        the smoke
Where you turned on the stinging lathes of Detroit and Lansing at
        night
And shrieked at the torch in your secret parts and the amorous
        tests,
But now with your eyes that enter the future of roads you forget;

You are all instinct with your phosphorous glow and your streak-
     ing hair.

And now when we stop it is not as the bird from the shell that I
     leave
Of the leathery pilot who steps from his bird with a sneer of de-
     light,
And not as the ignorant beast do you squat and watch me depart,
But with exquisite breathing you smile, with satisfaction of love,
And I touch you again as you tick in the silence and settle in sleep.

THE TWINS

(*March* 21, 1942. *At sea*)
Likeness has made them animal and shy.
See how they turn their full gaze left and right,
Seeking the other, yet not moving close;
Nothing in their relationship is gross,
But soft, conspicuous, like giraffes. And why
Do they not speak except by sudden sight?

Sisters kiss freely and unsubtle friends
Wrestle like lovers; brothers loudly laugh;
These in a dreamier bondage dare not touch.
Each is the other's soul and hears too much
The heartbeat of the other; each apprehends
The sad duality and the imperfect half.

The one lay sick, the other wandered free,
But like a child to a small plot confined
Walked a short way and dumbly reappeared.
Is it not all-in-all of what they feared,
The single death, the obvious destiny
That maims the miracle their will designed?

For they go emptily from face to face,
Keeping the instinctive partnership of birth

A ponderous marriage and a sacred name;
Theirs is the pride of shouldering each the same
The old indignity of Esau's race
And Dromio's denouement of tragic mirth.

FULL MOON: NEW GUINEA

These nights we fear the aspects of the moon,
Sleep lightly in the radiance falling clear
On palms and ferns and hills and us; for soon
The small burr of the bombers in our ear
Tickles our rest; we rise as from a nap
And take our helmets absently and meet,
Prepared for any spectacle or mishap,
At trenches fresh and narrow at our feet.

Look up, look up, and wait and breathe. These nights
We fear Orion and the Cross. The crowd
Of deadly insects caught in our long lights
Glitter and seek to burrow in a cloud
Soft-mined with high explosive. Breathe and wait,
The bombs are falling darkly for our fate.

WASHINGTON CATHEDRAL

From summer and the wheel-shaped city
That sweats like a swamp and wrangles on
Its melting streets, white mammoth Forums,
And political hotels with awnings, caryatids;
Past barricaded embassies with trees
That shed trash and parch his eyes,
To here, the acres of superior quiet,
Shadow and damp, the tourist comes,
And, cooled by stones and darkness, stares.

Tall as a lover's night, the nave
Broods over him, irradiates,
And stars of color out of painted glass
Shoot downward on apostles and on chairs
Huddled by hundred under altar rails.
Yet it is only Thursday; there are no prayers,

But exclamations. The lady invokes by name
The thousand-odd small sculptures, spooks,
New angels, pitted roods; she gives
The inventory of relics to his heart
That aches with history and astonishment:
He gives a large coin to a wooden coffer.

Outside, noon blazes in his face like guns.
He goes down by the Bishop's walk, the dial,
The expensive grass, the Byzantine bench,
While stark behind him a red naked crane
Hangs over the unfinished transept,
A Cubist hen rivalling the Gothic School.

Whether he sees the joke; whether he cares;
Whether he tempts a vulgar miracle,
Some deus ex machina, this is his choice,
A shrine of whispers and tricky penumbras.
Therefore he votes again for the paid
Clergy, the English hint, the bones of Wilson
Crushed under tons of fake magnificence.
Nor from the zoo of his instincts
Come better than crude eagles: now
He cannot doubt that violent obelisk
And Lincoln whittled to a fool's colossus.
This church and city triumph in his eyes.
He is only a good alien, nominally happy.

AUTO WRECK

Its quick soft silver bell beating, beating,
And down the dark one ruby flare
Pulsing out red light like an artery,
The ambulance at top speed floating down
Past beacons and illuminated clocks
Wings in a heavy curve, dips down,
And brakes speed, entering the crowd.
The doors leap open, emptying light;
Stretchers are laid out, the mangled lifted
And stowed into the little hospital.
Then the bell, breaking the hush, tolls once,
And the ambulance with its terrible cargo
Rocking, slightly rocking, moves away,
As the doors, an afterthought, are closed.

We are deranged, walking among the cops
Who sweep glass and are large and composed.
One is still making notes under the light.
One with a bucket douches ponds of blood
Into the street and gutter.
One hangs lanterns on the wrecks that cling,
Empty husks of locusts, to iron poles.

Our throats were tight as tourniquets,
Our feet were bound with splints, but now,
Like convalescents intimate and gauche,
We speak through sickly smiles and warn
With the stubborn saw of common sense,
The grim joke and the banal resolution.
The traffic moves around with care,
But we remain, touching a wound
That opens to our richest horror.
Already old, the question Who shall die?
Becomes unspoken Who is innocent?
For death in war is done by hands;
Suicide has cause and stillbirth, logic;
And cancer, simple as a flower, blooms.

But this invites the occult mind,
Cancels our physics with a sneer,
And spatters all we knew of denouement
Across the expedient and wicked stones.

THE FLY

O hideous little bat, the size of snot,
With polyhedral eye and shabby clothes,
To populate the stinking cat you walk
The promontory of the dead man's nose,
Climb with the fine leg of a Duncan-Phyfe
        The smoking mountains of my food
                And in a comic mood
        In mid-air take to bed a wife.

Riding and riding with your filth of hair
On gluey foot or wing, forever coy,
Hot from the compost and green sweet decay,
Sounding your buzzer like an urchin toy—
You dot all whiteness with diminutive stool,
        In the tight belly of the dead
                Burrow with hungry head
        And inlay maggots like a jewel.

At your approach the great horse stomps and paws
Bringing the hurricane of his heavy tail;
Shod in disease you dare to kiss my hand
Which sweeps against you like an angry flail;
Still you return, return, trusting your wing
        To draw you from the hunter's reach
                That learns to kill to teach
        Disorder to the tinier thing.

My peace is your disaster. For your death
Children like spiders cup their pretty hands

And wives resort to chemistry of war.
In fens of sticky paper and quicksands
You glue yourself to death. Where you are stuck
    You struggle hideously and beg
        You amputate your leg
    Imbedded in the amber muck.

But I, a man, must swat you with my hate,
Slap you across the air and crush your flight,
Must mangle with my shoe and smear your blood,
Expose your little guts pasty and white,
Knock your head sidewise like a drunkard's hat,
    Pin your wings under like a crow's,
        Tear off your flimsy clothes
    And beat you as one beats a rat.

Then like Gargantua I stride among
The corpses strewn like raisins in the dust,
The broken bodies of the narrow dead
That catch the throat with fingers of disgust.
I sweep. One gyrates like a top and falls
    And stunned, stone blind, and deaf
        Buzzes its frightful F
    And dies between three cannibals.

Winfield Townley Scott

WINFIELD TOWNLEY SCOTT *was born in Haverhill, Massachusetts, in* 1910 *and was graduated from Brown University in* 1931. *He is at present literary editor of the Providence Journal. His published volumes of verse are:* BIOGRAPHY FOR TRAMAN, WIND THE CLOCK, THE SWORD ON THE TABLE, TO MARRY STRANGERS, *and* MR. WHITTIER AND OTHER POEMS.

DEAR JEFF

D EAR JEFF: I will write this "statement" as a letter to you. You provide a good focus because we have known each other so long and because you are not a poet. It occurs to me that for longer than any contemporary friend you have read a lot of my poems; sometimes with more and sometimes with less satisfaction than I thought was deserved; but have read with good will always and a sort of reserved judgment as to how it will all come out. You suit me very well for this occasion—as for so many others.

How does a poet discover his difference from other poets? Probably in part through his talent, in part through his character, and never with complete consciousness. The more profound his difference the less likely that it be consciously attained. Indeed, he may be the slowest to recognize it, the last to know it—and, of course, the least useful in defining it. It is too near him; too much himself.

I think I suffered tardiness in overthrowing that falsest of reassurances in poetry: the reassurance of sounding like something already acclaimed. And I am thinking now not only of all those undergraduate verses and of all the boyhood stuff before that, but also of too many poems written afterwards.

I see now that one's "difference," if it exists, can be resisted. Of course the resistance does not present itself as resistance: it is rather a going along with something already there outside one's self and therefore not possibly wholly true for one's self.

I am not wishing away all the influences any young poet is

heir to. They are necessary in the learning of his craft; and perhaps the more the better up to a point. But I was always a "literary fellow" and I think in the long run I got farther than ever from knowledge of who I was. My first book is much disfigured by this; my later books progressively less so. I do not claim more than that.

For it is an easy thing to say that one's poems must come from within one's self, but it can be a very hard thing to *know* how to accomplish that. The knowing involves self-knowledge, and that involves character, and the whole enterprise involves time. And the end is not yet. This letter is no announcement.

Somebody—wasn't it Leigh Hunt?—said he had never seen anyone who looked so "conscious of a high calling" as John Keats. Most poets now tend to look sheepish or defensive. Yet I doubt if fewer people care about poetry and you will not tell me that life is more uncertain for us than it was for Keats. No: I think it is that poets should care more about poetry. Then we might obviate the kind of notion which just within your time and mine has so bedeviled the art; that it is all right to be Keats if you are a Humanist, or if you belong to such-and-such political party, or if you espouse neo-classicism, or if you write Americana, or if you enjoy a conversion to one of the high churches. But I cherish Hunt's remark as a reminder and say let us put first things first.

I am against footnotes in poetry, obscure sources of reference, misquotation of older poems, resort to foreign languages, and the general clutter which ensues when intellectuality attempts the primary position. But I am not against intellect. While I believe with everyone who has ever said it that poetry is made with words and not with ideas, I also believe that the size of the idea in any poem is relevant to the significance of the poem. Of course the emotional power of the poem *is* its power: effective or ineffective depending upon the technical craft.

I think you will agree—looking back over it all—that I have had at least one consistency, and that is the use of a basically simple vocabulary. Chalk it up to non-intellectuality if you want to. I know dazzling effects can be got with the strange and the esoteric, but they are not my kind of thing. For me the possibility of richness in the unexpected juxtaposition of common phrases, or of such phrases put at a fresh slant, is always exciting. (I admire Wallace Stevens at his distance—for example—but I love Thomas Hardy, warts and all).

And so—in short—you can see where I stand now, for whatever it is worth, out of these beliefs and disbeliefs: that ideally the poem is self-contained. Certainly the poem is meant to signify, meant to be understood. Whenever you say you want poetry you can understand, I always ask: When? I suppose one hopes the poem will have some quality which will tease the reader back a second time; if the poem is worth it and if the reader is worth it. But it cannot be my business to say how many readers. The poem asks only what any work of art asks: attention.

But I am bored with this. The effort of trying to explain what one is doing is not only dangerous but even unpleasant, as Hamlet discovered.

LANDSCAPE AS METAL AND FLOWERS

All over America railroads ride through roses.

I should explain this is thoroughly a matter of fact.
Wherever sandy earth is piled to make a road for train tracks
The banks on either side are covered with wild, sweet
Pink rambler roses: not because roses are pretty
But because ramblers grow in cheap soil and will hold
The banks firm against rain—therefore the railroad roses.

All over America the steel-supporting flowers,
Sometimes at village depots covering the shingled station,
Sometimes embracing watertanks, but mostly endless tendrils
Out of which locomotives and pullmans flash the morning—
And tunnels the other way into whose firm, sweet evening
The whistle fades, dragging freight cars, day coaches and the ca-
          boose.

SONNET

I watched the sea for hours blind with sun,
Hours and hours: all morning a dozen years
Racing and spent in the combers and beyond
Blown back in spume and seagulls' wings and still
Farther ash in the sky, shadowed then lost;
Wind-plowed-over the waves kept rolling in
Lashing salt air cold about my head,
Till the great wave where I saw all my dead
One moment as it stood and they within
As in dark glass which suddenly sun-crossed
Blazed with that luminosity which will
With first or last light raise all things in round
But far and foreign as though seen through tears
Once and forever before the wave shut down.

WE'LL ALL FEEL GAY

Even along the railway platform it was spring
And my uncle was coming on the noon train, back from the war.
I was nine that month. I had a new cap and no coat.
We walked around, my grandfather and I, and watched the tracks.

The tracks slid shining and quiet with the warm sun
And the station stayed very still. Hunched on the baggage-wagon
The blue baggageman smoked his pipe, said "How-do Mr. Scott,"
And my grandfather said "My son is getting back on this train";

And then it was coming. We stopped walking and listened, and
        then
The engine roared at the turn and raced at us and darkened
The whole station and shook it and I yelled "There he is!"
He leaned on a cane and stood very big in his khaki.

So we all sort of shook hands and the other people
Laughed and waved as they went by, and my uncle said
"Well, how's the new bus?" as we climbed into the
1919 green Cadillac touring.

We drove past the ballfield and up Pelham Street,
And they talked about the car, and into Spring Street and Broad-
        way,
And not about the hospital or the Argonne or France or
The Botches or anything like that; and my uncle

Looked at all the stores we went past—my grandfather's too,
With the seed packages bright in the window, and outside
Gilt-and-green lawn-mowers in a row where the elm trees
Cast a thin shade leafing across the brick sidewalk.

We drove through Friendship to our Street; my grandfather
Said the paint department yes should be moved, as they walked
Up the steps: but my uncle's cane crashed to the floor
And he was running all the way to the door where my grandmother
        stood.

THE U. S. SAILOR
WITH THE JAPANESE SKULL

Bald-bare, bone-bare, and ivory yellow: skull
Carried by a thus two-headed U. S. sailor
Who got it from a Japanese soldier killed
At Guadalcanal in the ever-present war: our

Bluejacket, I mean, aged 20, in August strolled
Among the little bodies on the sand and hunted
Souvenirs: teeth, tags, diaries, boots; but bolder still
Hacked off this head and under a leopard tree skinned it:

Peeled with a lifting knife the jaw and cheeks, bared
The nose, ripped off the black-haired scalp and gutted
The dead eyes to these thoughtful hollows: a scarred
But bloodless job, unless it be said brains bleed.

Then, his ship underway, dragged this aft in a net
Many days and nights—the cold bone tumbling
Beneath the foaming wake, weed-worn and salt-cut
Rolling safe among fish and washed with Pacific;

Till on a warm and level-keeled day hauled in
Held to the sun and the sailor, back to a gun-rest,
Scrubbed the cured skull with lye, perfecting this:
Not foreign as he saw it first: death's familiar cast.

Bodiless, fleshless, nameless, it and the sun
Offend each other in strange fascination
As though one of the two were mocked; but nothing is in
This head, or it fills with what another imagines

As: here were love and hate and the will to deal
Death or to kneel before it, death emperor,
Recorded orders without reasons, bomb-blast, still
A child's morning, remembered moonlight on Fujiyama:

All scoured out now by the keeper of this skull
Made elemental, historic, parentless by our
Sailor boy who thinks of home, voyages laden, will
Not say, "Alas! I did not know him at all."

THE HOUSE

When will violence shake, when break me—
Make me at last cry out? What loss
Heavy to crack my personal sky? What
Failure darken to bring me staring?
What good thing, evil thing—come either—
Split me and let the frozen blood?

I hear beneath the wind, beneath
The leaves' skating on the ground,
My ancestors' hair growing, whispering,
A tide out of the old men's skulls:
Think it flicks me, teases my fingers,
Writhes at my ankles, rejoices and grieves.

I walk up the stairs and walk down,
Hear news of murder and confront my death:
Death—death—death of love—a shape
Rocking a chair somewhere in this house.
Mirrors everywhere reflect me here
Going from room to room, lest I decrease.

If smaller, harder—then for what escape?
The sky grinning through the window
The hair furtive under the door—
What damnation damns me! And you:
I might speak of it and find it with you.
The air chokes my open mouth.

Haunted then? caught? snagged up
In a web of lies? dreaming?

Many questions for you and no answers.
I dare not and I know not what I dare not.
Then this is mad? and black blood wants peace?
Come peace. Come violence. Come violent peace.

BERMUDA SUITE

(For Eleanor)

1: The Voyage

The gray the vacant circle of the sea
Port and starboard sways among the clouds.
Like a slow metronome for timelessness
The centered ship creaks deeply down the east
Then slides against the west to tilt on clouds
That hold all this lolling quicksilver.

And thus eternity except for us;
Though keeled and waked obliterative in foam
Our interceptions of this pulsing void
Grew its existence and inhabitants,
And with salt tongue and all-pervading eye
Named the pastures of leviathan.

Marked by multitudinous hoofs of the wind
The waters of the world before the world
Have now become the landless skyless world,
And gray and cold and dumb and meaningless
Save for the mastery of our prow, and that
Advancing always rolls dead center still.

Southeast where morning showed beyond the prow,
Only the intermittent flaws in cloud—
Which mend and darken with a chilling zeal—
Admit light's vibrant archipelagoes.
Their brief creations on the ocean flash
Like glittering ghostly islands of the sun

2: The Green Moray

Fourteen miles off the land the sharp reefs fissure the water and
    at low-tide the water splits white on the coral bone;
None does, but a man could walk here.
What lurks here, deep and obscure in the swilling waters,
    is the great eel, the green moray.

This reef-arch, vertebrae revealed, locked skeletons where the
    volcanic spew shuddering away failed northwest to achieve
One island more,—
This guards the Eden of hibiscus, floating Bermudas, crescent of
    strung barges of flowers between the cobalt air and the zircon-
    melted sea.
All those islands in a dust of gold
Strewing on water their harebell-haunted hills
That change from morning to evening from blue to mauve,
Staked with cedar, paved with lily, branched with palm, and
    breathing freesia
Under the singing rings of scarlet birds.

Toward those the green moray lifts an indifferent eye long-learned
    in patient hate; slow and watchful amidst coral
Shifts the thick mass of his cold length;
Coiled in the dead defenses of the reefs he waits vicious for
    millennium,
When from the grottoes worms the landward march of the fathom-
    hidden,
Innumerable in a sluggish final seminal wave.

3: Portrait of Lizards

The lizard on the limestone wall
Shifts a noncommittal eye,
Innocently prehistorical.

Miss Moore remarked his heavy clay:
Miniature dinosaurian,
Ownerless, immortal toy.

Rust on cedar, blue on stone,
Green-mottle to the yucca spikes,
He poses frozen in the sun.

All afternoon is how he likes
Baking on his chilly buff:
So we assume: that what it takes

To stay so everlasting tough
Is thus desiring heat and light
While never getting quite enough.

He has not climbed far from the sight
And sound and savor of the sea,
Yet he has compromised the night

With undivulged facility.
He scuttles where the cacti sprawl
Across the rock; amidst them, he

Mounts a dome of brain coral:
There, self-fixed, triumphant, small,
The lizard's portrait of a moral . . .

Cold, chameleon, inexplicable.

4: Kites, Good Friday

> Upon mine honor, sir, I heard a humming,
> And that a strange one too, which did awake me.
> —*The Tempest*

Seven little boys like silhouettes dancing far on the headland
Salute the morning with the running and the rising of
their kites.
Uphill, drawing them, the soft brown hands paying out
string,
The boys have set them swinging in the wind on a rag-tailed
rocking and rising

And riding with a surge higher and east toward the sun and
    out on
Tauter string over the sea—far—stretched—rigid now—
    anchored and almost stilled
Stiffly balancing wind: each octagonal kite like a burning gem
Purple and gold and red; seal-centered with—invisibly—the bright
    paper heart;
The humming beginning now out of the strung-wedged Vs, a high
    keening across the Good Friday sun;
And cries on and on.

    Swiftly by ancient custom all over the Bermuda islands
The sky fills—thousands of many-colored kites staining like marvels
of windows the great blue air.
The sky sways with the glass of God, the whole dome throbbing
    with massed fretting of jewels, and their crying
Motored now to a diapason pulse, a humming roar drowning the
    wind;
And looped over the white shores and the outer reefs the foams
Break without sound.

    In this blazing dazzle of color all heaven moans
Reels in this spangling of spectrum; the air imbued
Purple and gold and red: ascending and singing day-dream strung
From the thousands of soft hands that have set sounding together
Multitudinous wires, space-filling harp tilting its mineral fires
    slant to the sun,
All fragmented are joined and woven, transformed, and the sky
    opening with transfigured blood.

Between all lifted hands and the kites such intense power strains,
Which holds? Which is held?
The power flows up the strings into the sky out of the hands that
    have set this glory there,
All faces lifted to love what they have made.
Even all the islands for this little while
Lifted between the waters and the sky.

5: Long. 60°50W; Lat. 32°15N

Flared down from broken cloud the calipered light
Stood strident, made exact embrace of land.
Brooched crescent upon platinum the islands
Curved gold-flecked emerald, and there was light
Only along the great bow of the islands
As though they swung burning alone in space.

Running out of the sea the man and woman
Flashed on the shore naked and beautiful,
And flung to sand as by a wave of air
They lay together breathlessly and then
They heard their hearts, and time resumed its beat.
Sand kept flickering with the ticking wind.

The sand swept high to a long wave of earth
That, wrought upon the rock, had rooted rock
Tendrilled in a gigantic grasp from air
Holding in perilous suspension
What cragged mass the sea once lifted up,
Conjoined from accident this miracle.

At its emergent line the man and woman
Stared at cloud-vexed sky, the chains of light.
They saw the flowered headlands shake and quiet
In criss-cross hammering of their sea-lashed hearts,
And remembered in wild wonder-eaten wisdom
That all the flowering was meant for them.

John Frederick Nims

JOHN FREDERICK NIMS *was born in Chicago in* 1914, *and studied at Notre Dame and the University of Chicago. He has taught at the University of Toronto and is now Associate Professor of English at Notre Dame. Mr. Nims has been one of the editors of Poetry, A Magazine Of Verse since* 1945. *He now lives in Niles, Michigan. His first volume,* THE IRON PASTORAL *was published in* 1947. *His second volume will appear in* 1950.

NOTES

THE FOLLOWING notes on poetic practice follow a form suggested by Mr. Ciardi. If there are found some inconsistencies between these opinions and the techniques actually employed in the poems by which I am here represented, perhaps it is because many of them, written quite a few years ago, were governed by principles and techniques I would now hesitate to endorse.

The oral quality of the poem? Oral?—I would rather say auditory. What happens in the mouth when we pronounce words or what we imagine happening there when we read them—clicks and hissings and stoppages—may involve us physiologically and therefore more fully in the experience of the poem. Perhaps poets take too little care of an effect which is more primitive and more intimate than the auditory experience. Poetry works through, implicates, and excites all the senses—first of all the sense of hearing, since poetry is first perceived (unless typography is meaningful) as a sound-continuum. The apprentice writer tries to make the continuum as pleasant as possible; he works for mellifluence and sonority; to these he is likely to sacrifice precision of diction, feeling, and idea. A more thoughtful attitude toward the sound-quality of a poem may lead the young poet to substitute the criterion of fitness for that of sweetness: "the sound must seem an echo to the sense." Instead of Pope's "echo" I would like a word that expresses simultaneity or antecedence, that would have the sound leading to the sense instead of following from it. It is this fitness

I would like to work for in what I write: at the extremes, the melli-
fluous *legato* when it fits the feeling; the harsh *staccato* when it
does.

Is it meant to be read aloud? I do not think about a poem's
actually being read aloud. But everyone who reads poetry should
surely hear it as he reads. Would you ask a painter: "Do you
expect people who look at your picture to notice the colors?"

The audience of the poem? This question has never occupied
me. When I write a poem, as I recall, I have no audience in mind:
there is no room there for anything except the poem. I suppose in
a sense I am writing for myself. But this solitaire has its rules.
Though I am writing for myself I am bound by the conventions,
or, better, by the possibilities of my language as it is used by men—
at least, by a kind of composite man, who is partly the man in the
street with his urgencies and vividnesses, partly the scholar with
his derivatives and polysyllables, partly the writer with his skills
and recollections. So, though I do not feel I am writing for an
audience, I feel that anyone who strays into the theater of the
poem should be able to find out what is going on there. Anyone,
that is, likely to stray into such a theater. That would include, I
suppose, people whose reactions and interests might be expected
to have something in common with my own. It would be comfort-
able to have a large audience, honestly won. But it would be shame-
ful for the writer to say anything less well than he knows how sim-
ply to gain more readers. Any of us in this book could write some-
thing that would bring him a hundred readers for every one he
has now. This would be failure.

When is a poem difficult? "Difficult . . . involving difficulties
(q.v.) in . . . understanding . . ." (Webster). It may be difficult
because it is badly written, because the writer has mismanaged
language. This kind of difficulty we cannot defend, though there
is some of it in high places. We will always have with us the
mâche-laurier whose reasoning apparently is: Some good writing
is obscure; therefore my obscure writing is good. Poetry may also
be difficult because the ideas and feelings of the poem are really
complex and profound: some of Dante, some of Shakespeare. This
kind we cannot blame; the limitation is ours. It may be difficult,
thirdly, because it is close-textured and original in expression: some

of Hopkins. This remains a difficulty only for the lazy reader who wants to work with easily achieved prefabricated reactions. It may be difficult because references are "private," almost solipsistic. But sometimes too much is made of this; cf. Auden's

> See him turn to the window, hearing our last
> Of Captain Ferguson.

Auden probably knows a Captain Ferguson; we don't. We can only construct a figure from the clues and situations of this poem; more than likely that is enough. Our Captain Ferguson may be as vivid and useful as Auden's. But when the whole meaning of a poem depends on an allusion, and when the only key to that allusion is in the mind of the writer and possibly of some of his friends, the writer has, perhaps snobbishly, constricted his poem. Constriction kills.

How difficult may a poem be? The choice is the writer's. If it is too difficult (in the unfavorable sense), the poem will not live, it will not even be born alive. Of course many "difficulties" of poetry (like that of Captain Ferguson) are irrelevant; they don't have to be solved. In this volume I have a poem called *Là ci darem la mano*. Most of its readers will remember the da Ponte lyric and the Mozart music. For me, the recollection provides a comment on, adds a dimension to, the theme of the poem. But if they don't recognize it, no matter; the poem does not require that recognition. Readers might guess, but need not know, that *Fairy Tale* came out of a reading of Jung's *Psychology of the Unconscious*. In the third line they may recognize a detail from *The Eve of St. Agnes;* in the fourth stanza they may recognize a line from Dekker. But the meaning is clear without these awarenesses, which only add little grace-notes of meaning. It is not necessary to understand the precise intent and force of every detail to "understand" a poem. The crowded eschatologies of Hieronymus Bosch, for example, are full of puzzles, yet the pictures as wholes are quite clear. Even essential difficulties can be by-passed for the sake of an objective. The most random and clotted cantos of Pound can be read for delight of phrase and cadence.

The language of the poem? Any special theories of diction? No special theories. I do not feel drawn, like Hopkins and Cummings (who are among my favorite poets) to formulate an idiom of my own. I would like to extract the strongest and raciest creatures from the zoo of language and harness these. What I would like always to find is what Conrad calls "the fresh usual word." It is so easy to be fresh:

> Life, an old gardener's fedora bleeding starlight. . . .

So easy to be usual:

> Oh morning like an exhalation rose . . .

But so difficult to be both at once.

Words are the poet's scales, the black and white keys he can strike. Ideally, he should know the keys from A to Z, should know the words he can use, and when; the words he cannot use— if there are any. He will be most wary of words whose habitat is literary—these will be the hardest to employ freshly.

Opening a page of the dictionary at random, I see words I like, words I dislike. I like *stack, stadium, staff, stag,* (though not at eve), *stage, stain, stagger.* The rare words are unusable: *stacher, stacte, staggard, staddle. Stactometer* and *stadiometer* are not for me. *Stagy* would take clever using. *Stagnant* is stagnant; a poet might stir it up. Sometimes a square word in a round hole is best.

Diction: an apparently natural arrangement of elements rich and right. Not "the language of men"; in actuality, that's often drab. But differing from it only in selectivity and expertness: the language of men as used by an expert in men's language.

The function of overtone? If by overtone is meant suggestion and association, then overtone is essential to good poetry. Without it we would have only a thin line of meaning, a kind of flat two-dimensional thing. A poem quite without it (were that possible) would be like a symphony orchestra in which each instrument played the very same note at the very same time. Overtone is depth and complexity; its pulls and tensions bring the poem to life, give it an activity and drama of its own. The thin poem over-simplifies and flattens. Let our mind stop the stream of reality at any moment and we are aware that any situation, however simple, is explosive with possibilities and divergencies, that it contains germs of its opposite. This vibrancy the poet aims at; the richer the associations and suggestions of the poem the more completely it has realized the ambiguous conditions of life itself.

Levels of meaning? The good poem will have levels of meaning whether the poet plans them or not. It will have levels of meaning as any situation in life, or any work of the painter, will have levels of meaning. Take Brueghel's *The Fall of Icarus*: for the simple beholder it may have meaning only as landscape. Some of the further depths and levels it has Auden has brought out in his *Musée des Beaux Arts*. We can look at any object; it will not long be simply itself. A lump of coal: blackness, warmth, diamond, ferns, Palaeozoic, evolution, creation, time, eternity—by abstraction and association through how many strata the mind works down to archetypes. In any poem, even a poor one, the levels of meaning are many; in the good poem, the tactfully written poem, the poet will lead the reader, as Beatrice Dante (who admitted four levels of meaning) to the planes most significant in the universe of the poem. He will lead him by hints and glances; he cannot pull him.

Subject Matter? Any predilections? "But how do you get your subjects?" I heard a student at a writers' conference ask Jessamyn West. "You don't get your subjects; they must get you." So with poetry: whatever sufficiently moves the poet is his subject. What moves one will of course not move another: that is one reason it is dangerous to imitate. What moves and interests a poet depends on the nature and subtlety of his perceptions and talents. Perhaps it comes back to Sidney's "Look in thy heart and write." At least (to save objective poetry) "Look with thy heart and write." In the past I have written what one reviewer called poems "about" things; I would rather have called them poems about "things." But at any rate the method no longer seems to be of interest to me unless the thing is the symbol of the sub-thing, the super-thing.

Restrictions? The only restriction is the limitation of the poet's ability. The subjects a poet would most like to write about may remain beyond the scope of his talents; he is lucky if he knows that scope. There are no objective restrictions: it was Van Gogh, wasn't it, who saw halos around the garbage heaps?

Imagery? Poetry is first of all a sound-continuum. This sound is one kind of imagery. The sounds this sound may represent are another. The tastes and fragrances and touches of a *St. Agnes Eve* give us other kinds. At least for me, the keenest imagery is visual. The ideal poem is almost a cinema reel of pictures, sometimes fading out for a moment so that the music can be heard, sometimes lost in a white light of thought—but poetry is never long without these images. *"Le monde est un ciel, une matière fluide et qui s'écoule, une longue étoffe diaprée."* The last four words are the world of poetry, *"une longue étoffe diaprée."* Jean Cassou goes on to show, in this appreciation of Dufy, how the images of the world fuse and unify; "une vague, des vagues, la mer. . . ." So should the images of a good poem. Never the image for the sake of the image; but the image for the sake of the last image and the next image and the whole poem. If one image is a wave, the whole must be the sea. To change the figure, the images of a good poem are all in the same key or right modulations of it.

Symbolism? I think what I have said on other topics implies an answer. A poem can hardly be without images; the best images are likely to be at the same time symbols, because of the levels of meaning they lead to. It is better if symbols are not identified as such; that is, if they seem at first simply to be images and let their deeper significance work into our consciousness. Otherwise, they fail as images. The poet should never have to say, "Look, this is a symbol, and it means. . . ." For a fine example of a contemporary symbolic poem, see Richard Wilbur's *Driftwood,* in which the reader feels (without being badgered) that the images are all richly symbolic.

Rhyme and its function in the poem? Rhyme I have not thought about deeply enough. I like it as musical and formal. Pleasant in itself, unless used clumsily, it encloses and shapes; it emphasizes. More subtly, it connects in our mind the rhyming words and hence can fuse or juxtapose or contrast.

Line length and the function (if any) of the line-end in guiding the reading of the poem? No comment really—any length that is right for the rhythm and feeling and form of the poem. I am afraid my own practice has been to regard the line too much as a unit and to fall into too great a uniformity of line-length.

The structure of the total poem? Formal, but with no show of formality. A poem should "sing in (its) chains like the sea."

Dylan Thomas's "Fern Hill" is especially wonderful in giving the effect of freedom while being most elaborately organized according to syllabic count. To risk an assailable figure, suppose we say bones should be rigid; flesh should not. I don't believe there is any single principle of unity in poetry; we would have to get down to cases to discuss this. In some poems it is feeling; in some imagery; it might sometimes be rhythm. Mere unity of thesis is, I think, not enough.

Rhythm and meter? Poetry should have a vital regularity like that of pulse or breathing, which vary with the needs and feelings of the organism; never a mechanical regularity, like a metronome. The individual rhythms of such poets as Hopkins and Thomas I greatly admire; I cannot (deliberately) use them because they are so clearly theirs. I have not worked out any rhythmical *system* that satisfies me, except a general feeling that it is better wantonly to break an established rhythm rather than keep to its tidy status quo. I am all for iambic fission; but it must be a fission somehow controlled. It is best if the compulsion of idea and feeling determine the variation of rhythm.

NEW YEAR'S EVE, 1938

Midnight the years last day the last
high hour the verge where the dancers comet
(loved water lapsing under the bridge
and blood dear blood by the bridged aorta
where the dreaming soul leans distant-eyed
long-watching the flood and its spoil borne seaward)

and I one fleck on the numbered face
one dot on the star-aswarming heaven
stand here in this street of all our streets
of all our times this moment only
the bells the snow the neon   faces
each our own but estranged and fleeing

from a bar all tinkle and red fluorescence
a boy in a tux with tie uneven
puppy-clumsy with auldlangsyning
plaintive so droll came crying Sally
Salleee again and Saalleee louder
a violin teased he passed in laughter

yet under the heart of each up vein
up brain and loud in the lonely spirit
rang desire for Sallys name
or another name or a street or season
not to be conjured by any horn
nor flavored gin nor the flung confetti

o watcher upover the world look down
through gale of stars to the globes blue hover
and see arising in troubled mist
from firefly towns and the dark between them
the waif appeal from lackland hearts
to Sallys name or perhaps anothers

CLOCK SYMPHONY

Time that brings children from the wizard den
Of books and cushions to the world above,
Boys to the desk of politics and rage,
Girls to the dream and bitter fact of love
(Both quickly to the paper veins of age),
Time that at last brings nothing good to men
We canonize with steeple, dial, and chest.
It spans, a leer of gold, the lender's vest;
In hickory hood, a dour monk eightfeet tall,
Lours in the hall;
From pillar of stone city directs all;
Judges the heel of athlete, saturnine,
Victor itself at last.
On delicate wrist of women, prisoned fast
With carat twine,
A golden beetle or ticking skull, the sharp insignia shine.

Sarcophagus your name: the vehicle wrist
You eat like yellow acid to the bone.
Ventriloquist: the nod of scholar bell,
Lank whistle or red gong or telephone.
Cruel to the poor: in tenement's dark cell
Your hard alarm at morning like a fist.
You mock the moneyed ear with alpine rime,
Hide wars in ormolu, death in a chime.
Ships, trains to you their black hosanna toss.
Watcher of loss,
Your fat and twitching grin is banker's boss.
Your favor more than moon all lovers want—
Two orbits' equinox.
Your cricket heart (physician's music box)
Is metal taunt
To limbs by thought or passion racked, with sin or grandeur gaunt.

The world: a sombre gallery of clocks:
Faces, the human dial; ruins that tell

The time of pride and politics and war;
The moon revolving to a rusty shell;
Pendulum pines; the flooded glass of shore
And terrible tick of shipwreck on the rocks.
At every chink the scoring eye of time.
Even man, the clockface doll with lips of rime
(Himself by deft and joking jeweler planned)
Whose nerve and gland
Run sweet, explode, and separate in sand,
Stares here: where Easter and dark Friday lie
In crystal, pins of gold,
Where tension of slow god in decades doled
Breeds ape and fly,
And through a tinsel gear of watch motors the heavy sky.

MADRIGAL

Beside the rivers of the midnight town
Where four-foot couples love and paupers drown,
Shots of quick hell we took, our final kiss,
The great and swinging bridge a bower for this.

Your cheek lay burning in my fingers' cup;
Often my lip moved downward and yours up
Till both adjusted, tightened, locksmith-true:
The flesh precise, the crazy brain askew.

Roughly the train with grim and piston knee
Pounded apart our pleasure, you from me;
Flare warned and ticket whispered and bell cried.
Time and the locks of bitter rail divide.

For ease remember, all that parted lie:
Men who in camp of shot or doldrum die,
Who at land's-end eternal furlough take,
On cots of harness with cropped bodies wake.

Mark it, young materialist: in crimson freeze
Or bloat and sallow with the blood's disease,
Virus of love, whose counter-dose alone
Is faucet of cut vein or ripsaw bone.

LOVE POEM

My clumsiest dear, whose hands shipwreck vases,
At whose quick touch all glasses chip and ring,
Whose palms are bulls in china, burs in linen,
And have no cunning with any soft thing

Except all ill-at-ease fidgeting people:
The refugee uncertain at the door
You make at home; deftly you steady
The drunk clambering on his undulant floor.

Unpredictable dear, the taxi drivers' terror,
Shrinking from far headlights pale as a dime
Yet leaping before red apoplectic streetcars—
Misfit in any space. And never on time.

A wrench in clocks and the solar system. Only
With words and people and love you move at ease.
In traffic of wit expertly manoeuvre
And keep us, all devotion, at your knees.

Forgetting your coffee spreading on our flannel,
Your lipstick grinning on our coat,
So gayly in love's unbreakable heaven
Our souls on glory of spilt bourbon float.

Be with me, darling, early and late. Smash glasses—
I will study wry music for your sake.
For should your hands drop white and empty
All the toys of the world would break.

DOLLAR BILL

The feathered thing of silver-grey and jade,
Her wing with sum and pompous annal spread,
Is strangest bird, world's wonder. Of more than stork
Or dove or jay or any eagle bred.
Her silver eggs explode with wine or milk,
Gardenia, limousine, or firework silk.

Her nature wild. Once captured, not a bird,
Heron nor Persian lark, is fed so fine.
Her Audubon, the banker, stalks and peers
Where audits bloom and grills of commerce twine.
She lives in leather nest or cote of steel.
In city migrates on the armored wheel.

Mallard and teal the fowler downs in fall.
But season is open always for green game.
All weapons used: hand or enchanting hair,
Instructed dice or dynamite or flame.
To pipe of organ some in chapel tread;
Others in alley with a pipe of lead.

Nameless. Her whims of voyage none can track.
Her legend lost; perhaps is charm or curse.
From chaw-stained overall she flutters straight
To the sweet nonsense of a lady's purse.
Wanton with rouge, with blood and beer defiled,
Is loved at Christmas by the snowy child.

She teems in steeple wall, or no bells ring;
In clinic roof, or all the patients die;
She lies with laurel on the captain's head
Or nations fall; their banners leave the sky.
Strange bird. Strange music from the poison breath.
Child of green lovebird and the raven death.

APOCALYPSE

I

And the sun became black as sackcloth of hair, and the whole moon
became as blood.

Turning from Plato to the rocky sergeant,
His mouth explosive with the sake of god,
Tatter your hate on targets, tear the sandbag,
Still fiercer in the whistling vitals prod.

This game is not the lamplit games of childhood.
Fair players are derided and shot through.
For black is white as lead and limb turn color;
And usual here is lightning from the blue.

Be tennis-nice, grin laud to the opponent --
A gunstock crushes on your open mouth;
Your tendons cut, you writhe on burning porches,
Hearing your honey torsoed in the bath.

Be hard: to win report and civic mention
Kick water from the teeth of dying men;
Brogan the wounded face, or never saunter
In innocent white the summer fields again.

II

Because thou sayest, I am rich and made wealthy and have need of
nothing.

But some in the bland spectacles of learning
With holy water sponge the blood away,
See pie in the sky and chortle hallelujah,
Yoo-hoo the silver lining, the new day.

Silver is Caesar's penny and coward's color.
Gilt Baalim, silver lining, both are sin
As Pilate heels away, as Herod darkens,
And hard at noon the blackest hours begin.

The cheerful are the round blank idiot faces;
Their hair is hanging frowzy in the beer;
They take their eyeballs out to play at marbles,
Scratching the catamite ilium of cheer.

As if, among the quiet sad of Calvary,
A third should yawn, and pick his teeth, and say:
Well, let's get going. I looked in the last chapter.
So take it easy, folks. He'll rise O.K.

III

Thy merchants were the great men of the earth; all nations have been deceived by thy enchantments.

Earth is our home: we shall not ride Niagara
Nor wander heavenward on the Disney road.
Too much will hold us here — our love for Hedy
Lamarr, Miss Otis, and the fair Isoude.

We, risen of froth, are creepers of the strata,
Are very earth, as currents are the sea.
So long as forest, gorge, and wailing bayou
Are native to this center, so are we.

This neighborhood between the map's four seasons,
The twelve addresses of the apartment clock,
Includes our city and we shall not leave it,
Nor any soft seduction slip the lock,

Unless he storm the stair and hurl the vases,
Hang one on the janitor, sideswipe the dray,
Unless Jehovah is handsome-tough as Gable.
Our souls are taken in the Sabine way.

IV

I will give him the morning star.

Fierce is the grin of suitors offering roses
With werewolf fingers in the polite glove.

We read in *Ranch Romances* and Krafft-Ebing
That gentleness is not the affair of love.

This season, that foils drowning and cirrhosis,
When lead instead of lechery burns the brain,
When slug and shrapnel are a streamline cancer,
And bombs supplant the beer-exploded vein,

Is quickening of life, the reel of being
Racing the spool, too quick for common eye;
Gears of the planet souped and a strong driver
Whizzing the sharp machinery of the sky.

His goggles scan the heaven, bright as lenses;
Us he abducts and dusenburgs away,
Headlight of fire x-raying earth our mistress:
December bones in a sweet whore of May.

TRAINWRECKED SOLDIERS

Death, that is small respecter of distinction,
 Season or fitness in an instant these
Tan casual heroes, floral with citation,
Scattered for blocks over the track
In lewd ridiculous poses, red and black.

These had outfaced him in the echoing valleys;
Thwarted like men of stone incredible fire;
Like dancers had evaded the snub bayonet;
Had ridden ocean or precipitous air.
Death turned his face aside, seemed not to see.
His unconcern made boyish melodrama
Of all that sergeant threatened, corporal bore,
Or captain shouted on the withering shore.

He watched the newsreel general pinning on their
Blouses the motley segments of renown;
Stood patient at the cots of wounded
Where metal pruned and comas hung;
Nodded to hear their plans: one with a child
His arms had never held; one with a bride;
One with a mere kid's longing for the gang
In green and ticking poolroom bluff with beer.
All these he herded through sargasso of mines
Back to the native field and Sunday steeple
Where only the russet hunters late in fall
Nitre the frosty heaven with abrupt smoke.
There he arose full height, suddenly spoke.

Spoke, and the four dimensions rocked and shattered;
Rearing, the olive pullmans spun like tops;
Corridors shrank to stairway and shot up;
Window, green pastoral lately, turned grenade;
The very walls were scissor and cut flesh.
The doors, the drinking fount, the studded trunk
Ruptured like booby-traps, a german's joke.
Captain and sergeant tumbled, wholly void
Their fortitude, muscle, and khaki fame
Like rules intended for another game.

Then death, the enormous insolence effected,
The tour de force pat and precisely timed,
Resumes his usual idiom, less florid:
A thousand men are broken at Cologne;
Elderly salesman falters on the landing;
Girl Slain in Park; Plane Overdue; Tots Drown.
But we who walk this track, who read, or see
In a dark room the shaggy films of wreck —
What do the carrion bent like letters spell
More than the old *sententiae* of chance? —
Greek easier (αιλινον αιλινον) than this fact.
You lie wry X, poor men, or empty O,
Crux in a savage tongue none of us know.

LA CI DAREM LA MANO

I

Since we are born in blood to be convinced
(As Juliet soon, then Brutus, Lear at last)
And no altimeter teaches like sheer fall,
Here is my hard memento, sermon for Sunday.

II

Scotch that incites us to each feminine face
Determined this. On rented linen
Under the rented stript walls of the bedroom
With many tongues the entire body begs.

But even upon your heart in the long progressive
Kiss that gropes in circle and never breaks
I move among lovers grotesquely dead.

All who threw themselves from hotels down
Or stumbled insane from love's path
In whose thorn-hedge psychosis and abortion
Gibber with tic for faces and fibrin hand;
All whom husbands or beefy police
Thudded upon with fists, hamstrung, or shot;
Middle-age bridegroom teasing the momentum
Of blood and sensitive vein, till his heart clotted,
Closed like a cramp in a grey runner's leg—
Joy his disease, orgasm too near center;
Or that salesman and the waitress with pretty red curls
In his night Ford in the winter-drifting lane
Whom stern monoxide in coition caught
And zero froze so (love's two-headed boy),
Lips, fingers, all shy reachers-out of sense
Stiffer than icicles on slate.

III

I deck our bed with these shapes and not flowers,
Seeing sprawled victims in a knot of chairlegs

And curtains shredded with clutch of plunging girls;
Feeling: on nostril, eartip, naked shoulder,
Chill of that twofold obscene icework camel.

For I remember that old marsh of Wasn't
And joy built up *toto caelo* from nothing
By God's art (best on Friday) sheer relievo.

By God's love, sheer relievo: in that chill
That hollow between shoulder and throat is warmer;
Deeper the spring-rain kisses; deeper, wilder
Our two bloods in the membrane-severed sea.

FOR MY SON

How the greenest of wheat rang gold at his birth!
How oaks hung a pomp in the sky!
When the tiptoeing hospital's pillowy arms
Godsped him in suns of July.

Then dizziest poplars, green-and-white tops,
Spun spinning in strings of the wind.
As that child in his wicker
With two great safeties pinned

Slept twenty-two hours with a Buddha-fine face
(His hands were palm-up like a dancer's).
Or his tragic mask's sudden pink-rubbery woe
Sent us thumbing four books for the answers.

And the grave clouds smiled over,
Smiled, flowing west to east, countering sun;
Fields at their leaving all spurted up green!
Old fences limped by at a run!

O elms, fling up up up corinthian fountains.
Fields, be all swirl and spangle, tangle of mirth:
Soon you will root in his woodbrook eyes more deeply
(O reborn poplars) than in Michigan earth.

FAIRY TALE

This is the hero; he is black or white,
Jewish or not-chosen, as you will.
He is villain too; porch-pillared from moonlight
And fondling with stub thumb the window sill.

Night wind laps back his hair; why, you all know him.
Eye a little pale, a yes-sir, no-sir mouth.
Disliked his heavy-hand pa; just to show him
He ran away from high school once down south.

He brings the laundry, brown purse a foot wide;
He rattles garbage cans, taxies you home.
Once when in rain you let him step inside
He looked beyond you to the living room.

Eyes narrowed, he hates *come* and *do* and *carry*.
Prince am I none, he feels, yet princely born.
Some stories read when he was ten and scary
Hard upon Shaftoe and the crumpled horn

Expressed him maybe; he didn't know; he forgot them
Glowering and drew secret maps in class.
Squirrels chuckled at him and by god he shot them.
His dreams have brought him here and cut this glass,

Or not his dreams. The imprisoned lady rather,
Her snow-white forearms bound, gazed and he came.
Gracious and golden-haired, unlike his mother.
Her hands were like his mother's just the same—

Not that he knew. He only knew the window
Tilted and stuck. Impatient, his blood cursed.
But his two secret words cónjured the window.
He thought a moment, swung his left leg first.

Once in, he heard them breathing. Slow, excited,
Clasping her image he made for their den.
A nervous click, the door rushed at him lighted,
All lamps and glass and draperies, the woman

Bolt upright, unbelieving. He came closer.
The ogre snored beside her, red mouth deep;
Disguised (as always) like Duffy the grocer,
He lay enchanted in a beery sleep.

And threshed and gurgled as the good scout-knife
Cut in, cut deeper, and the skin spread wide.
"She is half free," he thought, "this saves my darling."
And now for that witch-woman by his side.

But slow, but soft; this is liturgy. Once more
He saw the lady beckon, one arm free.
He flung back curtains, found the secret door;
Crooned as he swung it with the golden key.

The deacon two streets over under his steeple
Is dreaming this; his grating molars groan;
It runs with many faces through the people;
Dali will paint it with live telephones.

For this prince saw the ogre red and still;
Killed the enchantress (this was not *his* word);
A fountain of plumes, mounted the glass hill
Led by white reindeer and a silver bird.

Later, in alleys crouched, he never winces
As wheels skid shrieking, men shout, sirens wind.
A prince, he turns his back, smiles at the princess,
And both ride off together down his mind.

E. L. Mayo

E. L. MAYO *was born in Malden, Massachusetts. He has taught at Amherst, the U.S. Military Academy Preparatory School at Stewart Field, and Drake University, where he is at present on the English Faculty. His first book,* THE DIVER, *was published by the University of Minnesota Press. His second volume will be published in* 1950.

QUESTION AND ANSWER

THIS BUSINESS of trying to state some of the principles that guide me in the working of a poem has proved difficult—something like taking an X-ray of an ultra-violet light. To say how it *feels* to write a poem is of course comparatively easy. You simply take something that occurs to you—thought, attitude, or concept—*along with its native feeling tone,* and try to make something out of it, shape it into some sort of pattern or design that will bring it into sharper relief. You do this, furthermore, with the attendant notion that others have felt as you do, or will in the future, and that if you succeed in your task of imaginative realization and definition, the resulting poem will be a source of satisfaction to them.

But principles?

Fortunately, I am offered a number of specific questions to start with, and though offered only by way of suggestion, they are all good and pointed, and perhaps if I try to answer them they will lead me back to principles after all. The questions and my answers follow.

Should the poem be read aloud? On several occasions now I have read work of mine aloud to "good" audiences, audiences, that is, of well-informed, attentive people who seemed to be favorably disposed. My conclusions about results are rather mixed. The "easier" and "lighter" the poem, I should say, the better it goes over, unless (a) the poem is already well known to the audience, or (b) each member of the audience has a copy of the poem before him as you read.

It is also well, I think, for the reading poet to tell the audience what to watch for, to alert and prepare them. The reason for all

this jockeying for position is very simple: the average modern aud-
ience does not know how to *listen* to poetry; it has not been con-
ditioned. The most successful poetry on the radio in recent years,
that of Norman Corwin for example, purposely avoids density of
language and imagery and allows plenty of space between its cli-
maxes for the same reason. Even people who like poetry and know
a lot of it are accustomed to come to it *alone,* to take it, at their own
pace, from the pages of a book.

Yet in spite of these difficulties, I still think the supreme test of a
poem is test of oral reading. I do not agree that "melodies . . .
unheard are sweeter," not necessarily, that is. Γ. S. Eliot with his
quick flare for what is upmost in the contemporary mind entitles
his most recent long poem *Four Quartets,* implying, perhaps, that
the warmth and intimacy, as well as the density and intricacy, of
good chamber music are what modern poets are after; and such an
objective in turn implies not the big, cheering, stomping audiences
of which Vachel Lindsay dreamed—perhaps they will come later—
but small, thoughtful ones, no larger than you can gather around
the fireplace in your living-room. Modern poetry is not so much
proclaimed as it is insinuated: happy, then, the modern poet with
a living-room—or with friends to lend him theirs.

What are your working notions of the idiom of poetry? Robin-
son, Frost, and Eliot are to me the three great masters of poetic
idiom in our time; they are also the three great masters of the idiom
of modern speech where it enters the realm of poetic expressiveness.
A man might know all the great poetry of the world by heart and
be filled to the brim with inspiration and yet not be able to write a
modern poem. If he had no ear for the rhythm, diction, intona-
tions that accompany living, contemporary speech, he could not.
Now modern speech is no doubt a poor thing compared with
Shakespeare's, Melville's or even Mark Twain's but it is—heaven
help us—our own; and thin, anxious, *sotto voce,* tense, nervous,
brittle as it is, it is the only stuff good poetry can be made of in our
time. Or—perhaps I should qualify—good poetry cannot be made
without it. Poetic language is of course *heightened* language, and
so there is always room for the skilful modulator of words to em-
ploy the archaic when it serves his purpose; yet I am persuaded that
it draws its main blood-supply from the contemporary. In spite of

frequent resorts to the archaic, for example, Eliot succeeds in giv-
ing us living contemporary speech where Sandburg does not; pri-
marily, I think, because Sandburg captures language at its most ob-
vious and self-conscious, whereas Eliot snares it in the dry light
where it is most itself because it is most unconscious of itself. So
Frost, and so (in his great middle period) Robinson. A. E. Hous-
man was my first master, and a bad one because he "hoed and
trenched and weeded" too much; his diction has a false simplicity
that approaches emasculation. If I have any sense for the idiom of
poetry, at all, the credit must go to the three poets I have mentioned.

Of rhythm and meter? Effective meter is closely bound up with
the matter of living idiom just discussed. Frost's line from
"Birches,"

     /   /   /   /   /
Kicking my way down through the air to the ground

never fails to give me pleasure because it accommodates itself so
well to the purpose it serves in the poem (sudden activity after
inhibited movement) without violating American speech idiom
at any point. Some of the most casual and common idioms of the
language have strongly developed metrical elements; for example:

  ᴗ / ᴗ   / ᴗ / ᴗ   /
I told him half a dozen times

  /   ᴗ   ᴗ   / ᴗ ᴗ /
Whether you like it or not

  ᴗ   ᴗ   / ᴗ / / ᴗ   /   ᴗ   /
Is there any real reason why you can't?

(the list might be endlessly prolonged) and I conceive it the duty
of the poet who desires authenticity of sound and movement to
cultivate his ear, avail himself of these riches that lie so close to
hand whenever they serve his purpose. In this way his metrical ef-
fects become more than merely personal; they become *native*. He
thus clothes his naked uniqueness (no fear—it will be civilized
and intensified, not smothered by the clothing) in the real spoken
language of his time.

What I have said in this matter, I now realize, is quite in accord
with Shapiro's contention (in his *Essay On Rime*) that authentic
novelties in rhythm and meter in poetry are captured in prose be-
fore they are isolated in verse. My only proviso here would be that

the more direct and natural route for idiomatic and rhythmic innovations to take would be from *speech* to verse.

Speech, untutored and spontaneous, is almost always more rhythmic than written prose. Good dramatists (Sheridan as well as Odets) have always known this and have striven to keep their language unliterary and *breatheable*. They have always known, too, that the speech rhythms of twenty years ago were not the same as they are now. And they are always asking themselves, How do people really talk now? It is almost by this determination alone that Hemingway's prose, even though it is tainted with mannerism, touches greatness.

Of the level of diction? All human speech, when cleansed of the venal and commercial, is fit material for poetry. I have always blamed Frost for not letting Silas *say* anything in "The Death of The Hired Man." There, I think, his observation and his imagination failed. I myself avoid the dialect poem mostly because I dread the inevitable apostrophes and mangled spellings which so disfigure dialect poetry on the printed page. American dialect contains much rich poetic treasure I feel sure, but I wish that when it is placed before the public it could be done on phonograph records as Burl Ives's ballads are with all their native intonations *for the ear.*

Of subject matter? Anything. Whatever presents itself to me as charged with poetic interest. One may confidently expect to encounter poetry at every level of the Paradiso, at every declension of the Inferno, and everywhere in the murky Purgatory between. For poetry is the almost involuntary motion of the mind whereby we adopt an attitude or take up a position toward whatever we experience with sharpness and force. Nothing is unpoetic toward which it is possible for us to adopt a sincere attitude. Some of the best poems (see Hamlet's "To be or not to be") have been written about Nothing!

Of imagery? But the greatest thing by far is to be a master of metaphor. It is the one thing that cannot be learnt from others; and it is also a sign of genius, since a good metaphor implies an intuitive perception of the similarity in dissimilars. . . .

The words are Aristotle's, not mine, and it is of course a truism; it is also, however, true. Poetry is predominantly the world of likeness, Frost's "wave thrown back upon itself," the corrective of the second law of thermodynamics through whose action our intellectual as well as our physical possessions get more and more scattered about. Subjectively, a new metaphor or image comes to a writer not as a mere suitable "figure of speech," but as an instantaneous *clarification* of something which a moment before was a mere drift of emotion or tangle of concepts. One of the greatest psychic dangers of our time—due in part to the dizzying progress of physical science—is the falling apart of the conceptual and sensuous worlds. The star we see in the sky may have ceased to exist, the astronomer tells us, forty years ago. But imagery of its very nature *integrates,* and progressively, in the future, must intercede between the space-time continuum which the scientists report and the world of ham-on-rye which we can perceive for ourselves.

This does not mean, however, that we must strain to digest the indigestible or confine ourselves to rocket ships and radioactivity in our poetry as an earnest of our modernity. During the thirties, Auden and his circle worked very hard to inject Freud, coal-pits, pylons, and Marx into their poetry—not unsuccessfully, but nowadays there does not seem to be so much unction of salvation about these things as there seemed to be then.

If Donne could use a compass as the dominant image in a love poem, so can we use an alidade, a slide-rule, a pressure-gauge or an instrument board; thanks in some measure to the poets of the thirties, there are no longer any taboos on what we may use as raw material for our metaphors. But for that very reason we have no right to posture as "Courageous," "Radical," and "Ultra-modern" when we use them. Only as the attitude we take toward them is spontaneous, common, almost matter-of-fact, do they become suitable furniture of the imagination. The atom bomb is in everybody's thoughts these days, and the "flying saucer" recurs in the newspapers pretty frequently. I would say that they would be effective as images only if caught precisely in the social context and time perspective of the average well-informed person. The "saucers" are a joke; the A-bomb is not a joke—that's the size of it. It's perfectly possible that the A-bomb will never be employed in war, and that the flying saucers are an indication that The End Is at Hand; but how they are employed as imagery must depend on how

we feel about them *now*, not on what the future holds. The H. G.
Wells mind, shared in part by Blake, Shelley, and Kenneth Pat-
chen, has its place, but a subordinate place in modern poetry. In
my "The Pool," for example, I allude to Leonardo's Madonna of
the Rocks and comment:

> The rock she sits among
> Waits in a bombsight to be otherwise.

The "Bombsight" in this instance is a metonymy for the whole
technology of modern war and its threat to human values. Few of
us have seen a modern bombsight but most of us have heard, or
read, of its uncanny, superhuman accuracy. That is, enough of us
have a definite attitude toward it to make it accessible as poetic
imagery.

*Of line length and the function of the line in guiding the reading
of the poem?* Until our race grows more flat-chested or breathes
more deeply, the five-stress line will probably remain the standard
and typical line of English verse. It is notable I think that the
greatest innovator in English prosody in the past century, Gerard
Manley Hopkins, did his most notable work within the limits of
the five-stress line.

One reason for this dominance I have already hinted: its phy-
siological basis; the five-stress line remains a comfortable mouth-
ful of words. Another reason is sheer habit. As a glance through
"The Diver" will show you, I have followed along in the tradition
meekly enough, writing an occasional lyric in trimeter, tetrameter,
or the ballad stanza (for which, as being even older than the five-
stress line, I have a great affection) but employing the five-stress
line as a staple.

A third reason is the greater resiliency of the five-stress line,
which, because of the blank verse tradition, does not rely so heavily
as other lines do upon the end of the line in guiding the reading
of the poem. It is mainly by the placing of key or pivotal words
in the line, so that by their position or the extra metrical stress
that falls upon them they become more significant than they would
be in prose, that we "guide the reading" of a poem. Perhaps. Or
perhaps this is just one of those *ex post facto* notions that clutter
up the limbo of prosodic theory. At any rate, *except in drama,* the

regular placement of the pivotal word at the end of the line with too great frequency has been universally regarded as too bald a device. Look at the opening lines of *Paradise Lost*:

> Of Man's first *disobedience* and the fruit
> Of that *forbidden tree*, whose mortal taste
> Brought *death* into the world and all our woe,
> With *loss of Eden*, till one greater Man
> *Restore* us and regain the blissful seat,
> *Sing*, heav'nly Muse. . . .

It is notable that *none* of the words which I would consider pivotal occur at line-ends here. "Disobedience" and "forbidden tree" are given added prominence by coming just before the caesura, "death" by being placed in a metrical context of lighter stresses, "loss" "restore" and "sing" by being placed in a position to receive the first metrical stress in their respective lines.

Milton, of course is here adopting the long, easy pace of the distance runner. He has a long way to go and doesn't intend to strain things at the outset. But where thought is intense, turbulent, confused, as in the "Tomorrow" speech of Macbeth, note how frequently the pivotal word is placed at the *end* of the line as a sort of guide to the reader (or auditor) through the jungle of shifting metaphor. In the less passionate but more contemplative "mercy speech" of Portia, however, we find as much subtlety in the placing of the pivotal word as anywhere in Milton. The only rule I can extract from this excursion around Robin Hood's barn is:

> The more "difficult" your idea, the simpler should be the prosodic devices employed.

> The more direct and free from ambiguity your idea, the more you should avail yourself of all the varieties of metrical surprise and spatial emphasis which the five-stress line affords.

Such, at least, is my own rule of thumb.

Of overtones? Symbolism? Levels of meaning? This is ticklish ground. The three are closely related and fade into each other by indistinguishable degrees. Eliot's use of the word "light" in Coriolanus, for example, shifts to level after level and throws up associations with the Gospel of John and Dante as well as with the inveterate borrower of matches. All three depend for their effect upon the past, especially on the literature of the past, and are likely, if we are not careful in the use of them, to earn us the reputation of being literary prigs and academic Pharisees. Milton, Donne, Landor, and even Yeats could employ these devices with a hundred times more certainty of being understood than we can, and Eliot's *Waste Land* is a perpetual reminder to us of their perils as well as their enchantments. When Eliot wrote *The Waste Land,* he was acquainted with Pound and his circle. Eliot was a man of wide reading. Pound was a man of even wider, though more idiosyncratic, reading. With such an audience Eliot had no need to stint himself on allusion or to fear going "over the head" of his reader. For he knew that whatever he might refer to, Pound would arrive at instantaneously with the speed of light. No, Eliot did not write the poem primarily as a means whereby English majors might impress their friends; but unless we keep the facts firmly in mind we are likely to think so.

The magic of overtone and symbolism depends upon the reader's both knowing and not knowing. Doctor Johnson once defined "wonder" as the "impact of knowledge upon ignorance"; I should prefer to call it the impact of memory on parochial cocksureness. The thing known deeply but not too freshly or in too much scholastic detail, known in a sort of twilight awareness which is neither ignorance nor "information" makes the best allusion or overtone, as Hawthorne and Sophocles knew.

By way of illustration, I'll mention a couple of my own allusions, one rather remote and one comparatively familiar. In "The Pool," previously referred to, occur the lines:

> The numbered angels of Pythagoras
> Press in upon us from the upper air,
> Marrowless, cold,—how can they speak us true?

In a previous stanza I had referred to "bombsights," and my mind was still playing with the threat to culture of modern technology. But who was responsible for modern technology? Chiefly the mathematicians, and Pythagoras, so Whitehead informs us, was the father of modern mathematics. From him came the doctrine of the ultimate reality of *number,* as also the doctrine of the music of the spheres. And so our B-29's that fly like angels and are ruled by the mathematic laws that guide the sun and the other stars are at once a realization of the human dream and the most serious present menace to human survival. "How can they speak us true?" That, then, was what the phrase meant to me. Was there any "carry-over" for you?

My second allusion has at least familiarity to recommend it. Indeed, the poem "Wagon Train" is built upon it. We know that the wagon trains were orderly treks toward reasonably definite destinations, desperate sometimes because of the dangers along the way—and yet—most of them came through. And we are free and our country is great because they did. My strategy in the last stanza of the poem is to lead the reader to transfer some of his "wagon train attitude" not only to his own planet but to all the adventuring stars that make up this precarious universe.

Of the structure of the total poem? The structure of the poem comes out of writing it, usually. Somehow the poem carefully excogitated in advance always has a meretricious air of contrivance, like a knowingly-arranged shop window. Many's the time I've started a sonnet that turned into something else, and my "El Greco," included here, has only thirteen lines because that was the way it shaped itself at the time of writing. (I didn't notice the deficiency till long afterwards). This is not to say, however, that I am opposed to the writing of poetry in "standard" forms. On the contrary, I favor them as a stimulating discipline that forces the writer to take imaginative leaps. All the same, nobody writes well in the traditional forms until they have become a sort of second nature to him, until they are no longer metrical corsets and stanzaic straitjackets but a sort of *living tune in his ear.* As Samuel Daniel remarked, "They are not weights but wings."

Of rhyme and its function? Rhyme, though, remains a problem, especially to a writer like me, who venerates the old patterns as channels worn through the deserts of human speech by the form-hungry imagination. For nothing is more depressing than a banal rhyme. And the Norn who provided the English language with its miraculous resources, withheld—just to balance matters I suppose—one gift which most of the Romance languages take for granted: the gift of a multiplicity of rhyme words. Beginners in poetry are apt to adopt one of two mistaken courses: to employ rhyme-cliches until their verses jingle intolerably, or else to throw rhyme out of the window altogether and write prosy free verse (a poetic medium which requires above all a delicate and experienced "ear"). I am not sure which course is the more dangerous but I think likely the former; because at least the free-verser is brought up the more sharply against his own deficiency. All this by way of saying that inner rhyme, slant rhyme, assonance, consonance, alliteration and the rest seem to be the ways by which the best modern poets escape from this dilemma. My own practice is to employ enough true rhyme to *suggest* regularity but no more. Used thus, rhyme is helpful in establishing stanza form, as a device for emphasis and in general for the control of the overall sound structure. And perhaps, even now, I lean too heavily upon it. We should remind ourselves from time to time that Homer, Virgil, the *Beowulf*-poet, and Shakespeare (in the bulk of his poetry) did not employ it.

Of punctuation? It depends on the poem. The more "difficult" the poem, the more carefully I try to punctuate. By this I don't mean that the punctuation need be "standard." E. E. Cummings, I suspect, punctuates much more thoughtfully and carefully than Shelley ever did. Whatever, outside of the words themselves, aids in the communication of the precise thought, atmosphere, attitude intended, is legitimate. Simple spacing on the page, as employed by Mallarmé and MacLeish, may be of inestimable help in conveying fine shades of meaning.

Of communication? To whom is the poem written? The first question is indissolubly bound up with the second. "Masks" or no "masks," a poem is a kind of confession which says This is where my mind has been. And since this is so, I am minded to quote a passage from Augustine (*The Confessions, X, iv,* 5) in which he explains why he is writing his confessions and how he wants them to be taken. He says:

> Do they desire to joy with me, when they hear how near, by thy gift, I approach unto Thee? and to pray for me, when they shall hear how much I am held back by my own weight? . . . Let a brotherly, not a stranger mind, not that of the *strange children, whose mouth talketh of vanity, and their right hand is a hand of iniquity,* but that of the brotherly mind which when it approveth, rejoiceth for me, and when it disapproveth me, is sorry for me; because whether it approveth or disapproveth, it loveth me, to such will I discover myself. . . . My good deeds are Thine appointments

and Thy gifts; my evil ones are my offenses and Thy judgments. Let them breathe freely at the one; sigh at the other; and let hymns and weeping go up into Thy sight, out of the hearts of my brethren, Thy censors. And do Thou, O Lord, . . . have mercy upon me according to Thy great mercy for Thine own name's sake; and no way forsaking what Thou hast begun, perfect my imperfection.

Augustine's plea for an audience of "brotherly minds" in a world ripped and torn by theological controversy is understandable enough. He had his complement of malicious readers with noses only for scandal and heresy. The point is that he could never have brought himself to write as he did had he not visualized a company of minds similar to his own, sympathetic to pagan learning, rhetoric, and philosophy as his was, yet at the same time concerned above all things as his was with the problem of salvation. I do not mean by this to imply that the poet's quest is always basically a religious one—though it was for Hopkins and Dickinson. I mean that no poet can lift pen to paper until he has visualized a "brotherly" audience for what he is doing. His audience may be the stormy sea, as it was, on occasion, for Byron, or, as it was for Blake sometimes "the children of a future age"—but he cannot write for himself alone. Once, when I was eight years old, and feeling pretty puzzled about life (I was lying on my back in the grass, I remember, on the shady side of the gray double-decker where we lived then, looking up into the sky), I promised myself that when I grew up I'd remember myself as I was then and come back and explain what life was *really* like. There have been times in my writing when I have kept that appointment.

This is quite another matter from aiming one's poetry at a broad popular audience. I think that to do so must always be to cheapen it. The public despises even while it accepts the seer who comes too close to speaking its own language. *Communication* is a necessary concomitant of any artistic utterance whatsoever. This does not mean that the poem need be *clear* to the casual reader. Thus to be clear may be to sabotage the essence of what you are trying to say, may necessitate blackjack generalizations, treacle images, marcelled meter. Good poets do not aim at the market but create the appetite which they satisfy.

I SAW MY FATHER

I saw my father rising through the air
Higher than State House, Bunker Hill, and all—
From kissing earth ripped to a sky of fear . . .

Once, with straight black hair,
He sweated blood, I've heard my mother say,
Until there came a knocking at the door,
Heavy, peremptory.   Nobody

Nobody was there.

Thereafter he grew gray
Gently, quietly. At night, the dream
Stirring the roots of his hair, he would cry out,
A minister who had received his call . . .

Would he have answered me had I called?
Chewing a piece of grass, I stood there
In his green field waving frantically
"Goodbye! Goodbye! Goodbye! Goodbye!"

I shall not find his equal anywhere.

WAGON TRAIN

As pioneering children, when no rain
Made water brackish in the last canteen,
Went to sleep heedless, and as seldom knew
When guns were cocked and ready all night through,
So do we ride the earth's revolving wheel,
Moving across what prairies to what wars
Against what ambush eye does not reveal,
Nor do we know what loyal outriders
Swing on to clear our path across the plain,
But drift to sleep where canvas hides the stars
Of the long, planetary wagon train.

THE POOL

This is the pool that Plato visited
In the late Indian summer of his year
To eat the golden honey harvested
By his own bees in June and July sun.

The stench and smothering out of the wick of our time
Blackens, cracks, and dries
The calm Madonna with Leonardo's eyes;
The rock she sits among
Waits in a bombsight to be otherwise.

She sees the falling leaves, the dying leaves
That cling there still; above
Through the brown horror of the boughs she sees
The empty, arching skull.

But things above still find their counterparts
Under this water: tree responds to tree
And hill to hill; the smallest flake that flies,
Glassed in the pool, finds as it falls its own
Minutest properties.

The numbered angels of Pythagoras
Press in upon us from the upper air,
Marrowless, cold—how can they speak us true?
But in the pool, ugly or beautiful
All are compact of pity and of fear
As we are, only real.

THE UNINFECTED

I saw a man whose face was white as snow
Come slowly down the mall,
And he was followed by another one
Till there were seven in all.

Now this is very strange that lepers be
Allowed to walk abroad in broad daylight!
I shook myself, and quickly turned to call
A bluecoat, and as suddenly caught sight

Of one in blue ruling the thoroughfare,
Who made me passage through that brawling sea
With one raised hand. I spoke, and he inclined
To hear my word, the face of leprosy.

I turned and went straight on to search my own
Face in the next shop window mirror-glass—
Still no infection, not a single spot,
So I stood there and watched the lepers pass

Till four drove up to take me to a place
Where I live now, attended very well
By several strong male lepers dressed in white,
Eating what I like, sound as a bell.

IN THE WEB

What you desire not starlight nor tearose
Breathing at evening from the bush by the house
Tells, nor does the dialect of water
Hissing from the faucet or the hose
Gossip of your loss.

They keep your secret well until you die,
And as the colors of the evening sky
Burn to darkness down, each solemn color
That blesses you before it turns its shoulder
Is tacit with your ghost.

Huge as the night with stars above your house
These patterns laid on emptiness revolve
Beyond all searching; seeds you scatter strive,

Determined things, beyond the studious
Solicitudes of love.

This night and every night they dance in fire,
These patterns of the slayer and the slain,
And now a cock with half his feathers gone
Crows for a dawn he shall not see again
And cannot but desire.

LETTER TO KARL SHAPIRO

Where Athanase once hankered for a star
There was a bad odor; Poe's umbilical
Was never clean cut off: Virginia
Restless in tomb, Elaine unlovable
Supine in wandering barge, Beata in bed
Smell similarly water-lily-bad,
And have you ever had to wash by hand,
When the machine broke down, a baby's diapers?

Virginia, Elaine, and Beata
Assuredly did not, and did not see
How such chores lead two ways: to the corrupt
Winding-sheet considered much by Donne
And to the swaddlings wetted in a manger
By one who bleeds through all the firmament—
There being more room there than there was in the inn
For Word at once symbol and referent.

And such is poetry. Maybe we shall find
(Clawing through language till our fingers crack)
Blake's steel dividers drawing on chaos
Life's wiry line, or land in Rodin's vast
Hand squeezing succulent clay as many ways
As love has eyes or horror tongue to tell,
Or spy from Patmos on a Blue Monday
Earth's last diaper hung in the sun to dry.

EN ROUTE

The earth, that let us in, was soft as fern;
The sky that bars us out is hard as rock;
It has no knob to twist, no hinge to turn,
And knuckles bleed upon the slightest knock.

Earth, then! Do not look back. The sky's flare
Is Sodom, salt to you. Earth's mountains rise
Steep to foothills down; the crags bare
Teeth of stone to the singed refugees.

You in your hat and coat (gone, gone
The homestead where you put them on) take
What lies nearest, a book, a gnawed bone—
No souvenirs, no photos for God's sake.

The sky, a vortex passed already, leans
Hunched above us, waiting what earth means.

EL GRECO

See how the sun has somewhat not of light
Falling upon these men who stand so tall;
See how their eyes observe some inward sight
And how their living takes no room at all—
Their passing stirs no air, so thin they are.
Behind them see small houses with small doors;
The light comes from an unfamiliar star
That lights their walls and falls across their floors.
What shall we say when one of these men goes
Into his house and we no longer see
His eyes observing something that he knows?
And if their houses brim with radiancy
Why does no light come through as those doors close?

NAUSEA

How late the assassins ply their trade tonight;
The air is sweet with corpse-breath and the slight
Shivering in trees in starlight
Whispers death in nature. The old order
Changes, giving place to murder's
Breath in the night air—
Yet all my Lady's thoughts are centered here;

Here where above the city, on a girder,
Hamlet, his feathers ruffled in disorder,
Talks with his father's ghost. He tests the bare
Dissyllable "Revenge!" but on the stair
Descending to the pavement and the heat,
Where, under towers, ten thousand tired feet
Beat, rebeat, grows ill, and is sick in the street.

Still my Lady in her silver chair
Sees to its last minute particular
And sickening core the mystery of war,
And sees Prince Hamlet choose his rapier
Perpetually, and from her parapet
Above the world cries out with infinite
Heat, "Get about your business, Paraclete!"

ANGLO - SAXON

King Alfred sensed among his country's words
England's destiny;
But Caedmon, rapt, among his master's herds,
Felt all their history:
How all men, once, had owned a common tongue
And clumsy dialects the wide world over
Remember music that the first had sung,
And would discover,
Through cries confused, the excellent, true stem
And scattered vowels of Jerusalem.

THE D MINOR

Through what rock-strewn tunnels, O companions,
What wind-hurled clouds through passes in the mountains
You come!—sometimes moving overhead
And sometimes under; native to this ground

And natural guides over these rocks, but banished
By who knows what cabal
Of ancestors, atomic, integral,
Who took this ground and mapped it and are dead,

And it is well with them. The map indeed
Is beautiful and firmly drawn; the wood
Withdraws resemblance, as the lines of the hand
Change gradually, to their promised land . . .

Twangings as of sweet stringed instruments
On lone traverses heard, or chat-birds
Always unseen by man, by one man heard
In the dead-low and middle of the night

Speak, and the shiver of responding blood
Speaks the companion to the ancestor
Who Procne-like in his dry forest bed
Cannot speak again; his children

Blinkered, plated well with eyelid scorn
For what is not according to plan, hold on
To what is left of love like contraband;
And so the banished ones

Infiltrate the sad ranks. For one a door
Opens in singeing sun, another hears
Marching and counter-marching to a drum
At the earth's core; and one you sleep beside

Mutters in sleep: "Bridegroom, behold your bride."

ORACLE

I am just on my way tomb,
Several voices calling different things,
Such as, "Is it better to be kings
Without doms?" or "How
Having climbed clear to abstraction
To come back to our throne?"

Crystal by crystal, knowledge wonderful
Climbs from nothing upwards into cold—
And by what thievery? Who sucked up whose
Brains who has it? Will he keep it? You
Whose eyes' blue vacuum draws whirling in
More than heart can know, do you think so?

Does this make us more royal? You can tell
Who bathed in Shelley's radioactive
Contaminated waters once and heard
The death-boy crying down the Renaissance
"Never repent!" till B-14's like robins
Covered the children up in the deep wood.

Weep for them. Weep for yourself. But do not weep
For the New Men; they keep
Counsel on every level, dream, believe
Only this oracle: "Drink air   eye light
Touch fire   tongue water   greet these shifts of rock
With speech so large stars knock

"And though your talk be still
Honey and locusts to the general,
Scrambling slopes through ozones thin as doubt,
Though they pile mountain over mountain,
Speak! Who hear your voices in their mountains
Shall be ripped like mandrakes shrieking out."

Robert Lowell

ROBERT LOWELL *was born in Boston and attended Harvard University. He is at present engaged on a Guggenheim project. His first book,* LAND OF UNLIKENESS, *appeared in a limited edition and is now unavailable. His second book,* LORD WEARY'S CASTLE *won the Pulitzer Prize in Poetry for* 1946.

Editor's note: Robert Lowell writes: "I prefer reading poets on their own work to anyone else. However, your questionnaire comes to me at the wrong time. . . . I'm just getting back to writing and feel pretty numb about theorizing on old poems." Mr. Lowell then suggested that Randall Jarrell's long review of *Lord Weary's Castle* (in *The Nation*) contained technical analyses with which he was essentially in agreement. As a modest man, Mr. Lowell added that the praise contained in the review should be deleted as "inappropriate." The editor, not under the constraint of modesty, believes that the praise is both appropriate and merited, and the review is here reprinted in full by courteous permission of Mr. Jarrell and *The Nation*.

ROBERT LOWELL'S POETRY

by RANDALL JARRELL

MANY OF the people who reviewed *Lord Weary's Castle* felt that it was as much of an event as Auden's first book; I can think of no one younger than Auden who has written better poetry than Robert Lowell's. Anyone who reads contemporary poetry will read it; perhaps people will understand the poetry more easily and find it more congenial, if they see what the poems have developed out of, how they are related to each other, and why they say what they say.

Underneath all these poems "there is one story and one story only": when this essential theme or subject is understood, the unity of attitudes and judgments underlying the variety of the poems becomes startlingly explicit. The poems understand the world as a sort of conflict of opposites. In this struggle one opposite is that cake of custom in which all of us lie embedded like lung-fish—the stasis or inertia of the complacent self, the satisfied persistence in evil that is damnation. Into this realm of necessity the poems push everything that is closed, turned inward, incestuous, that blinds or binds: the Old Law, imperialism, militarism, capitalism, Calvinism, Authority, the Father, the "proper Bostonians," the rich who will "do everything for the poor except get off their backs." But struggling within this like leaven, falling to it like light, is everything that is free or open, that grows or is willing to change: here is the generosity or willingness or openness that is itself salvation; here is "accessibility to experience"; this is the realm of freedom, of the Grace that has replaced the Law, of the perfect liberator whom the poet calls Christ.

Consequently the poems can have two possible movements or organizations: they can move from what is closed to what is open, or from what is open to what is closed. The second of these organizations—which corresponds to an "unhappy ending"— is less common, though there are many good examples of it: "The Exile's Return," with its menacing *Voi ch' entrate* that transforms the exile's old home into a place where even hope must be abandoned; or that extraordinary treatment of the Oedipus complex, "Between the Porch and the Altar," with its four parts each ending in constriction and frustration, its hero who cannot get free of his mother, her punishments, and her world even by dying, but who sees both life and death in terms of her, and thinks at the end that, sword in hand, the Lord "watches me for Mother, and will turn / The bier and baby-carriage where I burn."

But normally the poems move into liberation. Even death is seen as liberation, a widening into darkness: that old closed system, Grandfather Arthur Winslow, dying of cancer in his adjusted bed, at the last is the child Arthur whom the swanboats once rode through the Public Garden, whom now "the ghost of risen Jesus walks the waves to run/ Upon a trumpeting black swan/ Beyond Charles River and the Acheron/ Where the wide waters and their voyager are one." (Compare the endings of "The Drunken Fisherman" and "Dea Roma.") "The Death of the Sheriff" moves from closure—the "ordered darkness" of the homicidal sheriff, the "loved sightless smother" of the incestuous lovers, the "unsearchable quicksilver heart/ Where spiders stare their eyes out at their own/ Spitting and knotted likeness"—up into the open sky to those "light wanderers" the planets, to the "thirsty Dipper on the arc of night." Just so the cold, blundering, iron confusion of "Christmas Eve Under Hooker's Statue" ends in flowers, the wild fields, a Christ "once again turned wanderer and child." In "Rebell-ion," the son seals "an everlasting pact/ With Dives to *contract/* The world that *spreads* in pain"; but at last he rebels against his father and his father's New England commercial theocracy, and "the world *spread* / When the clubbed flintlock broke my father's brain." The italicized words ought to demonstrate how explicitly, at times, these poems formulate the world in the exact terms that I have used.

"Where the Rainbow Ends" describes in apocalyptic terms the wintry, Calvinist, capitalist—Mr. Lowell has Weber's belief in the connection of capitalism and Calvinism—dead end of God's cove-nant with man, a frozen Boston where even the cold-blooded serpents "whistle at the cold." (The poems often use cold as a plain and physically correct symbol for what is constricted or static.) There "the scythers, Time and Death,/ Helmed locusts, move upon the tree of breath," of the spirit of man; a bridge curves over Charles River like an ironic parody of the rainbow's covenant; both "the wild ingrafted olive and its root/ Are withered" [these are Paul's terms for the Judaism of the Old Law and the Gentile Christianity grafted upon it]; "every dove [the Holy Ghost, the bringer of the olive leaf to the Ark] is sold" for a commercialized, legalized sacrifice. The whole system seems an abstract, rational-ized "graph of Revelations," of the last accusation and judgment brought against man now that "the Chapel's sharp-shinned eagle shifts its hold/ On serpent-Time, the rainbow's epitaph." This last line means what the last line in "The Quaker Graveyard"— "The Lord survives the rainbow of His will"—means; both are inexpressibly menacing, since they show the covenant as something that binds only us, as something abrogated merely by the passage of time, as a closed system opening not into liberation but into infinite and overwhelming possibility; they have something of the terror, but none of the pity, of Blake's "Time is the mercy of Eternity."

Then the worshipper, like a victim, climbs to the altar of the terrible I AM, to breathe there the rarefied and intolerable ether of his union with the divinity of the Apocalypse; he despairs even of the wings that beat against his cheek: "What can the dove of Jesus give/ You now but wisdom, exile?" When the poem has reached this point of the most extreme closure, when the infinite grace that atones and liberates is seen as no more than the bitter and useless wisdom of the exile, it opens with a rush of acceptant joy into: "Stand and live, / The dove has brought an olive branch to eat." The dove of Jesus brings to the worshipper the olive branch that shows him that the flood has receded, opening the whole earth for him; it is the olive branch of peace and reconciliation, the olive branch that he is "to eat" as a symbol of the eaten flesh of Christ, of atonement, identification, and liberation. Both the old covenant and the new still hold, nothing has changed: here as they were and will be are life and salvation.

Mr. Lowell's Christianity has nothing to do with the familiar literary Christianity of *as if*, the belief in the necessity of belief; and it is a kind of photographic negative of the faith of the usual Catholic convert, who distrusts freedom as much as he needs bondage, and who sees the world as a liberal chaos which can be ordered and redeemed only by that rigid and final Authority to Whom men submit without question. Lowell reminds one of those heretical enthusiasts, often disciplined and occasionally sanctified or excommunicated, who are more at home in the Church Triumphant than in the church of this world, which is one more state. A phrase like Mr. Lowell's "St. Peter, the distorted key" is likely to be appreciated outside the church and carefully overlooked inside it, *ad maiorem gloriam* of Catholic poetry. All Mr. Lowell's earliest poems would seem to suggest that he was, congenitally, the ideal follower of Barth or Calvin: one imagines him, a few years ago, supporting neither Franco nor the loyalists, but yearning to send a couple of clippers full of converted minutemen to wipe out the whole bunch—human, hence deserving. (I wish that he could cast a colder eye on minutemen; his treatment of the American Revolution is in the great tradition of Marx, Engels, and Parson Weems.) Freedom is something that he has wished to escape into, by a very strange route. In his poems the Son is pure liberation from the incestuous, complacent, inveterate evil of established society, of which the Law is a part—although the Father, Jehovah, has retained both the violence necessary to break up this inertia and a good deal of the menacing sternness of Authority as such, just as the poems themselves have. It is interesting to compare the figure of the Uncle in early Auden, who sanctifies rebellion by his authority; the authority of Mr. Lowell's Christ is sanctified by his rebellion or liberation.

Anyone who compares Mr. Lowell's earlier and later poems will see this movement from constriction to liberation as to his work's ruling principle of growth. The grim, violent, sordid constriction of his earliest poems—most of them omitted from *Lord Weary's Castle*—seems to be temperamental, the Old Adam which the poet grew from and partially transcends; and a good deal of what is excessive in the extraordinary rhetorical machine of a poem like "The Quaker Graveyard at Nantucket," which traps and twists to pieces the unwary reader—who rather enjoys it— is gone from his latest poems, or else dramatically justified and no longer excessive. The "Quaker Graveyard" is a baroque work, like *Paradise Lost,* but all the *extase* of baroque has disappeared— the coiling violence of its rhetoric, the harsh and stubborn intensity that accompanies all its verbs and verbals, the clustering stresses learned from accentual verse, come from a man contracting every muscle, grinding his teeth together till his shut eyes ache. Mr. Lowell's later work has moved in the direction of the poem's quiet contrast-section, "Walsingham"; the denunciatory prophetic tone has disappeared, along with the early satiric effects that were one of the poet's weaknesses. The later poems depend less on rhetorical description and more on dramatic speech; their wholes have escaped from the hypnotic bondage of the details. Often the elaborate stanzas have changed into a novel sort of dramatic or narrative couplet, run-on but with heavily stressed rhymes. A girl's nightmare, in the late "Katherine's Dream," is far more clear, open, and speech-like than the poet's own descriptive meditation in an earlier work like "Christmas at Black Rock." It is important to understand this development; the reviewers of *Lord Weary's Castle* did not realize that it exists.

Mr. Lowell has a completely unscientific, but thoroughly historical mind. It is literary and traditional as well; he can use the past so effectively because he thinks so much as it did. He seems to be condemned both to read history and to repeat it. His present contains the past—especially Rome, the late Middle Ages, and a couple of centuries of New England—as an operative skeleton just under the skin. (This is rare among contemporary poets, who look at the past more as Blücher looked at London: "What a city to sack!" Actually he said, "What a mix-up!" But this fits, too.) War, Trade, and Jehovah march side by side through all Mr. Lowell's ages: it is the fundamental likeness of the past and present, and not their disparity, which is insisted upon. "Cold / Snaps the bronze toes and fingers of the Christ / My father fetched from Florence, and the dead / Chatters to nothing in the thankless ground / His father screwed from Charlie Stark and sold / To the selectmen." Here is a good deal of the history of New England's ninetenth century in a sentence.

Of New England Mr. Lowell has the ambivalent knowledge one has of one's damned kin. The poems are crowded with the "fearful Witnesses" who "fenced their gardens with the Redman's bones"; the clippers and the slavers, their iron owners, and their old seamen knitting at the asylum; the Public Garden "where / The bread-stuffed ducks are brooding, where with tub / And strainer the mid-Sunday Irish scare / The sun-struck shallows for the dusky chub"; the faith "that made the Pilgrim Makers take a lathe / To point their wooden steeples lest the Word be dumb." Here his harshest propositions flower out of facts. But some of his earlier satires of present-day politics and its continuation have a severe crudity that suggest Michael Wigglesworth rewriting the "Horatian Ode"; airplanes he treats as Allen Tate does, only more so—he gives the impression of having encountered them in Mother Shipton. But these excesses were temporary; what is permanently excessive is a sort of obstinate violence or violent obstinacy of temperament and perception. In a day when poets wish to be irresistible forces, he is an immovable object.

Mr. Lowell's period pieces are notable partly for their details—which are sometimes magically and professionally illusionary—and partly for the empathy, the historical identification, that underlie the details. The period pieces are intimately related to his adaptations of poems from other languages: both are valuable as ways of getting a varied, extensive, and alien experience into his work. Dismissing these adaptations as misguided "translations" is like dismissing "To Celia" or *Cathay*, and betrays an odd dislike or ignorance of an important and traditional procedure of poets.

Mr. Lowell is a thoroughly professional poet, and the degree of intensity of his poems is equalled by their degree of organization. Inside its elaborate stanzas the poem is put together like a mosaic: the shifts of movement, the varied pauses, the alternation in the length of sentences, the counterpoint between lines and sentences, are the outer form of a subject matter that has been given a dramatic, dialectical internal organization; and it is hard to exaggerate the strength and life, the constant richness and violence of metaphor and sound and motion, of the language itself. The organization of the poems resembles that of a great deal of traditional English poetry—especially when compared to that type of semi-imagist modern organization in which the things of the poem seem to marshal themselves like Dryden's atoms—but often this is complicated by stream-of-consciousness, dream, or dramatic-monologue types of structure. This makes the poems more difficult, but it is worth the price—many of the most valuable dramatic effects can hardly be attained inside a more logical or abstract organization. Mr. Lowell's poetry is a unique fusion of modernist and traditional poetry, and there exist conjoined in it certain effects that one would hitherto have thought mutually exclusive; however, it is essentially a post- or anti-modernist poetry, and as such is certain to be influential.

This poet is wonderfully good at discovering powerful, homely, grotesque, but exactly appropriate particulars for his poems. "Actuality is something brute," said Peirce. "There is no reason in it. I instance putting your shoulder against a door and trying to force it open against an unseen, silent, and unknown resistance." The things in Mr. Lowell's poems, have, necessarily, been wrenched into formal shape, organized under terrific pressure, but they keep to an extraordinary degree their stubborn, unmoved toughness, their senseless originality and contingency: no poet is more notable for what, I have read, Duns Scotus calls *haeccitas*—the contrary, persisting, and singular thingness of every being in the world; but this detailed factuality is particularly effective because it sets off, or is set off by, the elevation and rhetorical sweep characteristic of much earlier English poetry. Mr. Lowell is obviously a haptic rather than a visual type: a poem like "Colloquy in Black Rock" has some of the most successful kinaesthetic effects in English. It is impossible not to notice the weight and power of his lines, a strength that is sometimes mechanical or exaggerated, and sometimes overwhelming. But because of this strength the smooth, calm, and flowing ease of a few passages, the flat and colloquial ease of others, have even more effectiveness than they ordinarily would have: the dead mistress of Propertius, a black nail dangling from a finger, Lethe oozing from her nether lip, in the end can murmur to the "apple-sweetened Anio":

> . . . Anio, you will please
> Me if you whisper upon sliding knees:
> "Propertius, Cynthia is here:
> She shakes her blossoms when my waters clear."

Mr. Lowell, at his best and latest, is a dramatic poet: he presents people, their actions, their speeches, as they feel and look and sound to people; the poet's generalizations are usually implied, and the poem's explicit generalizations are there primarily because they are dramatically necessary—it is not usually the poet who means them. He does not present themes or generalizations but a world; the differences and similarities between it and ours bring home to us themes, generalizations, and the poet himself. The "personality" of the poet is usually not exploited; the *I* who stands meditating by Hooker's statue is closer to the different *I*'s of the dramatic monologues than to the man who wrote them. It is partly because of this that atheists are vexed by his Catholic views (and Catholics by his heretical ones) considerably less than they normally would be.

But there are other reasons. The poet's rather odd and imaginative Catholicism is thoroughly suitable to his mind, which is so traditional, theocentric, and anthropomorphic that no images from the sciences, next to none from philosophy, occur in his poems. Such a Catholicism is thoroughly suited to literature, since it is essentially literary, anthropomorphic, emotional. It is an advantage to a poet to have a frame of reference, terms of generalization, which are themselves human, affective, and effective as literature. *Bodily Changes in Fear, Rage, Pain and Hunger* may let the poet know more about the anger of Achilles, but it is hard for him to have to talk about adrenalin and the thalamus; and when the arrows of Apollo are transformed into a "lack of adequate sanitary facilities," everything is lost but understanding. (This helps to explain the dependence of contemporary poetry on particulars, emotions, things—its generalizations, where they are most effective, are fantastic, though often traditionally so). Naturally the terms of scientific explanation cannot have these poetic and emotional effects, since it is precisely by the exclusion of such effects that science has developed. (Many of the conclusions of the sciences are as poetic as anything in the world, but they have been of little use to poets—how can you use something you are delighted never to have heard of?) Mr. Lowell's Catholicism represents effective realities of human behavior and desire, regardless of whether it is true, false, or absurd; and as everyone must realize, it is possible to tell part of the truth about the world in terms that are false, limited, and fantastic—else how should we have told it? There is admittedly no "correct" or "scientific" view of a great many things that a poet writes about, and he has to deal with them in dramatic and particular terms, if he has foregone the advantage of pre-scientific ideologies like Christianity or Marxism. Of course it seems to me an advantage that he almost necessarily foregoes; I remember writing about contemporary religious poems, "It is hard to enjoy the ambergris for thinking of all those suffering whales," and most people will feel this when they encounter a passage in Mr. Lowell's poetry telling them how Bernadette's miraculous vision of Our Lady "puts out reason's eyes." It does indeed.

It is unusually difficult to say which are the best poems in *Lord Weary's Castle*: several are realized past changing, successes that vary only in scope and intensity—others are poems that almost any living poet would be pleased to have written. But certainly some of the best things in the book are "Colloquy in Black Rock," "Between the Porch and the Altar," the first of the two poems that compose "The Death of the Sheriff," and "Where the Rainbow Ends"; "The Quaker Graveyard at Nantucket" and "At the Indian-

Killer's Grave" have extremely good parts; some other moving, powerful, and unusual poems are "Death from Cancer," "The Exile's Return," "Mr. Edwards and the Spider," and "Mary Winslow"—and I hate to leave entirely unmentioned poems like "After the Surprising Conversions," "The Blind Leading the Blind," "The Drunken Fisherman," and "New Year's Day." But no poem in *Lord Weary's Castle* is so good as that long dramatic monologue of a New Brunswick nun which was published in the *Kenyon Review* in 1948.

When I reviewed Mr. Lowell's first book I finished by saying, "Some of the best poems of the next years ought to be written by him." The appearance of *Lord Weary's Castle* makes me feel less like Adams or Leverrier than like a rain-maker who predicts rain, and gets a flood which drowns everyone in the county. One or two of these poems, I think, will be read as long as men remember English.

THE EXILE'S RETURN

There mounts in squalls a sort of rusty mire,
Not ice, not snow, to leaguer the Hôtel
De Ville, where braced pig-iron dragons grip
The blizzard to their rigor mortis. A bell
Grumbles when the reverberations strip
The thatching from its spire,
The search-guns click and spit and split up timber
And nick the slate roofs on the Holstenwall
Where torn-up tilestones crown the victor. Fall
And winter, spring and summer, guns unlimber
And lumber down the narrow gabled street
Past your gray, sorry and ancestral house
Where the dynamited walnut tree
Shadows a squat, old, wind-torn gate and cows
The Yankee commandant. You will not see
Strutting children or meet
The peg-leg and reproachful chancellor
With a forget-me-not in his button-hole
When the unseasoned liberators roll
Into the Market Square, ground arms before
The Rathaus; but already lily-stands
Burgeon the risen Rhineland, and a rough
Cathedral lifts its eye. Pleasant enough,
Voi ch' entrate, and your life is in your hands.

COLLOQUY IN BLACK ROCK

Here the jack-hammer jabs into the ocean;
My heart, you race and stagger and demand
More blood-gangs for your nigger-brass percussions,
Till I, the stunned machine of your devotion,
Clanging upon this cymbal of a hand,
Am rattled screw and footloose. All discussions
End in the mud-flat detritus of death.

My heart, beat faster, faster. In Black Mud
Hungarian workmen give' their blood
For the martyre Stephen, who was stoned to death.

Black Mud, a name to conjure with: O mud
For watermelons gutted to the crust,
Mud for the mole-tide harbor, mud for mouse,
Mud for the armored Diesel fishing tubs that thud
A year and a day to wind and tide: the dust
Is on this skipping heart that shakes my house,

House of our Savior who was hanged till death.
My heart, beat faster, faster. In Black Mud
Stephen the martyre was broken down to blood:
Our ransom is the rubble of his death,

Christ walks on the black water. In Black Mud
Darts the kingfisher. On Corpus Christi, heart,
Over the drum-beat of St. Stephen's choir
I hear him, *Stupor Mundi,* and the mud
Flies from his hunching wings and beak—my heart,
The blue kingfisher dives on you in fire.

THE QUAKER GRAVEYARD
IN NANTUCKET

(*For Warren Winslow, dead at sea*)

*Let man have dominion over the fishes of the sea and the fowls of
the air and the beasts and the whole earth, and every creeping
creature that moveth upon the earth.*

I

A brackish reach of shoal off Madaket,—
The sea was still breaking violently and night
Had steamed into our North Atlantic Fleet,
When the drowned sailor clutched the drag-net. Light

Flashed from his matted head and marble feet,
He grappled at the net
With the coiled, hurdling muscles of his thighs:
The corpse was bloodless, a botch of reds and whites,
Its open, staring eyes
Were lustreless dead-lights
Or cabin-windows on a stranded hulk
Heavy with sand. We weight the body, close
Its eyes and heave it seaward whence it came,
Where the heel-headed dogfish barks its nose
On Ahab's void and forehead; and the name
Is blocked in yellow chalk.
Sailors, who pitch this portent at the sea
Where dreadnaughts shall confess
Its hell-bent deity,
When you are powerless
To sand-bag this Atlantic bulwark, faced
By the earth-shaker, green, unwearied, chaste
In his steel scales: ask for no Orphean lute
To pluck life back. The guns of the steeled fleet
Recoil and then repeat
The hoarse salute.

II

Whenever winds are moving and their breath
Heaves at the roped-in bulwarks of this pier,
The terns and sea-gulls tremble at your death
In these home waters. Sailor, can you hear
The Pequod's sea wings, beating landward, fall
Headlong and break on our Atlantic wall
Off 'Sconset, where the yawing S-boats splash
The bellbuoy, with ballooning spinnakers,
As the entangled, screeching mainsheet clears
The blocks: off Madaket, where lubbers lash
The heavy surf and throw their long lead squids
For blue-fish? Sea-gulls blink their heavy lids
Seaward. The winds' wings beat upon the stones,

Cousin, and scream for you and the claws rush
At the sea's throat and wring it in the slush
Of this old Quaker graveyard where the bones
Cry out in the long night for the hurt beast
Bobbing by Ahab's whaleboats in the East.

III

All you recovered from Poseidon died
With you, my cousin, and the harrowed brine
Is fruitless on the blue beard of the god,
Stretching beyond us to the castles in Spain,
Nantucket's westward haven. To Cape Cod
Guns, cradled on the tide,
Blast the eelgrass about a waterclock
Of bilge and backwash, roil the salt and sand
Lashing earth's scaffold, rock
Our warships in the hand
Of the great God, where time's contrition blues
Whatever it was these Quaker sailors lost
In the mad scramble of their lives. They died
When time was open-eyed,
Wooden and childish; only bones abide
There, in the nowhere, where their boats were tossed
Sky-high, where mariners had fabled news
Of IS, the whited monster. What it cost
Them is their secret. In the sperm-whale's slick
I see the Quakers drown and hear their cry:
"If God himself had not been on our side,
If God himself had not been on our side,
When the Atlantic rose against us, why,
Then it had swallowed us up quick."

IV

This is the end of the whaleroad and the whale
Who spewed Nantucket bones on the thrashed swell
And stirred the troubled waters to whirlpools
To send the Pequod packing off to hell:

This is the end of them, three-quarters fools,
Snatching at straws to sail
Seaward and seaward on the turntail whale,
Spouting out blood and water as it rolls,
Sick as a dog to these Atlantic shoals:
Clamavimus, O depths. Let the sea-gulls wail

For water, for the deep where the high tide
Mutters to its hurt self, mutters and ebbs.
Waves swallow in their wash, go out and out,
Leave only the death-rattle of the crabs,
The beach increasing, its enormous snout
Sucking the ocean's side.
This is the end of running on the waves;
We are poured out like water. Who will dance.
The mast-lashed master of Leviathans
Up from this field of Quakers in their unstoned graves?

V

When the whale's viscera go and the roll
Of its corruption overruns this world
Beyond tree-swept Nantucket and Wood's Hole
And Martha's Vineyard, Sailor, will your sword
Whistle and fall and sink into the fat?
In the great ash-pit of Jehoshaphat
The bones cry for the blood of the white whale,
The fat flukes arch and whack about its ears,
The death-lance churns into the sanctuary, tears
The gun-blue swingle, heaving like a flail,
And hacks the coiling life out: it works and drags
And rips the sperm-whale's midriff into rags,
Gobbets of blubber spill to wind and weather,
Sailor, and gulls go round the stoven timbers
Where the morning stars sing out together
And thunder shakes the white surf and dismembers
The red flag hammered in the mast-head. Hide,
Our steel, Jonas Messias, in Thy side.

VI
Our Lady of Walsingham

There once the penitents took off their shoes
And then walked barefoot the remaining mile;
And the small trees, a stream and hedgerows file
Slowly along the munching English lane,
Like cows to the old shrine, until you lose
Track of your dragging pain.
The stream flows down under the druid tree,
Shiloah's whirlpools gurgle and make glad
The castle of God. Sailor, you were glad
And whistled Sion by that stream. But see:

Our Lady, too small for her canopy,
Sits near the altar. There's no comeliness
At all or charm in that expressionless
Face with its heavy eyelids. As before,
This face, for centuries a memory,
Non est species, neque decor,
Expressionless, expresses God: it goes
Past castled Sion. She knows what God knows,
Not Calvary's Cross nor crib at Bethlehem
Now, and the world shall come to Walsingham.

VII

The empty winds are creaking and the oak
Splatters and splatters on the cenotaph,
The boughs are trembling and a gaff
Bobs on the untimely stroke
Of the greased wash exploding on a shoal-bell
In the old mouth of the Atlantic. It's well;
Atlantic, you are fouled with the blue sailors,
Sea-monsters, upward angel, downward fish:
Unmarried and corroding, spare of flesh
Mart once of supercilious, wing'd clippers,
Atlantic, where your bell-trap guts its spoil
You could cut the brackish winds with a knife

Here in Nantucket, and cast up the time
When the Lord God formed man from the sea's slime
And breathed into his face the breath of life,
And blue-lung'd combers lumbered to the kill.
The Lord survives the rainbow of His will.

IN MEMORY OF ARTHUR WINSLOW

I. DEATH FROM CANCER

This Easter, Arthur Winslow, less than dead,
Your people set you up in Phillips' House
To settle off your wrestling with the crab—
The claws drop flesh upon your yachting blouse
Until longshoreman Charon come and stab
Through your adjusted bed
And crush the crab. On Boston Basin, shells
Hit water by the Union Boat Club wharf:
You ponder why the coxes' squeakings dwarf
The *resurrexit dominus* of all the bells.

Grandfather Winslow, look, the swanboats coast
That island in the Public Gardens, where
The bread-stuffed ducks are brooding, where with tub
And strainer the mid-Sunday Irish scare
The sun-struck shallows for the dusky chub
This Easter, and the ghost
Of risen Jesus walks the waves to run
Arthur upon a trumpeting black swan
Beyond Charles River to the Acheron
Where the wide waters and their voyager are one.

II. DUNBARTON

The stones are yellow and the grass is gray
Past Concord by the rotten lake and hill
Where crutch and trumpet meet the limousine

And half-forgotten Starks and Winslows fill
The granite plot and the dwarf pines are green
From watching for the day
When the great year of the little yeomen come
Bringing its landed Promise and the faith
That made the Pilgrim Makers take a lathe
And point their wooden steeples lest the Word be dumb.

O fearful witnesses, your day is done:
The minister from Boston waves your shades,
Like children, out of sight and out of mind.
The first selectman of Dunbarton spreads
Wreaths of New Hampshire pine cones on the lined
Casket where the cold sun
Is melting. But, at last, the end is reached;
We start our cars. The preacher's mouthings still
Deafen my poor relations on the hill:
Their sunken landmarks echo what our fathers preached.

III. FIVE YEARS LATER

Th ; Easter, Arthur Winslow, five years gone
I came to mourn you, not to praise the craft
That netted you a million dollars, late
Hosing out gold in Colorado's waste,
Then lost it all in Boston real estate.
Now from the train, at dawn
Leaving Columbus in Ohio, shell
On shell of our stark culture strikes the sun
To fill my head with all our fathers won
When Cotton Mather wrestled with the fiends from hell.

You must have hankered for our family's craft:
The block-house Edward made, the Governor,
At Marshfield, and the slight coin-silver spoons
The Sheriff beat to shame the gaunt Revere,
And General Stark's coarse bas-relief in bronze
Set on your granite shaft

In rough Dunbarton; for what else could bring
You, Arthur, to the veined and alien West
But devil's notions that your gold at least
Could give back life to men who whipped or backed the King?

IV. A PRAYER FOR MY GRANDFATHER TO OUR LADY

Mother, for these three hundred years or more
Neither our clippers nor our slavers reached
The haven of your peace in this Bay State:
Neither my father nor his father. Beached
On these dry flats of fishy real estate,
O Mother, I implore
Your scorched, blue thunderbreasts of love to pour
Buckets of blessings on my burning head
Until I rise like Lazarus from the dead;
Lavabis nos et super nivem dealbabor.

"On Copley Square, I saw you hold the door
To Trinity, the costly Church, and saw
The painted Paradise of harps and lutes
Sink like Alantis in the Devil's jaw
And knock the Devil's teeth out by the roots;
But when I strike foɪ shore
I find no painted idols to adore:
Hell is burned out, heaven's harp-strings are slack.
Mother, run to the chalice, and bring back
Blood on your finger-tips for Lazarus who was poor."

MARY WINSLOW

Her Irish maids could never spoon out mush
Or orange-juice enough; the body cools
And smiles as a sick child
Who adds up figures, and a hush
Grips at the poised relations sipping sherry
And tracking up the carpets of her four

Room kingdom. On the rigid Charles, in snow,
Charon, the Lubber, clambers from his wherry,
And stops her hideous baby-squawks and yells,
Wit's clownish afterthought. Nothing will go
Again. Even the gelded picador
Baiting the twinned runt bulls
With walrus horns before the Spanish Belles
Is veiled with all the childish bibelots.

Mary Winslow is dead. Out on the Charles
The shells hold water and their oarblades drag,
Littered with captivated ducks, and now
The bell-rope in King's Chapel Tower unsnarls
And bells the bestial cow
From Boston Common; she is dead. But stop,
Neighbor, these pillows prop
Her that her terrified and child's cold eyes
Glass what they're not: our Copley ancestress,
Grandiloquent, square-jowled and wordly-wise,
A Cleopatra in her housewife's dress;
Nothing will go again. The bells cry: "Come,
Come home," the babbling Chapel belfry cries:
"Come, Mary Winslow, come; I bell thee home."

CHARLES THE FIFTH
AND THE PEASANT

(*After Valéry*)

Elected Kaiser, burgher and a knight,
Clamped in his black and burly harness, Charles
Canters on Titian's sunset to his night;
A wounded wolfhound bites his spurs and snarls:
So middle-aged and common, it's absurd
To picture him as Caesar, the first cause
Behind whose leg-of-mutton beard, the jaws
Grate on the flesh and gristle of the Word.

The fir trees in the background buzz and lurch
To the disgruntled sing-song of their fears:
"How can we stop it, stop it, stop it?" sing
The needles; and the peasant, braining perch
Against a bucket, rocks and never hears
His Ark drown in the deluge of the King.

BETWEEN THE PORCH
AND THE ALTAR

I. MOTHER AND SON

Meeting his mother makes him lose ten years,
Or is it twenty? Time, no doubt, has ears
That listen to the swallowed serpent, wound
Into its bowels, but he thinks no sound
Is possible before her, he thinks the past
Is settled. It is honest to hold fast
Merely to what one sees with one's own eyes
When the red velvet curves and haunches rise
To blot him from the pretty driftwood fire's
Facade of welcome. Then the son retires
Into the sack and selfhood of the boy
Who clawed through fallen houses of his Troy,
Homely and human only when the flames
Crackle in recollection. Nothing shames
Him more than this uncoiling, counterfeit
Body presented as an idol. It
Is something in a circus, big as life,
The painted dragon, a mother and a wife
With flat glass eyes pushed at him on a stick;
The human mover crawls to make them click.
The forehead of her father's portrait peels
With rosy dryness, and the schoolboy kneels
To ask the benediction of the hand,
Lifted as though to motion him to stand,

Dangling its watch-chain on the Holy Book—
A little golden snake that mouths a hook.

II. ADAM AND EVE

The farmer sizzles on his shaft all day.
He is content and centuries away
From white-hot Concord, and he stands on guard.
Or is he melting down like sculptured lard?
His hand is crisp and steady on the plough.
I quarrelled with you, but am happy now
To while away my life for your unrest
Of terror. Never to have lived is best;
Man tasted Eve with death. I taste my wife
And children while I hold your hands. I knife
Their names into this elm. What is exempt?
I eye the statue with an awed contempt
And see the puritanical facade
Of the white church that Irish exiles made
For Patrick—that Colonial from Rome
Had magicked the charmed serpents from their home,
As though he were the Piper. Will his breath
Scorch the red dragon of my nerves to death?
By sundown we are on a shore. You walk
A little way before me and I talk,
Half to myself and half aloud. They lied,
My cold-eyed seedy fathers when they died,
Or rather threw their lives away, to fix
Sterile, forbidding nameplates on the bricks
Above a kettle. Jesus rest their souls!
You cry for help. Your market-basket rolls
With all its baking apples in the lake.
You watch the whorish slither of a snake
That chokes a duckling. When we try to kiss,
Our eyes are slits and cringing, and we hiss;
Scales glitter on our bodies as we fall.
The Farmer melts upon his pedestal.

III. KATHERINE'S DREAM

It must have been a Friday. I could hear
The top-floor typist's thunder and the beer
That you had brought in cases hurt my head;
I'd sent the pillows flying from my bed,
I hugged my knees together and I gasped.
The dangling telephone receiver rasped
Like someone in a dream who cannot stop
For breath or logic till his victim drop
To darkness and the sheets. I must have slept,
But still could hear my father who had kept
Your guilty presents but cut off my hair.
He whispers that he really doesn't care
If I am your kept woman all my life,
Or ruin your two children and your wife;
But my dishonor makes him drink. Of course
I'll tell the court the truth for his divorce.
I walk through snow into St. Patrick's yard.
Black nuns with glasses smile and stand on guard
Before a bulkhead in a bank of snow,
Whose charred doors open, as good people go
Inside by twos to the confessor. One
Must have a friend to enter there, but none
Is friendless in this crowd, and the nuns smile.
I stand aside and marvel: for a while
The winter sun is pleasant and it warms
My heart with love for others, but the swarms
Of penitents have dwindled. I begin
To cry and ask God's pardon of our sin.
Where are you? You were with me and are gone.
All the forgiven couples hurry on
To dinner and their nights, and none will stop.
I run about in circles till I drop
Against a padlocked bulkhead in a yard
Where faces redden and the snow is hard.

IV. AT THE ALTAR

I sit at a gold table with my girl
Whose eyelids burn with brandy. What a whirl
Of Easter eggs is colored by the lights,
As the Norwegian dancer's crystalled tights
Flash with her naked leg's high-booted skate,
Like Northern Lights upon my watching plate.
The twinkling steel above me is a star;
I am a fallen Christmas tree. Our car
Races through seven red-lights—then the road
Is unpatrolled and empty, and a load
Of ply-wood with a tail-light makes us slow.
I turn and whisper in her ear. You know
I want to leave my mother and my wife,
You wouldn't have me tied to them for life . . .
Time runs, the windshield runs with stars. The past
Is cities from a train, until at last
Its escalating and black-windowed blocks
Recoil against a Gothic church. The clocks
Are tolling. I am dying. The shocked stones
Are falling like a ton of bricks and bones
That snap and splinter and descend in glass
Before a priest who mumbles through his Mass
And sprinkles holy water: and the Day
Breaks with its lightning on the man of clay,
Dies amara valde. Here the Lord
Is Lucifer in harness: hand on sword,
He watches me for Mother, and will turn
The bier and baby-carriage where I burn.

Randall Jarrell

RANDALL JARRELL *was born in* 1914 *and grew up in California and Tennessee. He attended Vanderbilt University. He has taught at Kenyon College, The University of Texas, Sarah Lawrence College, and the Salzburg Seminar in American Civilization. He was for a year literary editor of The Nation. He is at present Associate Professor of English at the Woman's College of the University of North Carolina. He has published three volumes of poetry:* BLOOD FOR A STRANGER, LITTLE FRIEND, *and* LOSSES.

ANSWERS TO QUESTIONS

I. (ORAL QUALITY). All my poems are meant to be said aloud; many of them are dramatic speeches or scenes.

2. (audience). I don't know whom they are written for—for the usual audience that reads poetry from age to age, I believe, and not for the more specialized audience that reads modern poetry. It seems to me that the poet's responsibility is to his subject-matter, but that one of the determining conditions of the poem is the hypothetical normal audience for which he writes it. No one would say that a mathematician or scientist is chiefly or directly responsible to his readers; it is a mistake to say that a poet is.

3. (language). I try to make the language fit the poem. Since the poem is one of my actions, it will have a family resemblance to other actions and poems of mine, but I do not try to make it have one. As the cartwright in Chuangtse says, "When I make the spokes too tight, they won't fit the wheel, and when I make them too loose, they will not hold. I have to make them just right. I feel them with my hands and judge them with my heart. There is something about it which I cannot put down in words. I cannot teach that feeling to my own son, and my own son cannot learn it from me." And he finishes as anyone would like to finish: "Therefore, at the age of seventy, I am good at making wheels."

4. (overtones). If the poem has a quiet or neutral ground, a delicate or complicated figure can stand out against it; if the

ground is exaggerated and violent enough, no figure will.

5. (levels of meaning). It is better to have the child in the chimney-corner moved by what happens in the poem, in spite of his ignorance of its real meaning, than to have the poem a puzzle to which that meaning is the only key. Still, complicated subjects make complicated poems, and some of the best poems can move only the best readers; this is one more question of curves of normal distribution. I have tried to make my poems plain, and most of them are plain enough; but I wish that they were more difficult because I had known more.

6. (subjects). Half my poems are about the war, half are not. Some of their usual subjects are: airplanes and their crews, animals, ballet, carriers, children, concentration camps, the dead and dying, dreams, forests, graves, hospitals, letters, libraries, love, *Märchen*, moralities, people in extreme situations, prisoners, soldiers, the State, training camps, Western scientific and technical development—in short, *la condition humaine*. Some of these I enjoy writing about, others I could not help writing about. Ordinarily the poems are dramatic or have implied narratives; few are pure lyrics.

7. (imagery). Images seem to me means, not ends; I often reread Proust, and almost never reread Virginia Woolf.

8. (symbols).In works of art almost anything stands for more than itself; but this *more*, like Lohengrin, vanishes when it names itself.

9. (rhyme). Rhyme as an automatic structural device, automatically attended to, is attractive to me, but I like it best irregular, live, and heard.

10. (line-endings). I assume that the reader will indicate line-endings when he reads the poem aloud; if he doesn't he is reading it as prose.

11. (the structure of the total poem; what makes its unity?). An answer would take too many pages.

12. (meter). Most of my poems are written in ordinary iambic verse, regular or irregular according to the poem. Once upon a time I wrote accentual verse; I've used irregular anapests for special-case poems, syllabic verse for translations of Corbière, and so on.

The questionnaire also says that *Any statement you make about the ethical-philosophical relation of the poet to his writing will be most welcome.* My poems show what this relation actually is for me; what I say that it should be matters less. I *think* that I am relatively indifferent to the poem-as-performance-of-the-poet, and try to let the poem have a life of its own; the reader of the poem can know whether or not this is true.

To write in this way about one's own poetry is extremely unpleasant and unnatural. A successful poem says what a poet wants to say, and more, with particular finality. The remarks he makes about his poems are incidental when the poem is good, and embarrassing or absurd when it is bad—and he is not permitted to say how the good poem is good, and may never know how the bad poem is bad. It is better to write about other people's poetry. But to be in this anthology one had to write about one's own; and to have you read the poems, I was willing to write this prose.

THE STATE

When they killed my mother it made me nervous;
I thought to myself, it was *right*:
Of course she was crazy, and how she ate!
And she died, after all, in her way, for the State.
But I minded: how queer it was to stare
At one of them not sitting there.

When they drafted Sister I said all night,
"It's healthier there in the fields";
And I'd think, "Now I'm helping to win the War,"
When the neighbors came in, as they did, with my meals.
And I was, I was; but I was scared
With only one of them sitting there.

When they took my cat for the Army Corps
Of Conservation and Supply,
I thought of him there in the cold with the mice
And I cried, and I cried, and I wanted to die.
They were there, and I saw them, and that is my life.
Now there's nothing. I'm dead, and I want to die.

A CAMP IN THE PRUSSIAN FOREST

I walk beside the prisoners to the road.
Load on puffed load,
Their corpses, stacked like sodden wood,
Lie barred or galled with blood

By the charred warehouse. No one comes today
In the old way
To knock the fillings from their teeth;
The dark, coned, common wreath

Is plaited for their grave—a kind of grief.
The living leaf
Clings to the planted profitable
Pine if it is able;

The boughs sigh, mile on green, calm, breathing mile,
From this dead file
The planners ruled for them. . . . One year
They sent a million here:

Here men were drunk like water, burnt like wood.
The fat of good
And evil, the breast's star of hope
Were rendered into soap.

I paint the star I sawed from yellow pine—
And plant the sign
In soil that does not yet refuse
Its usual Jews

Their first asylum. But the white, dwarfed star—
This dead white star—
Hides nothing, pays for nothing; smoke
Fouls it, a yellow joke,

The needles of the wreath are chalked with ash,
A filmy trash
Litters the black woods with the death
Of men; and one last breath

Curls from the monstrous chimney . . . I laugh aloud
Again and again;
The star laughs from its rotting shroud
Of flesh. O star of men!

PORT OF EMBARKATION

Freedom, farewell! Or so the soldiers say;
And all the freedoms they spent yesterday
Lure from beyond the graves, a war away.
The cropped skulls resonate the wistful lies
Of dead civilians: truth, reason, justice;
The foolish ages haunt their unaccepting eyes.

From the green gloom of the untroubled seas
Their little bones (the coral of the histories)
Foam into marches, exultation, victories:
Who will believe the blood curled like a moan
From the soaked lips, a century from home—
The slow lives sank from being like a dream?

THE DEAD WINGMAN

Seen on the sea, no sign; no sign, no sign
In the black firs and terraces of hills
Ragged in mist. The cone narrows, snow
Glares from the bleak walls of a crater. No.
Again the houses jerk like paper, turn,
And the surf streams by: a port of toys
Is starred with its fires and faces; but no sign.

In the level light, over the fiery shores,
The plane circles stubbornly: the eyes distending
With hatred and misery and longing, stare
Over the blackening ocean for a corpse.
The fires are guttering; the dials fall,
A long dry shudder climbs along his spine,
His fingers tremble; but his hard unchanging stare
Moves unacceptingly: *I have a friend.*

The fires are grey; no star, no sign
Winks from the breathing darkness of the carrier
Where the pilot circles for his wingman; where,
Gliding above the cities' shells, a stubborn eye
Among the ashen nations, achingly
Tracing the circles of that worn, unchanging No—
The lives' long war, lost war—the pilot sleeps.

EIGHTH AIR FORCE

If, in an odd angle of the hutment
A puppy laps the water from a can
Of flowers, and the drunk sergeant shaving
Whistles *O Paradiso!*—shall I say that man
Is not as men have said: a wolf to man?

The other murderers troop in yawning;
Three of them play Pitch, one sleeps, and one
Lies counting missions, lies there sweating
Till even his heart beats: One; One; One.
O murderers! . . . Still, this is how it's done:

This is a war. . . . But since these play, before they die,
Like puppies with their puppy; since, a man,
I did as these have done, but did not die—
I will content the people as I can
And give up these to them: Behold the man!

I have suffered, in a dream, because of him,
Many things; for this last saviour, man,
I have lied as I lie now. But what is lying?
Men wash their hands, in blood, as best they can
I find no fault in this just man.

SIEGFRIED

In the turret's great glass dome, the apparition, death,
Framed in the glass of the gunsight, a fighter's blinking wing,
Flares softly, a vacant fire. If the flak's inked blurs—
Distributed, statistical—the bombs' lost patterning
Are death, they are death under glass, a chance
For someone yesterday, someone tomorrow; and the fire
That streams from the fighter which is there, not there,
Does not warm you, has not burned them, though they die.
Under the leather and fur and wire, in the gunner's skull,
It is a dream: and he, the watcher, guiltily
Watches the him, the actor, who is innocent.
It happens as it does because it does.
It is unnecessary to understand; if you are still
In this year of our warfare, indispensable
In general, and in particular dispensable
As a cartridge, a life—it is only to enter
So many knots in a window, so many feet;
To switch on for an instant the steel that understands.
Do as they said; as they said, there is always a reason—
Though neither for you nor for the fatal
Knower of wind, speed, pressure: the unvalued facts.
(In Nature there is neither right nor left nor wrong.)

So the bombs fell: through clouds to the island,
The dragon of maps; and the island's fighters
Rose from its ruins, through blind smoke, to the flights—
And fluttered smashed from the machinery of death.
Yet inside the infallible invulnerable
Machines, the skin of steel, glass, cartridges,
Duties, responsibility, and—surely—deaths,
There was only you; the ignorant life
That grew its weariness and loneliness and wishes
Into your whole wish: "Let it be the way it was.
Let me not matter, let nothing I do matter
To anybody, anybody. Let me be what I was."

And you are home, for good now, almost as you wished;
If you matter, it is as little, almost, as you wished.
If it has changed, still, you have had your wish
And are lucky, as you figured luck—are, really, lucky.
If it is different, if you are different,
It is not from the lives or the cities;
The world's war, just or unjust—the world's peace, war or peace;
But from a separate war: the shell with your name
In the bursting turret, the crystals of your blood
On the splints' wrapped steel, the hours wearing
The quiet body back to its base, its missions done;
And the slow flesh failing, the terrible flesh
Sloughed off at last—and waking, your leg gone,
To the dream, the old, old dream: *it happens,*
It happens as it does, it does, it does—
But not because of you, write the knives of the surgeon,
The gauze of the theatre, the bearded and aging face
In the magic glass; if you wake and understand,
There is always the nurse, the leg, the drug—
If you understand, there is sleep, there is sleep. . . .
Reading of victories and sales and nations
Under the changed maps, in the sunlit papers;
Stumbling to the toilet on one clever leg
Of leather, wire, and willow; staring
Past the lawn and the trees to nothing, to the eyes
You looked away from as they looked away: the world outside
You are released to, rehabilitated
(*What will you do now? I don't know*)—
It is these. If, standing irresolute
By the whitewashed courthouse, in the leafy street,
You look at the people who look back at you, at home,
And it is different, different—you have understood
Your world at last: you have tasted your own blood.

A GAME AT SALZBURG

A little ragged girl, our ball-boy;
A partner—ex-Afrika-Korps—
In khaki shorts, P.W. illegible.
(He said: "To have been a prisoner of war
In Colorado is a *privilege.*")
The evergreens, concessions, carrousels,
And D. P. camp of Franz Joseph Park;
A grey-green river, evergreen-dark hills.
Last, a long way off in the sky,
Snow-mountains.

Over this clouds come, a darkness falls,
Rain falls.
        On the veranda Romana,
A girl of three,
Sits licking sherbet from a wooden spoon;
I am already through.
She says to me, softly: *Hier bin i'.*
I answer: *Da bist du.*

I bicycle home in my raincoat
Through the the ponchos and pigtails of the streets,
Bathe, dress, go down four flights of stairs
Past Maria Theresa's sleigh
To the path to the garden, walk along the lake
And kick up, dreamily, the yellow leaves
Of the lindens; the pigeons are cooing
In the morning-glories of the gardener's house,
A dragonfly comes in from the lake.
The nymphs look down with the faces of Negroes,
Pocked, moled with moss;
The stone horse has sunk in marsh to his shoulders.

But the sun comes out, and the sky
Is for an instant the first rain-washed blue
Of becoming: and my look falls

Through falling leaves, through the statues'
Broken, encircling arms
To the lives of the withered grass,
To the drops the sun drinks up like dew.
Life, life everywhere.
In anguish, in expectant acceptance
The world whispers: *Hier bin i'*.

VARIATIONS

I

"I lived with Mr. Punch, they said my name was Judy,
I beat him with my rolling-pin, he hit me with his cane.
I ran off with a soldier, he followed in a carriage,
And he drew a big revolver and he shot me through the brain.
But that was his duty, he only did his duty—"

Said Judy, said the Judy, said poor Judy to the string.

"O hear her, just hear her!" the string said softly.
And the string and Judy, they said no more.
Yes, string or Judy, it said no more.
But they hanged Mr. Punch with a six-inch rope,
And "Clap," said the manager; "the play is over."

II

"I lay like a swan upon the down of Heaven.
When the clouds came the rain grew
Into the rice of my palaces, the great wits
Were the zithers of my garden, I stood among sedge
And held to the peoples the gold staff of God."

Said Grace, said Good, O said the son of God.

The wives and wise, the summer's willows
Nodded and were fed by the wind; when the snow fell
And the wind's steps were pink in the pure winter,
Who spared his charcoal for the son of God,
The vain wind failing at the pass to Hell?

III

"I lived in a room full of bears and porridge,
My mother was dead and my nurse was horrid.
I sat all day on a white china chamber
And I lay all night in my trundle bed.
And she wasn't, she wasn't, O not a bit dead!"

The boy said, the girl said—and Nurse she said:

"I'll stew your ears all day, little hare,
Just as God ate your mother, for you are bad,
Are bad, are bad—" and the nurse is the night
To wake to, to die in; and the day I live,
The world and its life are her dream.

IV

"I was born in a hut, my wit is heavy.
My sister died, they killed my father.
There is no time I was not hungry.
They used me, I am dying.
I stand here among graves."

The white, the yellow, the black man said.

And the world said: Child, you will not be missed.
You are cheaper than a wrench, your back is a road,
Your death is a table in a book.
You had our wit, our heart was sealed to you:
Man is the judgment of the world.

BURNING THE LETTERS

*(The wife of a pilot killed in the Pacific is speaking several years
after his death. She was once a Christian, a Protestant.)*

Here in my head, the home that is left for you,
You have not changed; the flames rise from the sea
And the sea changes: the carrier, torn in two,
Sinks to its planes—the corpses of the carrier
Are strewn like ashes on the star-reflecting sea;
Are gathered, sewn with weights, are sunk.
The gatherers disperse.

                                       Here to my hands
From the sea's dark, incalculable calm,
The unchanging circle of the universe,
The letters float; the set yellowing face
Looks home to me, a child's at last,
From the cut-out paper; and the licked
Lips part in their last questioning smile.
The poor labored answers, still unanswering;
The faded questions—questioning so much,
I thought then—questioning so little;
Grew younger, younger, as my eyes grew old,
As that dreamed-out and wept-for wife,
Your last unchanging country, changed
Out of your own rejecting life—a part
Of accusation and of loss, a child's eternally—
Into my troubled separate being.

A child has her own faith, a child's.
In its savage figures—worn down, now, to death—
Men's one life issues, neither out of earth
Nor from the sea, the last dissolving sea,
But out of death: by man came death
And his Life wells from death, the death of Man.
The hunting flesh, the broken blood
Glimmer within the tombs of earth, the food
Of the lives that burrow under the hunting wings

Of the light, of the darkness: dancing, dancing,
The flames grasp flesh with their last searching grace—
Grasp as the lives have grasped: the hunted
Pull down the hunter for his unused life
Parted into the blood, the dark, veined bread
Later than all law. The child shudders, aging:
The peering savior, stooping to her clutch,
His talons cramped with his own bartered flesh,
Pales, flickers, and flares out. In the darkness—darker
With the haunting after-images of light—
The dying God, the eaten Life
Are the nightmare I awaken from to night.

(The flames dance over life. The mourning slaves
In their dark secrecy, come burying
The slave bound in another's flesh, the slave
Freed once, forever, by another's flesh:
The Light flames, flushing the passive face
With its eternal life.)

The lives are fed.

Into the darkness of their victory;
The ships sink, forgotten; and the sea
Blazes to darkness: the unsearchable
Death of the lives lies dark upon the life
That, bought by death, the loved and tortured lives,
Stares westward, passive, to the blackening sea.
In the tables of the dead, in the unopened almanac,
The head, charred, featureless—the unknown mean—
Is thrust from the waters like a flame, is torn
From its last being with the bestial cry
Of its pure agony. O death of all my life,
Because of you, because of you, I have not died,
By your death I have lived.

The sea is empty.

As I am empty, stirring the charred and answered
Questions about your home, your wife, your cat
That stayed at home with me—that died at home
Gray with the years that gleam above you there

In the great green grave where you are young
And unaccepting still. Bound in your death,
I choose between myself and you, between your life
And my own life: it is finished.

                                   Here is my head
There is room for your black body in its shroud,
The dog-tags welded to your breastbone, and the flame
That winds above your death and my own life
And the world of my life. The letters and the face
That stir still, sometimes, with your fiery breath—
Take them, O grave! Great grave of all my years,
The unliving universe in which all life is lost,
Make yours the memory of that accepting
And accepted life whose fragments I cast here.

THE DEAD IN MELANESIA

Beside the crater and the tattered palm
The trades, the old trades, sigh their local psalm:
But their man-god in his outrigger,
The boars' tusks curling like a nautilus,
Fell to the schooners cruising here for niggers.
To the Nature here these deaths are fabulous;

And yet this world works, grain by grain, into the graves
Till the poor *ronin* in their tank-sealed caves
Are troubled by its alien genius
That takes uncomprehendingly the kites, the snow—
Their decomposing traces. And the conquerors
Who hid their single talent in Chicago,

Des Moines, Cheyenne, are buried with it here.
The including land, mistaking their success,
Takes the tall strangers to its heart like failures:
Each missionary, with his base and cross,
Sprawls in the blood of an untaken beachhead;
And the isles confuse him with their own black dead.

A COUNTRY LIFE

A bird that I don't know,
Hunched on his light-pole like a scarecrow,
Looks sideways out into the wheat
The wind waves under the waves of heat.
The field is yellow as egg-bread dough
Except where (just as though they'd let
It live for looks) a locust billows
In leaf-green and shade-violet,
A standing mercy.
The bird calls twice, "*Red* clay, *red* clay";
Or else he's saying, "Directly, directly."
If someone came by I could ask,
Around here all of them must know—
And why they live so and die so—
Or why, for once, the lagging heron
Flaps from the little creek's parched cresses
Across the harsh-grassed, gullied meadow
To the black, rowed evergreens below.

They know and they don't know.
To ask, a man must be a stranger—
And asking, much more answering, is dangerous;
Asked about it, who would not repent
Of all he ever did and never meant,
And think a life and its distresses,
Its random, clutched-for, homefelt blisses,
The circumstances of an accident?
The farthest farmer in a field,
A gaunt plant grown, for seed, by farmers,
Has felt a longing, lorn urbanity
Jailed in his breast; and, just as I,
Has grunted, in his old perplexity,
A standing plea.

From the tar of the blazing square
The eyes shift, in their taciturn

And unavowing, unavailing sorrow.
Yet the intonation of a name confesses
Some secrets that they never meant
To let out to a soul; and what words would not dim
The bowed and weathered heads above the denim
Or the once-too-often washed wash dresses?

They are subdued to their own element.
One day
The red, clay face
Is lowered to the naked clay;
After some words, the body is forsaken. . . .
The shadows lengthen, and a dreaming hope
Breathes, from the vague mound, *Life*;
From the grove under the spire
Stars shine, and a wandering light
Is kindled for the mourner, man.
The angel kneeling with the wreath
Sees, in the moonlight, graves.

THE DEATH OF THE BALL
TURRET GUNNER

From my mother's sleep I fell into the State,
And I hunched in its belly till my wet fur froze.
Six miles from earth, loosed from its dream of life,
I woke to black flak and the nightmare fighters.
When I died they washed me out of the turret with a hose.

LADY BATES

The lightning of a summer
Storm wakes, in her clay cave
At the end of the weeds, past the mock-orange tree—
Where she would come bare-footed, curled-up-footed
Over the green, grained, rotting fruit
To eat blackberries, a scratched handful—
The little Lady Bates.
You have played too long today.
Open your eyes, Lady.
                        Is it a dream
Like the ones your mother used to talk away
When you were little and thought dreams were real?
Here dreams are real.
There are no more dreams, no more real—
There is no more night, there is no more day.

When the Lord God and the Holy Ghost and the Child Jesus
Heard about you, Lady,
They smiled all over their faces
And sang like a quartet: "Lady Bates,
Is it you, the little Lady Bates
Our minister, one Sunday evening,
Held down in the river till she choked
In a white dress like an angel's, red
With the clay of that red river? Lady,
Where are the two we sent to fetch your soul:
One coal-black, one high-yellow angel?
Where is night, where is day?
Where are you, Lady Bates?"

They looked for you east, they looked for you west,
And they lost you here in the cuckoo's nest
Eating the sweet white heart of the grass. . . .
You died before you had even had your hair straightened
Or waited on anybody's table but your own.
You stood there helping your step-mother

Boil clothes in the kettle in the yard,
And heard the girls go by, at play,
Calling to you in their soft mocking voices:
"Lady-Bug, Lady-Bug, fly away home."

You are home.
There is a bed of your own
Here where a few stones
Stick up in the tall grass dried to hay—
And one willow, at the end of summer,
Rustles, too dry to weep for you,
And the screech-owl sheers away
And calls, *Who, who*—you are afraid
And he is afraid: who else could see
A black ghost in the dark?
A black, bare-footed, pig-tailed, trifling ghost
With eyes like white clay marbles,
Who haunts no one—who lies still
In the darkness, waiting
While the lightning-bugs go on and off?
The darning-needles that sew bad girls' mouths shut
Have sewn up your eyes.
If you could open your eyes
You would see nothing.
                      Poor black trash,
The wind has blown you away forever
By mistake; and they sent the wind to the chain-gang
And it worked in the governor's kitchen, a trusty for life;
And it was all written in the Book of Life;
Day and Night met in the twilight by your tomb
And shot craps for you; and Day said, pointing to your soul,
"This *bad* young colored lady,"
And Night said, "Poor little nigger girl."

But Death, after the habit of command,
Said to you, slowly closing his hand;
"You're a big girl now, not even afraid
Of the dark when you awake—

When the day you sleep through
Is over, and you awake,
And the stars rise in the early evening
An inch or two over the grass of your grave—
Try to open your eyes;
Try to reach to one, to the nearest,
Reach, move your hand a little, try to move—
You can't move, can you?
You can't move. . . .
You're fast asleep, you're fast asleep."

John Holmes

JOHN HOLMES *was born in Somerville, Massachusetts, in* 1904. *He was educated at Tufts and Harvard and has taught at Lafayette College. He is at present Assistant Professor of English at Tufts College. He has published a book of notes on poetry,* THE POET'S WORK, *and three volumes of poetry:* ADDRESS TO THE LIVING, FAIR WARNING, *and* MAP OF MY COUNTRY. *His fourth volume will be published in* 1950.

THE MYTH IN THE MIRROR

MY POEMS have never been written according to a program of literary, political, or technical belief. Such poems, I have thought, would be only a little better than occasional verse, without a date but soon dated. But my way, as much as I know it even at forty-five, with several books, and the unmade makings of several more, is the hard way. I have tried for a long time to find out how and why I write, at the same time that I do not really want to know. Circling myself more or less warily, I have made guesses that become more and more provable. I know now that I have certain convictions, certain blind areas, certain over-used images, and certain rhythms that are mine the way my hands and feet are mine, for better or for worse. I have come to the conclusion that writing poetry has been a long (twenty-five years is a long time) self-discovery. It is literally true that I often do not know what I think about things until I see what I will write about them. Thus the beginnings of my poems, the starters, come by accident, but they prick a sensitive nerve, or lay open a memory. Without enough variety of form, I think, or a very large vocabulary either of word or image, I begin to try to begin a poem.

The poems I have chosen to represent my writing here seem to me to reveal a rather dark and in-turned habit of feeling and thinking. Even this act of choice for this book has been exploratory, a little surprising, and not easy during or after the process. I find that the pieces I want to exhibit show my tribal, or family, or self-rooted

[202]

way of thinking, my dark and fearful preoccupations; and a kind of aloneness, though I value and seek togetherness. One of the conclusions I have come to lately is that I have always been a myth-maker, and that I am my own best myth; I have invented myself. Poetry is becoming for me one way of either destroying the myth or making it truth. I think this accounts for a tight rhythm, a harsh metaphor, a disturbed or deliberately ambiguous or very private reference.

Self-explanatory prefaces, and autobiographical pieces, usually bring out the worst in writers, and more so in poets than in novel-ists. In all the books I have read, where this sort of thing is done, the accounts are silly, evasive, coy, untruthful, desperate, or helpfully accurate, which is rare, and what I am trying to be: des-perately and helpfully accurate, but I cannot be sure that I'm not making some of the other errors.

The fact is that I do not really want to know how and why I write, and I had rather keep my ways and means to myself. A miner, a carpenter knows what he has to work with, and what he can do. Poets don't know; at any rate, I don't. As an additional handicap to my deliberate ignorance, I teach college students how to write po-etry. This year-in-year-out gamble is sometimes good for them, sometimes for me. They get the thrill, which I deprecate, of studying poetry with me, an actually published poet, and they get a certain amount of useful suggestion, and not very much severity. I always mean to be severe, and never am. I get from them a depressing rea-lization of what it means to begin from the bottom of September; but they do it once, and I do it every year. All this doesn't help. One has too many strands of life to rope and handle anyway, with-out teaching the writing of poetry, which is being a kind of stand-in for one's self. But it happens that I like to teach, and I think that by this time I know all the risks and penalties of being a writer who teaches writing, and I know the rewards and privileges.

I do not really know how I write a poem, and do not even want to tell how I would begin; but I am a teacher, and I have learned how to play a part, to make-believe I am telling how. There are some things you must never tell, and never do. And it may be that when you open the last locked closet door there is nothing at all in-side; some dust, some empty boxes. I think not, but I'd rather keep that key in my pocket.

The only poem I ever talked about before I wrote it was a long section of an autobiographical poem called "Map of My Country"; this section was to come about midway, and I had finished most of the other parts. But I described the unwritten part so many times that it became almost impossible to set it down, and I had to do it in a different meter and therefore a different tone from the one I had meant to use, to break my own block. The greatest difficulty I suffer is interruption. I have become expert at being interrupted, and find something wildly funny in the instant and continuous result of touching my typewriter, as if a thousand radars were focused on my desk, waiting. Some day, for posterity, I'll deposit in Charles Abbott's great manuscript collection at the library of the University of Buffalo a set of worksheets, with indications of every ring of the telephone, every errand, every call to dinner, every visit by loving wife and child, every plumbing crisis, or furnace need, or whatever. But I would not reverse night and day, as some poets do, to gain uninterrupted quiet. I write very slowly, and can perhaps better afford interruptions than some, or have grown a thick skin.

Most of the poems in my book, *Address To The Living,* 1937, which is not represented here, look to me to be straight-edged blocks of stanzas—as if the letters in each line were counted, and four lines to a stanza, and five stanzas to a poem, a slightly dull effect. Now I am pretending to tell how I write. I think this block effect resulted from using the typewriter, and from a habit of neatness, even when I wrote in pencil in a big heavily bound notebook such as law students use. It looked highly regular on the page. Then I made some recordings of poetry, and I began to read poems to audiences, and I discovered the need of much wilder and wider rhythms—a poem ought to be a good fat part for an actor, I said. I recorded several discs for Professor Packard of the Harvard Vocarium, and was dismayed at my monotone, my dullness and my own poor diction. I had an opportunity to hear other poets make recordings, and to listen to a great many. When I made the three twelve-inch discs published by the Harvard Vocarium (which include "Map of My Country" and "Evening Meal in the Twentieth Century") I had learned not only to speak poetry to be heard, but to write poems to be spoken to be heard. And I noted that they looked different on the page, irregular as to line-length, stanza-shape, and so on, because the pattern was for the ear. I still use the typewriter for composition, but it is as natural an instrument as the pencil, and I hear rather than see what I write.

It seems to me that the origin of a poem is in some unexpected stimulus to long-accumulated emotion and belief. The stimuli are bombarding the poet all the time, but for reasons of other occupation, or tiredness, he may not be hit at all; when he is in a state of receptiveness—of being well, being highstrung, being extra wide-awake, being very angry, very much in love—he will start a poem from almost any stimulus. But with me this stimulus is almost always one that awakes impressions and acts and memories stored away in the margins and back rooms of the subconscious. I do not believe in "inspiration." I believe only in a stubborn, decade-long, deeply necessary desire to write, and the flashes of ignition that come when the poet is inflammable. And it is more a matter of physical condition that one might think. The response to the flash requires a great output of energy, and the right combination of readiness and occasion does not happen often or predictably.

My habit is to begin with a sheet in the typewriter, and a two-fingered two or three lines, or six or eight lines. Then come some and less successful attempts at more lines, and the page is full. Out it comes, in goes a new sheet, and I take another running start up a hill that will steepen sharply from here on. For people who say they cannot use a typewriter because it is a machine, and makes a noise, I have no sympathy, and to them I pay no attention. I am as lost without my own typewriter as one might be without a pipe, a dish, a gun, a hat. It is at once a real comfort and a familiar tool; I'd rather have the telephone or the stove break down than the typewriter. I rarely write letters in longhand, or anything, and I would as soon think of wearing another man's shoes as using another man's typewriter. I work away at the poem by an incremental sort of process, slow, slow, and hard. Each new sheet begins with the first lines of the new poem, and each carries a few more than the last, with revisions or elimination in each new copying. Sometimes, when the sheet lies on the desk, I make some changes in pencil, but these are immediately typed on the next sheet. I can be impersonal or objective enough to number these worksheets, and show them to students, or so I have done now and then. When in earlier years I wrote in the law-school notebooks, in pencil, the pages filled up with columns of rhyme-words, with doodles, with remembered fragments, with lists of homework, painting and repairs, to be done. I should not have blamed the telephone and the family for interrupting, because I am one of my own best interrupters; I can think of more things to keep me from writing than any two living authors, and I never forget I am spending valuable energy that way.

The process of writing a poem quickens toward the end, as it comes to be the poem it is meant to be, God willing. I am much too apt to stuff the last draft into an envelope and mail it to an editor; in a few hours I am revising again. I cannot learn to wait for a poem to finish itself, in spite of being a slow word-by-word writer. I send a good many copies of new poems to my many correspondents, and the physical act of re-typing them leads to tightening and shortening. This, I think, is the actor rehearsing his good fat part, and cutting out the mumbles and the involved grammar that will prevent him from making a public success. One has always the audience in mind, whether a real audience facing the platform, or the larger one reading the magazine or book. But beyond these readers is always the anthologist, the professor, and the enthusiast, who has undisputed right to say No, and No, and No; and then maybe Yes, once in a hundred or more poems. What makes him say Yes? It is brevity, clarity, timelessness, sincerity. It is greatness of thinking, and greatness of style, and greatness of the performance as a whole. How can one achieve this greatness, this permanence, in a rented room, on a piece of cheap paper rolled into a small typewriter? What makes immortality? Well, devotion makes it, and skill makes it, and there is always the spirit. One does not describe the spirit. One does not estimate skill. Humility and experience intervene. The best one can do is done alone.

The simple fact is that I had rather be writing a poem than doing anything I have ever done—with one or two exceptions. I said I have no program, no code, and I must by now have been sufficiently personal, wilful, and without guide other than intuition and accident, to prove it. I want to say that I had rather be writing a poem *again* etc., but that sounded as though I was assuredly the author of one or more successful poems. I have had the experience a few times of writing a thing that made me pound the desk with my fist, and say, "That's it!" One talks aloud in an empty room less as time goes on; or is it more? At any rate, to have had the feeling once, even once, of getting it right, makes one want to repeat that deep satisfaction. There are two states, for me, of the great pleasure of making a poem. One is the first long excited newness of the poem's coming to life; the other is the longer, more cared-over, probably more exciting revision. I know of no more satisfying work—and work is the word—than the revision of a draft of a piece of writing. It is a great happiness. It is only human nature to wish to have again, and again, a happiness as great as any one has known.

In such a state, one does not ask what audience the poem is meant for, or what school of poetry one will be indexed in, or what fashion of words one must follow. Nothing matters but the poem. And so all prefaces, especially this one, are pleasant indulgences and somehow lies. I should simply have begun and ended by saying, "One ruthless purpose, and that poetry," a motto I made years ago, very selfish, very difficult for anyone else to live with, which has turned out to be so. No one can teach the writing of poetry, any more than love can be taught; these are matters of pigment, inheritance, of height and body-heat—as selfish as that—and the imagination and the intellect and the energy. I believe that a poet's works show all his physical nature, his whole social and economic background, and his riches equally with his poverty in these respects; nothing is concealed, nothing unused. I would and usually do jeer at poets who proclaim a platform, and sound off from that rigidly timbered structure. Those who really have one hardly know it, and never mention it. Those who have none define themselves too elaborately, and change the definition next year. It would be better to write the poems.

This soliloquy should include observations of the methods of other poets, if only to show that I know my methods are mine, and not to be imitated, a lesson that these several pages may have been worth writing, if I have been determined, and secretive, and sufficiently unhelpful. Some poets walk their poems into being. They keep all the words and the lines in their head, or heads, for weeks and months, talking to themselves as they go to meet their friends, or do their shopping. When they put the poem on paper, they know it by heart; heart here is an important word. Some poets are stricken with inspiration, or the Muse's wing brushes their brow; I have heard them say so, but I doubt it. Most poets do not and can not tell how the poem happens, and like me, they waste their time trying to set it forth. The one truth to be salvaged from the beach-drift of the dozen essays in this book will be that poets are their own men, and go their own way, and that if you think you are a poet, you had better go your own way, and quit listening to poets. Their voices make a wind that howls down your own voice. My ideas are mine, as ridiculous, as noble, as topical or as specially verbalized as any. And no one told me how to write poetry.

Having been at some pains to be myself, to the point of seeming simpleminded, I can make some amends by commenting on the accompanying poems. But I mistrust such comment, and am sure only that I do not know the whole story of the origin and making of any of these poems.

The section of "Map of My Country" in this group is an example of my effort, referred to earlier, to write for the voice, not the eye. It is a poem I can say effectively; the cadences were built deliberately, and I felt freed of rhyme into a more sweeping music of balanced and repeated phrase-lengths. The difficulty in composition, of course, is that there is no model, and no guide but one's ear, for such poetry; this one happens to run the way my speaking voice runs, as naturally (for me) as my hair grows. It is also a miniature version of the poem it begins; an introduction, a preview. The references happen all to be real people and places, though I alone know what they are; it seemed to me that they were not secretive or obscure, but common to human experience. The poem that pairs with this, for the same oral qualities is "Evening Meal in the Twentieth Century." In it I satisfied myself that I had matched tone of voice to the emotion of the subject-matter. It was written in the middle nineteen-thirties, when the violence in Europe was thought by too many to be safely distant; I felt that it was in the room with me and those I loved. A reviewer spoke of it as a poem of humility; I know only that it is a poem about my family, terribly exposed to a danger of which I was acutely, grievously aware, and they were not. I knew, of course, that I was putting into words what any thoughtful citizen and father was thinking then— or should have been thinking.

I'm afraid I dragged my son unfairly into the piece called "Metaphor for My Son." It was a pretty deliberate construction, and is intended to be about art and the artist, a subject I repeat myself on; I chose flying for its overtones of speed, courage, and pride in skill. The device of addressing the poem to my son is of course a symbol; I am sending forward in time a message about a thing I love to those I love, and he represents the future audience. Much more directly (but again no one else knows it) the poem "The New View" draws my family in; it is about my father. Poetry being a discovery of my emotions and motives and problems and awarenesses, I used it is an outlet for my remorse once when I had had sharp words with my father, then old and ill; he had come back at me with the old fire and authority, and I knew who was in command. I remembered then the tree I describe, and the sting I got from hornets in it, and made the likeness in this poem; an act of repentance, I suppose. Years later it was used for an examination question for the freshmen in their finals in English, and I briefed my colleagues as above. We were all unexpectedly given about half the answers in terms of social revolution, and the necessarily attendant pains. This delighted me, because it showed me that my image worked on at least two levels, the private and the public, and probably more.

"The Fear of Dying" is autobiographical, and a piece of middleaged self-therapy; I had the new and hardly pleasant fear, and tried to get rid of it by an act of exorcism, by saying it aloud. More obscurely, even to myself, I think that the poem "But Choose" is also a defiant, purging, exorcising sort of thing. I recounted the bitterest, the most painful, the most desperate things I knew, and let myself rage at those who also knew them but evaded them in ordinary conversation—as if I were not as guilty as the most boring babbler. I was frightened, and found my fear unbearable. I turned on others, an imagined audience, and berated them for their concealments, their lies, the "Very well, thank you," in response to the "How are you?" Of course, I was talking to myself; I was working up part of the myth, myself as Job, and by indirection wailing out not imaginary woes. It is in such a poem that the stanza pattern does not matter much, but the rhythm a great deal; I think that in this one every harshness and rapidity, every effect of crowded syllable, every wrenched and wrung line and violation of a normal meter is an important part of what I wanted to get said—the grimness, the horror, the beating against the invisible bars of silence.

I had looked at a large and invaluable collection of shells, the same color and pattern recurring the world over—at extraordinary photographic enlargements of cross-sections of more shells—and at an album of the almost infinite variety of seaweeds to be found in a limited part of the shore of Scotland, these beautiful and delicate ribbons of green and red and glassy gelatin carefully mounted on pages, labelled, named, all known. All this humbled me as nothing had, as no human relationship ever had. What is man, that Thou rememberest him? I never felt that way before that day. And as I ground out the lines, I found them spiralling from in to out, as the shells do; it can be noted in the rhyme-scheme. I make no claim here to mysticism, but this poem wrote itself, and went beyond what I knew. In another way, "Herself" reached into an area I had not known; the instances of telepathy were told me by a young girl who had experienced them, but I discovered suddenly the knowledge that that sensitivity or receptivity is part of what it is to be a girl. The delicacy of the body, female naked beauty, is a force, almost apart from any one girl with any one name. I wanted to evoke a partly erotic sense of that, then used the device of several names to mean all girls. I am painfully aware of having repeated my subject-matter in other poems, so some of the excitement in getting this one said was its strangeness, its newness.

While "The Core" would seem to be about my son, and I would seem to have started from him, from a child's voice, and to have been moved on through the poem by that impetus, it was the form of the poem that was the stronger motive. "The New View" is autobiographical, a record of a family thing that happened, and "The Core" looks as though it belonged in the family category. But the simple fact is that I felt I had been roughening my meters too much, writing too much cadenced verse, and wanted the satisfaction of writing a poem in a tight form, a strict rhyme-pattern, and an absolutely regular beat. I committed myself to requirements even more severe than I had intended, with the very short lines, and the necessity of matching exactly the rhyme-sounds always at the same place—even the length of the poem, twelve four-line stanzas in three equal parts, was required, as I soon saw, but I was determined to fulfill the form, or to submit to the form but move with as much energy and freedom as possible within it. My own emotion was certainly four parts for the construction to one for the boy. Actually I am so superstitious, and so fond, that it is disturbing to read the poem aloud. But I still think the emotional experience of this one was technical and not dynastic.

Searching for the sensuous pleasure of composition, to have again a joy I had had before, to be given away and lost in making words make lines make a poem make a feeling and a meaning, I tried in "Grass" to be, and not think. I wanted a wholly physical sensation, green, wet, bone, body, smell. The sound of the syllables as they came was like eating, like love, like swimming. No intellect, nothing but feel. Yet I suppose much of the pleasure I wanted a reader to have is intellectual—a pleasure in the words as words, their sound, their overtones, their not-quite-rhymes. I had my own pleasure in the making of it; perhaps that is all there is to it. Perhaps all the talking we do about theories of writing is a disguised confession of experience of selfish joy.

But if "Grass" is sensuous, and to its author satisfying, "The Broken One" is philosophical. The poem is a record of a real encounter. I saw the bird in a big nest on a small island. I was told about it before I saw it by Richard Eberhart. It is really his bird and should be his poem; after all, I was visiting him at his place in Maine. He and I talked a good deal about it, and on several levels, the practical, the ethical, the symbolic. For me it was one of those starters I have mentioned before; the years had accreted compassion for the failure, the one fated to fail. I do not think that the economy of the nation, or its spirit, would fall apart if Eberhart's osprey were left in its open nest, nor that the world would be saved if he or I or the game-warden saved the bird. Not actually; but symbolically, yes. I feel (think is not the right word here) I feel that it is no use to save a crippled bird, no use whatever, and that it is a great pity not to try. It is a symbolic guilt; why should I differentiate between a sea-osprey and a Lithuanian? Be consistent, be honorable, do as well by ants and birds and strangers as you would by your own best-beloved. The Golden Rule. Also it is the story of the Good Samaritan again, a symbol and a legend that has come to mean more to me than any ancient story. And so my friend, the poet Dick Eberhart, and I, had a concern, as the Quakers say, about this osprey. If we did nothing about it, would we also do nothing about the broken ones of our own kind? We knew we would, but we knew we would rest easier at night if we hadn't the dead osprey to think about. I had to write the poem, whether or not Dick did. This is one more use of poetry, a confessional that may be a lesson.

By my own kind of indirection, I have responded to most of the suggestions the editor has made; I hope. As I do this really diffi-cult job of self-examination, I feel good about the discovery that sometimes subject-matter and sometimes form have been my motiv-ations, though the revelation dismays me a little. I am not really very happy about my findings, but I think it has been a good thing, like going to the sulphur-baths in the old days, or to a psychia-trist. I hope I have not told all. I want to keep a few things to my-self. But as I examine myself, and my poems, I have a new idea: it may be that vocabulary is more important than form or theme. Words. The words of a poem, not the lines or the sound. At the anthologist's end of the twentieth century, I may have something important to say about vocabulary. Until then, I shall be too busy; I have poems to write.

HERSELF

Herself listening to herself, having no name,
She walked in an airy April sun, clothes close on her
And thin and of some printed green;
A girl came nearer and nearer, came
Carrying white and yellow flowers.

Girls are smooth with sleep in the morning
And, before they dress, up out of naked bed,
Stand open to all airs,
Next to the world's body as the world's to theirs.
In the evening and at midnight, light
Curves round a girl, reaches to brush her cheek,
Her lips, loose hair, or breast or knee.
Outlining her with shining that cannot speak.

Ann at midnight and three midnights heard a voice
Saying, When you come back you will not find me here.
Or Hulda. Not Ruth, perhaps Elizabeth,
Who read next year's news in a letter, all the accidents
Postmarked, and lost it. No one believed her.

It was a dead man, if you know what it is to be dead.
Eleanor, he said, or Janet Janet Janet do you dream me?

THE BROKEN ONE

The torn book we burn, and the dead tree
Silent of sap and wind, we cut down.
What space can we spare for an osprey,
Islanded with a wing hurt, or not grown?

We intervene by boat, summer human beings
Capture it in a net, we shout. Spread care

Over its whiteness, bring it to the station
For study. Is not the sea-osprey rare?

The mother will die of feeding it, or fly
South from winter later, the broken one
Shrink, crying and flapping and left by
As the slow must be. Already all is done.

Yet we steer steadily into it, sunburned
And laughing to meet water. Today is the day
We die all a little, leaving the bird to be
Sea-wreck, moss, bones. It will drift away,

Turned in a wilderness of wind and sun
Where nothing happens, as we are careless
Of one another, and of the broken one
To be blest, although we do not bless.

What happened was that the game-warden
Was told, who in official kindness came,
Saw, and carried the big bird off, a pardon
For no crime, for which there is no name.

MAP OF MY COUNTRY

A map of my native country is all edges,
The shore touching sea, the easy impartial rivers
Splitting the local boundary lines, round hills in two townships,
Blue ponds interrupting the careful county shapes.
The Mississippi runs down the middle. Cape Cod. The Gulf.
Nebraska is on latitude forty. Kansas is west of Missouri.

When I was a child, I drew it, from memory,
A game in the schoolroom, naming the big cities right.

Cloud shadows were not shown, nor where winter whitens,
Nor the wide road the day's wind takes.

None of the tall letters told my grandfather's name.
Nothing said, Here they see in clear air a hundred miles.
Here they go to bed early. They fear snow here.
Oak trees and maple boughs I had seen on the long hillsides
Changing color, and laurel, and bayberry, were never mapped.
Geography told only capitals and state lines.

I have come a long way using other men's maps for the turnings.
I have a long way to go.
It is time I drew the map again,
Spread with the broad colors of life, and words of my own
Saying, Here the people worked hard, and died for the wrong
                          reasons.
Here wild strawberries tell the time of year.
I could not sleep, here, while bell-buoys beyond the surf rang.
Here trains passed in the night, crying of distance,
Calling to cities far away, listening for an answer.

On my own map of my own country
I shall show where there were never wars,
And plot the changed way I hear men speak in the west,
Words in the south slower, and food different.
Not the court-houses seen floodlighted at night from trains,
But the local stone built into housewalls,
And barns telling the traveler where he is
By the slant of the roof, the color of the paint.
Not monuments. Not the battlefields famous in school.
But Thoreau's pond, and Huckleberry Finn's island.
I shall name an unhistorical hill three boys climbed one morning.
Lines indicate my few journeys,
And the long way letters come from absent friends.

Forest is where green fern cooled me under the big trees.
Ocean is where I ran in the white drag of waves on white sand.
Music is what I heard in a country house while hearts broke,
Not knowing they were breaking, and Brahms wrote it.

All that I remember happened to me here.
This is the known world.
I shall make a star here for a man who died too young.
Here, and here, in gold, I shall mark two towns
Famous for nothing, except that I have been happy in them.

GRASS

Mouth down in the timothy,
Belly flat, knees dug
Into the dark earth,
Tastes more birth than death.

World green and wet,
Not with tears, rides up.
All grass pushes up
Under no one, no I.

Here for the lying on is
Green grown wild and always.
Give up to the grass.
It forgives you wholly.

Where your father drowned,
After all the men
Before him, and women,
You not last in that line,

Flung and gone down
To the grassy underlands,
You wash in that green,
That grass in your hands.

THE SPIRAL

The infinite orderliness of the natural world
Is past all wonder. Only I, ignorant, wonder
At common and colored and never-repeated curled
Slow growth of shells above the sea and under.
A scum of seaweed is a jungle a green inch wide,
A man's lifetime long for seeing, naming, caring
To map it in one page. Spread there and dried,
It is one pattern for the mind's comparing
With Mind that remembers everything It made.

Caverns of almost nothing, and heavens, discover
Alike a little of the great calm of law obeyed.
Sun casts the year's same shadow over and over.

Out of shadow I, but no longer saying I,
Move myself from myself in an opening spiral,
Drawn toward the light in understanding why
One cell may be one cell yet see the spiral
Whole, and what slow accretion shapes a whole.

But there is more, a world in a tall fountain's
One waterdrop, fire in a crumb of coal,
And worlds more in the grains that make mountains.

METAPHOR FOR MY SON

I hope when you're yourself and twice my age
Still you'll rake your heart in unreasonable rage
At the imperfect praise of perfect things,
If in all the weathers of your mind and power
You work to stretch the best of fliers' wings.
I've seen the landsmen tire their legs in an hour.

And I hope you'll have a son a flier who fights
Your old-fashioned praise of earlier heights.

But may his son remember the three of us,
And understand our impatient angry pride.
Let the wind blow in our lifetime long to bless
Good wings, and you be one to see them ride

As I see them soar up the bright streams of air,
Hang, wing away, shine in the shine of bare
Sunlight pouring toward earth in middle day.
You'll see man's power alive in grace; then see
The grounded watchers stare up and turn away.
I say, Curse them. And may you always be

Angry as I am when the tough, the rare, the tall
Fliers with all their wisdom burn and fall.
I hope you'll live to learn to rage at their death
Too young by unnatural causes away from the field.
I want you to measure as I have measured breath
Then, and to keep the deep wells of grief sealed.

This will be hard on you, but high is hard.
I want you to tell our sons I cursed; I cared.
And forget me. Tell them it was not always so
That all men clambered on any climbing thing
To drag it down. You'll tell them, once you know,
Even once, air running over and under the wing,

Wind trying and shaping the immeasurable air
To a map of the coasts of heaven forever clear.
Fear will be tied around your wrist. But fliers
Before our time have had that weight there, too,
And heard the long wind screaming through the wires,
And have done what they have told themselves to do.

THE NEW VIEW

There was an old stump of an old tree standing
All naked of bark, and brown, and ten feet tall
In the wrong place for our summer pleasure.
I pushed it over. I was glad to see it fall.

Let it lie there in the high grass till it rotted.
The roots broke when I rocked it where it stood,
The trunk split, and the shell in half-round pieces
Opened, and let fall something that had been wood.

But there were bees in it. Bees have a business
Not safely suddenly outraged by anything.
Nothing is left to an old man but his anger,
And I had hurried death that needs no hurrying.

The stump gone, we could look further and greener.
It was two June days before my wound was well.
That was all we got, and we had the spoiled honey
For sorrow, and a new view past where the tree fell.

EVENING MEAL IN THE
TWENTIETH CENTURY

How is it I can eat bread here and cut meat,
And in quiet shake salt, speak of the meal,
Pour water, serve my son's small plate?
Here now I love well my wife's gold hair combed,
    Her voice, her violin, our books on shelves in another room,
The tall chest shining darkly in supper-light.
I have read tonight
The sudden meaningless foreign violent death
Of a nation we both loved, hope
For a country not ours killed. But blacker than print:
For the million people no hope now. For me

A new hurt to the old health of the heart once more:
That sore, that heavy, that dull and I think now incurable
Pain:
Seeing love hated, seeing real death,
Knowing evil alive I was taught was conquered.
How shall I cut this bread gladly, unless more share
The day's meals I earn?
Or offer my wife meat from our fire, our fortune?
It should not have taken me so long to learn.
But how can I speak aloud at my own table tonight
And not curse my own food, not cry out death,
And not frighten my young son?

BUT CHOOSE

Judgment and cash and health and faith in God go wrong.
Venus the queen of love and lovely Mrs. Adams age.
Of which men weary. Water gets in behind the stone,
A stain: and the wars that were to end the wars rage.

When was it we spoke saying terrible things aloud,
And any honorable man could beat his breast for woe?
The meat at my table lies cold on the plates, uncut,
And ruin of himself. There he was; who else would go?

Nobody wants to hear of hard times the heart has,
How grief stops it, how it fails when an only son
Stiffens in paralysis, how death has taken it aback
Doing to a dear friend what elsewhere death has done.

Old Testament Job is my familiar respectable neighbor.
Who would have thought his fortune could fall so low?
I went to see him sitting dirty, crazy, in a rubbish
And ruin of himself. There he was; who else would go?

Shall I not name him? May I not speak of the spirit
He burned with, so like fire consuming a hard wood,
And the wood the world burning, and the flame my hurt?
But uncomfortable. Not usual. As conversation not good.

Outlaw it, then: Keep your sweet selves to yourselves.
Yet I know a dreadful story you must stay to hear.
Sit on the rock. Suicide. And by what act of faith
Have you never heard music smoking the midnight air?

I heard water open open like an upturned tree. Have you heard
Water that green way? Have you dived naked into a tree?
I know an intelligence like a torch in a slow wind,
Feeding itself on joy, on its pride brightening to be.

Sirs, ladies and sirs, the wind hears you, do you not
Hear the wind of time listening to everything you are?
Time troubles its course with your color of glory.
My own ribs under the glass skin of history stare.

You were there when the map crawled, the flower spoke.
You broke your own heart and bandaged up your hand
That struck blood. I stood a tidemark in the sea-tide.
I had mountains under me once. The great air drowned

The distance from me down, three hundred miles an hour
From west east toward home, as if from doom to life.
I flew through my own brain-cap, arched over the world.
And you. You blew there. You know. What can we save?

But I'll tell nothing, or talk like you in nothings
Of no pain, no unwordable wild delight, of life no news.
Have you read Yeats? Have you heard Job? Or Ariel?
Die as you are, or living speak like them. But choose.

THE FEAR OF DYING

All men know it, the young when the enemy in them,
Or an enemy armed, reveals a little its real wrath.
Older men speak of it to men of their age only after
They search the pain secretly, the shortened breath.
It comes as a cough in winter rudely, or it waits
Behind dawn, at the edge of the sleep it illuminates.

All men suffer pangs not to be slept away, soreness
Some for the lame world, but more for this new hurt
Indifferently durable and cruel, so dull, so patient
At kidneys, or head, or the heart the heart the heart.
Every day men die. Not every day a man a man knows.
But they die. The vague ache returns after it goes.

Or seems a veil, each voice possibly the last speaking.
Or superstition seems as good a rule as any rule.
At forty five I think how my thin father at eighty
Died without any of this wordiness about his soul,
His bowels, his world-sorrow. But it is my own death
I count kisses toward. Or is it mine? Or my breath?

Where is there consolation? I'll imagine my funeral—
No, not mine, but yours, my father's, the ceremonials
Of the sad unwinding of the world, the fading. This
All attend, honorably dressed in good dark clothes,
This end of Ming and Elizabethan effort, this stop
To colonial Roman and American history. All this goes
Down with me if I must go down, and I say No to death,
No death. Let them stand, the walls of my house. I'll
Be angry I cannot sit there angry at such time's waste,
The music, bad poetry, then friends busy in daylight,
And my light out, and a slowness to my furious haste.
It is enough to make a man think twice before dying.
I'll send myself a green wreath, I'll send a wreath
All green, deserved, but not be there for that death.

THE CORE

All children sound the same.
Walking today, I came
Near small boys counting loud
The words of a game.

A voice there seemed my son,
Again and again the one
I would know in any crowd.
But I knew none.

I thought, if he were dead
How always in my head
Would sound in any street
Something he said,

Until I could not bear
To walk out anywhere,
For fear that I might meet
His voice in air.

The calendar of light
Gives walls again their white
At the same hour of year
That they stood bright

A year of sun ago.
The night and noontide flow
From once to now and here,
On a deep-bent bow.

I thought then how the hand
Quickens to understand
The shape of solid things
In shape as planned.

. I thought then how the mind
Goes out to its own kind
In slowly opening rings,
To seek, to find.

In my own history caught,
I am what I have taught,
But turned and turned in more,
My need is naught.

The blue globe on its pin
Whirls all the voices in
To color and light, the core
Where sounds begin,

And whirling spins it out
Wider and wide about,
A wave—of many, one—
An echoing shout

From children in a game,
To tell me that the name
Of One was always one,
And sounds the same.

Richard Eberhart

RICHARD EBERHART *was born in Austin, Minnesota, in* 1904. *He attended Dartmouth as an undergraduate, went to Cambridge on a Rhodes Scholarship, and returned to do graduate work at Harvard. He has taught at St. Marks, and is at present an executive of the Butcher Wax Company. His published titles are*: BRAVERY OF EARTH, READING THE SPIRIT, SONG AND IDEA, POEMS NEW AND SELECTED, BURR OAKS, *and* BROTHERHOOD OF MEN. *He was co-editor of* WAR AND THE POET, *an anthology of war poetry from* 1800 B.C. *to* 1945 A.D.

NOTES ON POETRY

A POET DOES what he can do. Poetry is dynamic, Protean. In the rigors of composition it seems to me that the poet's mind is a filament, informed with the irrational vitality of energy as it was discovered in our time in quantum mechanics. The quanta may shoot off any way. (You breathe in maybe God). If you dislike the word inspiration, say then that the poet in a creative state of mind is in a state different from that of his ordinary or logical state. This leads on not to automatic writing, but to some mysterious power latent within him which illuminates his being so that his perceptions are more than ordinarily available for use, and that in such moments he has the ability to establish feelings, ideas and perceptions which are communicable in potential degree and with some pleasure.

Poetry is a defense of the most intimate parts of man. It is an evocation, a crystallization from a cloud of unknowing of his individuation. By its performance the poet learns his own nature. By its reception the reader may focus his own attitudes. The art once set exists on an impersonal plane for judgment, not by the poet, nor perhaps by his most intimate reader, but judgment by critics. The best critics are the arbiters of value, themselves necessarily contained within the areas of sensibility allowed by the kind of society of which they are a product and a reflection. Here too change is of the essence. Criticism itself is changeable, Protean,

[225]

always shifting and turning, always, like the artist, seeking the truth, whose absolutes in turn become relative.

The finalities of poetry are ultimately mysterious. One would not write poetry if one had perfect understanding. There would be nothing to communicate. It is a compulsive matter. Poetry is an aberration from perfection. It is shadows and nuances standing for definition. Words are sensitive tools which exteriorize the mind. If the mind were clear, it would write logic or mathematics. Mind is not the whole of the human being; there are other, and problematical, and quixotic, and mysterious reaches. But at his peak the poet writes with a whole clarity. Groddeck in theory and Blake in poetry have spoken for realizations superseding those which we posit as of the mind alone. Poetry is a complement to complexity, a resource of the Imagination. It honors the deep, the nameless resources of the Psyche. It makes the world in its own image.

ON MOTIVE

The motive for writing is to make up for some sense of lack in oneself, an obscure and earthly realization that must be as old as man. This includes, of course, the excess of energy common to the artist, his direct and violent perceptions. Divisive man can know unity only at death (or so he can speculate), and he cannot know what kind of unity that is. He lives in continuous struggle with his imperfection and the imperfection of life. If one were only conscious of harmony, there would be no need to write. The drive to create art is to create something delectable, possibly permanent (within the limits of permanence); it is an example of extreme will in man which pretends that it can bend the fierce primordial nature to intelligent use; that it can erect an arbitrary world beyond the normal chaos of man. Order may itself seem anachronistic, but in art it is through order that the pleasure comes.

The aim of the poet is a world of suggestion. He defines himself as he goes along. The definitions are never absolute. What is not said in poetry is a deep value to it. The implications reward the reader each in his own way. A one-to-one relationship would devastate the impeccable rarities. If the impeccability is such, the rarities are none the less evasive, to charm the senses. If one could know anything definitely, accurately, or perhaps "scientifically" (in the lesser sense of measure, not in the greater sense of imagination, where science and poetry join, as in Einstein's Unified Field Theory) one would not write a poem. The poem is an erection from primitive complexities, involvements and engagements. Antennae-like intuitions are compulsively exercised toward the gain of meanings, of significance, of new relationships.

A motive of the poet is by delving in his senses to clarify his understanding of life, to enlarge it, to mask it, to metamorphose it, to beguile it in metaphor, and to enact its perturbation in the reader in canny, cunning, manifold ways. His motive, of many, is none less than nor other than truth, a word still consanguineous to ultimate perplexity, strife, and aspiration. From a numberless despairs and stark realizations, a numberless unfathomable joys, a numberless confrontations of tragedy he hopes by the most exciting, exacting and unpredictable divination to set down in a rhythm, a phrase, a stanza, a whole poem, anywhere in the exalting reaches of language known as peculiar to his blood, an urgency of faith, a nuance of explosive or soft-ramifying verity, a symbolic urgency. His motive is by subtlety and definition to capture the whole heart of man. His claim is as deep as life and death. And his reason for writing springs from a purity beyond every instance of evil, existing as a total admission and confrontation of it. The motive is to draw the possibility of pleasure from the general suffering which is the mortal estate; an arbitrary pleasure, erect and cognizant art, not unmindful of that complexity and that error essential to man's understanding.

Excavations toward salvation: the saving grace of a poem may light the reader likewise out of some darkness, and art is essentially social. The inspiration of the artist is from the reservoir that makes the geyser; style is the cap that lets it flow in a certain form.

Christ is the poem absolute, as Shakespeare is the poet resolute, showing merely the whole world of sensation. Christ is impossible to overhaul, while Shakespeare can be contained in imagination alongside. The meanings of Dante always jump beyond him, making the previous sentence mandatory. Yet we are pleased with lesser poets than Shakespeare or Dante, and study the masters of our century on not so exalted grounds, because any excellence is a blessing.

The motive of the reader, not a poet, should be to commit himself to a ceaseless, life-long examination of values, and to embody in his character, or at least to hold in his mind, the best poetry that has been written.

ON STRUCTURE

Each poem has a structure of its own; structure is closely allied to the nature of the poet's mind: the poem looks like the poet. But the poet did not know how he would look in it before the poem was written. He only knows toward the end of his life what he looks like in the poems he has written. The structure of the poetry goes into history as a part of the structure of the mind of the period. Each age has its style and tone which it is the delight of students to detect and savor.

ON RHYTHM AND METER

Rhythm is dictated to the poet by his inner being. It reflects his peculiarity. It is like something symbolically grasped out of the sky while walking; it comes is a quick realization, inevitably (but subject to change), a gift, provoking a force of words. Meter is the control of innate rhythms.

ON LEVELS OF MEANING

Pleasure increases with ambiguity. But there is a point where ambiguity thrashes its thresher. At this point, the poet must ease off, or the reader will revolt, deny, accuse him of unintelligibility. Somewhere between subtlety of evocation and statements of plain sense the most engaging poetry will be determined.

ON STYLE

Style begins by an exacerbation of the inelastic essences and ends in the possibility of a lucid continuum of varying meanings.

ON DOGMA

On any topic of poetry one should not be dogmatic. There is greater freedom in the tentative.

ON THE INELUCTABLE

It is a grant of sanctity.

ON FORTUNE

Fortune favors the grave.

A LEGEND OF VIABLE WOMEN

I

Maia was one, all gold, fire, and sapphire,
Bedazzling of intelligence that rinsed the senses,
She was of Roman vocables the disburser,
Six couturiers in Paris sat to her hats.

There was Anna, the cool Western evidencer
Who far afield sought surrender in Sicily,
Wept under the rose window of Palma de Mallorca,
For she thought fate had played a child in her hand.

There was Betty the vigorous; her Packard of Philadelphia
Spurred she; she was at home in Tanganyika,
Who delighted to kill the wild elephant,
Went Eastward on, to the black tigers of Indochine.

There was Margaret of Germany in America, and Jerusalem,
Of mild big eyes, who loved the blood of Englishmen,
Safely to voyage the Eros battlements of Europe,
Protectress to be of young and home, massive the mother.

There was Helen the blond Iowan, actress raddled,
Who dared learning a little, of coyness the teacher,
Laughing subtleties, manipulator of men, a Waldorf
Of elegant fluff, endangering to the serious.

There was Jeannette the cool and long, bright of tooth,
Lady of gay friendship, and of authentic song,
Beyond and indifferent to the male seduction
Who to art pledged all her nature's want and call.

There was the sultry Emma of West Virginia,
Calf-eyed, velvet of flesh, mature in youngness,
Gentle the eager learner of nature's dimensions,
Always to her controlling womanhood in thrall.

There was Sue, the quick, the artful, the dashing,
Who broke all the laws; a Villager in her own apartment,
She was baffled by the brains of Plato and Aristotle,
Whose mind contained most modern conceptions.

There was Maxine, a woman of fire and malice
Who knew of revenge and subterfuge the skills,
A dominator, a thin beauty, a woman of arts and letters;
She of many psychological infidelities.

There was savage Catherine, who leaped into the underground,
Her female anger thrown at abstract injustice.
And she could match her wits with international man,
A glory, a wreaker, alas, who now posthumous is.

There was Madge the sinister, who raged through husbands three.
She was somdel Groddckian, a spendthrift of morality;
Existentialist that with men was dexterous
And would be in ten years after thirty, thirty three.

There was a nun of modesty, who with service was heavy
And big with sweet acts all her sweet life long;
Enough wisdom she had for twenty ordinary women
Who percepted love as a breath, and as a song.

II

Where is Kimiko, the alabaster girl of Tokyo,
Living in bamboo among rustling scents and innuendoes,
To whom from Hatteras, the Horn, or Terra del Fuego
Returned as to a starry placement the sea voyager?

Where has time cyclic eventuated Vera
The proud noblewoman of Vienna? Among opera lights
She lived in a gayety of possessive disasters,
Abandoned to the retaliatory shores of music.

Where is the naked brown girl of the nipa hut,
Under fronds, to Mount Mayon's perfect symmetry,

From the wash of the sea, looking from Legaspi?
Where in nature is this form, so brown, so fair, so free?

Where, who, sold into slavery in white Shanghai,
Walked and breathed in grace on Bubbling Well Road,
Subject to ancient sinuosities and patience,
Whose power was to represent unquestioning obedience?

Where is Hortense, the hermetically sealed?
Where is Hermione, haunted by heavens, who hesitated?
Where is Lucy, of bees and liberty the lover?
Where is Eustacia, of marionettes and Austrian dolls?

III

There were prideful women; women of blood and lust;
Patient women who rouged with scholarship's dust;
There were women who touched the soul of the piano;
Women as cat to mouse with their psychoanalyst.

There were women who did not understand themselves
Locking and unlocking misery's largess yearly;
Fabulous women who could not manumit the world
And babbled in syllables of the past and of money.

There were women committed to sins of treachery
The aborters of privilege and of nature's necessity;
There were the sinners in acedia of frigidity
Who negated even the grossness and grandeur of fear.

There were women without tenderness or pity
There were those more male than feminine men
Who rode the horses of their strident fury,
To whom subtle time made a passing bow.

There were independent women of society
Whose proud wisdom was their father's will.
There were mysterious women, Egyptian as a scarab
To whom scent and sound were a mysterious recall.

IV

Women are like the sea, and wash upon the world
In unalterable tides under the yellowing moon
Whose essential spirit is like nature's own,
To man the shadowy waters, the great room.

They come and go in tides of passion, and show
The melancholy at the heart of fullness,
Time crumples them, these vessels of the generations
Are crushed on the rocks as the green sea urchins.

They are the flesh in its rich, watery symbol,
A summer in July under the tenderest moon,
An island in the sea invincible to touch,
A refuge in man against refulgent ideation.

Women have gone where roll the sea bells
In the long, slow, the wide and the clear waters;
Their flesh which is our love and our loss
Has become the waste waters of the ocean swell.

They are the mothers of man's intelligence
To whom he is held by umbilical time,
And far though he roam, to treat with imagination,
He is brought home to her, as she brings a child.

FOR A LAMB

I saw on the slant hill a putrid lamb,
Propped with daisies. The sleep looked deep,
The face nudged in the green pillow
But the guts were out for crows to eat.

Where's the lamb? whose tender plaint
Said all for the mute breezes.
Say he's in the wind somewhere,
Say, there's a lamb in the daisies.

THE GROUNDHOG

In June, amid the golden fields,
I saw a groundhog lying dead.
Dead lay he; my senses shook,
And mind outshot our naked frailty.
There lowly in the vigorous summer
His form began its senseless change,
And made my senses waver dim
Seeing nature ferocious in him.
Inspecting close his maggots' might
And seething cauldron of his being,
Half with loathing, half with a strange love,
I poked him with an angry stick.
The fever arose, became a flame
And Vigour circumscribed the skies,
Immense energy in the sun,
And through my frame a sunless trembling.
My stick had done nor good nor harm.
Then stood I silent in the day
Watching the object, as before;
And kept my reverence for knowledge
Trying for control, to be still,
To quell the passion of the blood;
Until I had bent down on my knees
Praying for joy in the sight of decay.
And so I left; and I returned
In Autumn strict of eye, to see
The sap gone out of the groundhog,
But the bony sodden hulk remained.
But the year had lost its meaning,
And in intellectual chains
I lost both love and loathing,
Mured up in the wall of wisdom.
Another summer took the fields again
Massive and burning, full of life,
But when I chanced upon the spot
There was only a little hair left,

And bones bleaching in the sunlight
Beautiful as architecture;
I watched them like a geometer,
And cut a walking stick from a birch.
It has been three years, now.
There is no sign of the groundhog.
I stood there in the whirling summer,
My hand capped a withered heart,
And thought of China and of Greece,
Of Alexander in his tent;
Of Montaigne in his tower,
Of Saint Theresa in her wild lament.

"IF I COULD ONLY LIVE AT THE PITCH THAT IS NEAR MADNESS"

If I could only live at the pitch that is near madnes
When everything is as it was in my childhood
Violent, vivid, and of infinite possibility:
That the sun and the moon broke over my head.

Then I cast time out of the trees and fields,
Then I stood immaculate in the Ego;
Then I eyed the world with all delight,
Reality was the perfection of my sight.

And time has big handles on the hands,
Fields and trees a way of being themselves.
I saw battalions of the race of mankind
Standing stolid, demanding a moral answer.

I gave the moral answer and I died
And into a realm of complexity came
Where nothing is possible but necessity
And the truth wailing there like a red babe.

FROM FOUR LAKES' DAYS

Summery Windermere, sweet lake!
Where eyes wake wide to see again
And the fields, O clover earth-breath take
On the roads, in the warmed-away rain;
Then Far, and then Near Sawrey
Are; foot-increasing Esthwaite
Water is, O the green! far, see
What you will, walk. There's a late
Spell on the hills, will break not,
A gentlest mystery like a fate,
Something serene, you cannot take not
On Hawkshead Hills. Blare on the air,
Bagpipes! 'tis the merry-hearted note—
Thus you change, hill and valley share,
Feel each, know none by rote.

Young ferns by time-retaining tarn
Lose something of goldenness: height
Down-dooms, moves along the tarn;
(In poised fragility, my fright)
My heart leapt down, so with gloom
Leaded and time-encased, I shied
From the tremor, the small room
Of (bleak tarn!) all that has died.
Glen Mary unsilences; slight
Whispery waterfall, then such
Tossing laughter as can fight
Rocks, and overcome them much.
On heart-beat and feet go, he, I,
Who than happiness happier be
Keeping earth joined to the sky,
Locking, in love, earth and the sea.
But, topped, stop. Somehow
Miser it, lest the mind
Race beyond the senses' pace
And the whole being nothing find.

Valley-volleying blackbird (how new)
Another flier has; sheep can
With a strange passion bleat; there grew
In spider's earth-sight something of man.

In air-shiver against white wall
A flower, blue, incandescent
Does dance on the eye-ball;
It makes beauty effervescent.
At Fell Foot (charm) farm. Rob
This, clover-over-the-dales;
Smells of cows; good hob-
Nail, spike my ear! and kissing pails.

Till the twilight folds and all's
As blue as the bluewashed walls.

THE FURY OF AERIAL BOMBARDMENT

You would think the fury of aerial bombardment
Would rouse God to relent; the infinite spaces
Are still silent. He looks on shock-pried faces.
History, even, does not know what is meant.

You would feel that after so many centuries
God would give man to repent; yet he can kill
As Cain could, but with multitudinous will,
No farther advanced than in his ancient furies.

Was man made stupid to see his own stupidity?
Is God by definition indifferent, beyond us all?
Is the eternal truth man's fighting soul
Wherein the Beast ravens in its own avidity?

Of Van Wettering I speak, and Averill,
Names on a list, whose faces I do not recall
But they are gone to early death, who late in school
Distinguished the belt feed lever from the belt holding pawl.

"I WALKED OUT TO THE GRAVEYARD TO SEE THE DEAD"

I walked out to the graveyard to see the dead
The iron gates were locked, I couldn't get in,
A golden pheasant on the dark fir boughs
Looked with fearful method at the sunset,

Said I, Sir bird, wink no more at me
I have had enough of my dark eye-smarting,
I cannot adore you, nor do I praise you,
But assign you to the rafters of Montaigne.

Who talks with the Absolute salutes a Shadow,
Who seeks himself shall lose himself;
And the golden pheasants are no help
And action must be learned from love of man.

THE CANCER CELLS

Today I saw a picture of the cancer cells,
Sinister shapes with menacing attitudes.
They had outgrown their test-tube and advanced,
Sinister shapes with menacing attitudes,
Into a world beyond, a virulent laughing gang.
They looked like art itself, like the artist's mind,
Powerful shaker, and the taker of new forms.
Some are revulsed to see these spiky shapes;
It is the world of the future too come to.
Nothing could be more vivid than their language,
Lethal, sparkling and irregular stars,
The murderous design of the universe,
The hectic dance of the passionate cancer cells.
O just phenomena to the calculating eye,
Originals of imagination. I flew
With them in a piled exuberance of time,

My own malignance in their racy, beautiful gestures
Quick and lean: and in their riot too
I saw the stance of the artist's make,
The fixed form in the massive fluxion.

I think Leonardo would have in his disinterest
Enjoyed them precisely with a sharp pencil.

A MAN OF SENSE

Evil was dangled in front of him like an apple,
A winesap. He saw the apple-crush in the cider mill
Like the mesh of blossom on the trees; draining off
More evil as the amber oozed, he would drink it down,
Becoming a part of the blossom and the fruit;
So surely the wine went back to earth in him.

He became aware of evil in the very air,
In time, and while he breathed the delight of June,
He knew not what to make of the evil of the air.
Things screen us; books do; museums filled with art,
The rich success of shale-stood city towers;
War's bloody hiatus, its true or demented dreams.

To live in luxury, to love the difficult,
And clarify the ways of man to men in thought,
Perturbed by God and evil, but letting them be,
Was what the world allowed him, a special plane,
Genius for friendship with the deft and debonair,
But not to go mad over inscrutability.

Imagination was that formative intelligence
That shaped him less to action than to contemplation;
Imagination it was, the inexhaustible source,
That blessed him in luminous, suspended swirls.
He was the recipient of the ages' thought.
He knew the pleasure of an antique loss.

To a man of meditation the memorable
Makes the marmoreal; skunk cabbages can too.
He is the defender of the library cults;
Cut off from agriculture, and from locomotion
In a sense, his eye distills the fluctuant scene,
And he can be the farmer of Horace undebited.

He is for pure merriment and for pure fun.
A cynical joke with a lavender tinge, or an
Irish bull a yard long, or minuscule bombast in
Disruption of the over or the underdog
Infect the air with his suitable laughter.
Laughter is innocence where before there was none.

Precisely he is mysterious, but offends no man;
Talents he has, that is to have no talent unduly.
He averts from his gaze the awkward, the ugly,
A triumph of sheer character; if he is favored
It is because the times allowed an elegant fate.
Somebody else made the money, he made the manners.

To be fervent, he thought, is not to be true.
To be detached, the observer, is to be true.
The spectator of life is superior to the actor;
The actor, embroiled, does not control the action.
An impersonal eye controls its speculation,
Losing, apparently, the illusion it is in.

He triumphed, delicately, and walked along the Charles.
The old airs of Paris hung about his head.
There was no use doing anything about man.
In China the rice was coming up again.
The boats turned and curved upon the water
Not knowing the mathematical lines they were making.

He thought of poetry, and of St. John the Divine;
He thought he had known, one time, as index,
The voluminous interstices of the Inferno,

The Purgatorio, and lessly the Paradiso.
It was not this that was to be his guide.
It was a dream, a secret, a pure idea in time.

He was not a clear soul;
Clarity, perforce, was juvenile.

Often he had thrown himself away
To be sure he was not there to stay.

Espousing the inextricable
Made his temerity immiscible.

He sought in everything quality,
Which deviates into policy.

Every action involves criticism
For not being another action.

And every criticism is an instinct
For being in the inner self.

And every effort is a struggle
To evaluate and predict.

And every man loves and loses
In the guilt of experience.

He would not accept any definition of taste
Knowing that change was certain to violate it.
To live in a fluid ambience of the possible
Brought him joy; he gave it back the tentative.

To evade the substratum of one's life,
Those fixed and barnacle-encrusted pilons,

Was not a linguistic feat, but a conceptual.
Water can look like air; disturbed, it becomes flighty.

He had rejected the romantic, as was expected.
Time was when he gorged on gorgeous effect
And never understood, so stuffed, the spectacle.

What then one could not command or do
One said time's perspective would surely show.
That devil of lovers would ruin and debase

An ancient menace which exalted to confound.
At least time would make plain the issue,
Time tragedian become time comedian.

But see his corpse in the ground,
Be sure some massive stain will adhere to it.

But see his soul ascend,
Be sure in the air he will not quite see it.

The very present world was pat.
A classicist. He could get along with that.

If this was to be classical,
To accept a golden evenness
And ease the tension off the eyelids,
Order the blood, be well balanced,

He approved a modern classical stance
And thought, by St. George, that he had it.
Certain dragons of recalcitrant years
He had conquered, and was glad of it.

It was his doughtiness to imagine pure harmony,
Holding the past in fee, the future not fearing,

Walking by water of suicides, swimmers, and sailors,
Dealing out his rich increase on the air
In private meditation: a whole man,
Wholeness describing imaginary society.

If it was Athens he thought he was in,
It was cool and clean, knowledge after tragedy,
And if the ideal Christian commonwealth
It was a prized and inner unity,
And if it was the actual world he was walking in
He made it in his senses by imagination free.

THE TOBACCONIST OF
EIGHTH STREET

I saw a querulous old man, the tobacconist of Eighth Street.
Scales he had, and he would mix tobacco with his hands
And pour the fragrance in a paper bag.
You walked out selfishly upon the city.

Some ten years I watched him. Fields of Eire
Or of Arabia were in his voice. He strove to please.
The weights of age, of fear were in his eyes,
And on his neck time's cutting edge.

One year I crossed his door. Time had crossed before.
Collapse had come upon him, the collapse of affairs.
He was sick with revolution,
Crepitant with revelation.

And I went howling into the crooked streets,
Smashed with recognition: for him I flayed the air,
For him cried out, and sent a useless prayer
To the disjointed stones that were his only name:
Such insight is one's own death rattling past.

John Ciardi

JOHN CIARDI *was born in Boston in* 1916 *and attended Bates College, Tufts College, and the University of Michigan. He has taught at the University of Kansas City, and is at present Assistant Professor of English at Harvard. His published titles are:* HOMEWARD TO AMERICA, OTHER SKIES, *and* LIVE ANOTHER DAY. *He is editor of this collection, and his fourth volume of poems,* THE STATISTICIAN'S EYE, *will appear in* 1950.

TO THE READER OF (SOME) GENERAL CULTURE

I

WHO IS THE reader of general culture? I am willing to apply the term to any man who meets most of the following specifications. He goes to symphony. He likes to spend an afternoon at the museums and galleries and he has some notion of what he looks at there. He knows part of the difference between the Ballet Russe and a chorus-line. He has read enough psychology to know that only an expert should tamper with Freud. He is aware that ideas have histories, and that the ideas held by the people about him are usually retrograde in the best history of things. He has browsed through philosophy in a general way. He knows other societies have come before his, that others will come after his, and that none have been absolute and that none will be, but that some common dynamics of the human spirit has shone through them all, and that the best name anyone has found to give to that dynamics is Art. He entertains ideas and seeks to place them in perspective. He tries, as best the world and his checkbook will let him, to keep up with the best prose available, and he does not confuse the best prose with the book club selections. He knows some of the poetry of the past and values it, and would like to know more about the poetry of his own times, but has found over and over that the books he picks up to read simply baffle him.

Or he is, if you prefer, a man at least as well educated as the

[244]

poet (usually no incredible feat), but not in a literary specialty. I mean to stress the word "educated" and I mean it to exclude the technicians. Technicians are not educated; they are trained. Education does not occur except where questions of human value are invoked. Only technology could have produced for us that laboratory primitive in our midst, the push-button Neanderthal. I do not mean that a technician cannot be educated, but that education seldom happens as part of his intrinsic training. Those are vacuum tubes that were his eyes. They glow, and when they are not destroying us they seem to point new directions. But we must learn to value only the civilized man.

Can the poet address himself to that notion of the civilized man, or must he think only of the literary specialist? Must he forever be Mr. Eliot writing for Mr. Pound and Mr. Pound writing for Mr. Eliot? Eliot and Pound have both, or at least Eliot has, earned a considerable share of that license no intelligent man would withhold from genius. Their influence, however, has gone far beyond their personal interchanges, and however valuable much of that influence has been in making poetry more venturesome, it is reasonable to ask if their influence toward greater and greater specialization does not add to more ill than good. I cannot escape the conviction that my reader of general culture is more important to the future of poetry than either Eliot or Pound.

Both of these writers are baroque poets. By baroque I mean simply that sort of writing that addresses itself inward to other writing, rather than outward to the lives of men. Robert Graves, another baroque poet, recently invoked the parable of the Scilly Islanders in his defense of the baroque: the islanders live by taking in each other's washing. "They never," adds Graves, "upset their carefully balanced island economy by trying to horn into the laundry trade of the mainland, and nowhere in the Western Hemisphere was washing better done."[1]

The best counter-statement I know appeared in the best written newspaper in the United States today. It is a translation by H. L. Davis from the writings of the Spanish poet, Antonio Machado.[2]

---

1. Robert Graves, *Poems*, 1938-1946. New York, Creative Age Press.

2. H. L. Davis, "From the Far West," *Rocky Mountain Herald*, Denver, Colorado, April 2, 1949.

Really creative art never turns its back on nature, and by nature I mean all parts of life and of earth that have not yet been transformed into art, including, obviously, the mind and soul of the poet himself. To create, an artist must transform some part of this raw material into a work of art. Obviously, this cannot be done with material that has been transformed already. It is true that there exists a form of aesthetic apathy which undertakes to find its material in the work of past artists rather than in nature, and insists that one can be creative merely by rearranging it. This is as if bees should spend their working hours gathering honey from the comb at one side of the hive and carrying it to the comb on the opposite side, instead of going out and gathering it from flowers. True, they deal in honey, the same as the older-fashioned bees did, but whose? And to what purpose?

Baroque poetry with its frigid vehemence, its exhibitionistic forcefulness and false dynamism, its arbitrary twistings and distortions, its carefully-arranged denaturalizing of living speech into a dead language, its strained mannerisms and calculated artificialities, can, in a period of exhaustion or perversion of taste, produce an effect superficially resembling aesthetic emotion. What it can never attain to is grace. Grace can come only when an art achieves complete forgetfulness of itself, of its means and techniques and methods, and this can happen only in the hands of a great artist. . . .

Excellent arguments are always possible in favor of the baroque. Whatever happens on the mainland, Graves is incontrovertible within his island kingdom. And his Scilly Islanders undoubtedly are champion launderers. But that kingdom *is* an island, and therein lies the central weakness of the baroque—not in the coherence of its argument nor in the skill of its performance, but in the simple fact that when that argument and method conquer, art imbreeds itself to death and exile, for in art the exile from human immediacy is always death. *Poetry, A Magazine of Verse,* carries on the back cover of every issue, a sentence from Whitman: "To have great poets, there must be great audiences too." The poet who values his are in human terms must accept this concern for his audience.

One cannot, however, bring the poetry to the audience: the audience must be brought to the poetry. The poet must write to his own standard of excellence. If this necessarily implies puzzling his audience at times, there is no help for it. But neither must one make a virtue of this loss. And by loss I mean any failure of communication. For it is nonsense to believe that poets write for any reason except to be read. If a Rossetti makes the gesture of burying his love poems with his beloved, you may be sure he will exhume them later—unless he has taken the professional precaution of making copies. Yet even in the work of poets who are writing well today, I have frequently found a strange mood of self-enclosure, as if anything less than deliberate evasion of the reader constitutes a debauchery of artistic integrity. The name of this trend, at its extreme, is Coterie.

But perverse or not, the poet's sense of artistic integrity is his indispensable rite. My concern is not with ways of watering his standards down to mass taste, but with any means available for preparing the potential reader to perceive the poem that follows from those standards. Traditionally, this function has been largely left to reviewers, critics, and teachers. The poets would do better to retain a considerable part of this function for themselves. Far too many reviewers lack qualification; the critics have succeeded too often in making the discussion of poetry more private and more specialized than is even the most esoteric poetry; and the teachers of English have too often exhibited themselves as historians of the external aspects of poetry with a hawk's eye for a neo-platonic doctrine or for obscure sources, but with little or no attention to the real issue of "what makes this poem a poem, and what makes it the poem it is rather than the poem to which we are comparing it?"

The poet's responsibility to declare himself and his working principles is especially urgent today when the cultural world lacks a central tradition, and when scholarship has made so many traditions available to any poet, that only a specialist can be expected to know which side of Parnassus the poet grew up on, and whether it was indeed Parnassus or only a bibliography of references to it.

For myself, I will accept a simplification. Of the poets of the past whose works I am able to read in the original I admire most Dante, Chaucer, of course Shakespeare, and Donne. I should be happy to think that I have learned anything at all from these authors. Of the poets of this century, I have been most moved by (and, I hope, somewhat indebted to) Yeats, the early Eliot, Spender, and MacLeish. I admire the triumph of many individual pieces by many other authors, but these are the men whose vision has seemed to speak to me in more than fragments. I think MacLeish's theories of poetic communication, though they lack the monumental quality of Eliot's criticism, hold forth a better hope for poetry than I can find in Eliot, if by poetry we mean fewer Ph. D. theses and more of what Emily Dickinson called "that desirable gooseflesh." I hasten to add that my admiration for Eliot, though qualified, is great. But I am a specialist: I make my living by writing and by teaching others to write, and the world has allowed me to find my bread in books. Or my crumbs in books and my bread in student papers. Nevertheless, I am not compelled to make a living *before* I can be free to turn to literature. I see no reason for asking my reader to be a specialist, or any more of a specialist than I am at Symphony Hall. Stravinsky does not ask me to be Stokowski before permitting me to find pleasure in his compositions. I would not ask any of my readers to be Kenneth Burke.

II

The following principles are not intended for the critic: they set forth nothing that will appear new to him. They are intended, rather, for the general reader I have been describing. I believe them to be a basic smplification of the general outlook and techniques from which I try to write poems. They are presented here too briefly to appear as more than rules of thumb, but I am willing to defend them in greater detail. Obviously no such formalization is without a second motive: I believe that the baroque has already gone so far in our literature that only a reassertion of these sound and enduring principles and practices can offer a hope and future for poetry.

1. *A poem should be understandable.*

By understandable I do not mean paraphrasable. No poem should ever be read as an exercise in running paraphrase. The reader must bring a metaphoric sense to the reading, just as a listener to music must bring some sensitivity to the musical idiom. But a good poem should deliver a living observation in an emotional way. The poem cannot do this immediately for all readers, but neither should it require endless scholarly dissection and a special code book. Nevertheless a poem may be "difficult," but only in proportion to its power to lure the reader back to a re-reading. The lures are: sound, evocation, imagery, phrase, symbol, rhythm, personality, and the total impact of all these things plus the perceived fragment of the "meaning."

Most poems "mean" several things at once (as does *Moby Dick* for instance), and an interesting part of each level of meaning should reveal itself at each reading. Each level of meaning, must, further, maintain its wholeness. (As *Moby Dick* is a well resolved adventure story on the level at which it is an adventure story, a carefully sustained symbolic parable on the level at which it is a symbolic parable, etc.) The best reader is the one who captures most of these levels most quickly, but the poem should have pleasure to give at each level, and it is never necessary to capture all the levels of meaning in order to enjoy a poem.

2. *Poetry should be read aloud.*

It should, accordingly, be written to be read aloud, and no typographical eccentricity should be permitted to usurp the function of the speaking voice. Conversely, any typographical device that guides the reader toward reading the poem as the poet intended it to be read, is valuable.

3. *Poetry should be about the lives of people.*

4. *Poetry should be specific.*

Obviously, poetry must be free to deal with evocative half-states and evasive moods, but the evocation must be produced by sensory stimuli *over which the poet exercises some control.* I do not think it is possible for the poet to control the response to abstract labels. Therefore he must give himself to the perceivable. This is especially true of the use of symbolism. Some of the worst poems written today are bad because they use abstractions as symbols.

5. *There is no subject not fit for poetry and no word not fit for poetry.*

As noted, I believe the specific is better stuff for the evocation of mood than is the abstract. It is also true that some words (beauty, truth, justice, in one class; sarabande, alabaster, crepuscular in another) have been so overused that they are dangerous when employed by an unsceptical mind. In any case, the language of common speech is preferable to enlarged rhetorical constructions, and the "pretty" should be approached willingly but with caution.

6. *Art from which no personality emerges is dead.*

7. *In a successful poem the subject must create its own form.*

The structure of poetry exists in the same way as the structure of music. Both begin by stating a theme, both develop that theme by delays and complications (other themes), and both must lead the expectancies they have created to a resolution unique to the particular development of the poem or piece of music itself. The strong and right resolution of the "Ode on a Grecian Urn," for example, cannot provide a meaningful resolution for the "Ode to a Nightingale" or for any other poem. That resolution may be a tonic, a meaningful and controlled discord, or a dying fall. There is no other satisfactory analogy between music and poetry, and it is a confusion of terms to speak of the mellifluousness of some poetry as "musical."

8. *Whenever a poem seems to be saying two things at once, it is saying two things at once, and should be so understood.*

For example, "a way of wishing well," the last phrase in "Composition for a Nativity," is intended to mean both "well-wishing" and "wishing-well." It is my sense that the wistfulness of tossing the sentimental penny into those childish waters of superstition is a right counterpoint to the seriousness of well-wishing, itself a forlorn enough gesture in our times. Similarly, "star hurlers" in "In the Year of Many Conversions and the Private Soul" is intended to mean both those larger-than-life romantics would like to hurl stars, and "star hurlers" (baseball pitchers) who invariably seem to be temperamental and non-mental children.

9. *There is no such thing as a poem that does not affirm.*

Accusing a conscientious artist of intellectual negation is simple nonsense. Whatever the subject, or its mood, or the poet's rationalized philosophy of zeal or despair, his devotion to his form is *per se* a declaration of faith that allegiance to the art form is a better, truer, and deeper way of living.

10. *A line of poetry is a conceived unit, not a typographical fragment.*

It should have wholeness. A pause is normally anticipated at the end of a line. If the line means one thing with an end pause, and another thing when the reading is run on to the next line, both meanings should function together.

11. *A poem is not a syllogism, and its essential unity and progression are psychological rather than logical.*

12. *Rhyme (internal as well as line-end) is not an appliquéd ornamentation, but part of the total voice-punctuation of the poem.*

It is one way (along with "sense," line length, punctuation, and rhythm) that the poet controls the reader's voice, leading him to speak the piece as the poet heard it. In many cases, this effect is best achieved by irregular rather than regular rhyme.

13. *The norm of English metrics is the iambic pentameter line, but the best poetry is written less out of a strict observance of that line, than out of a sensitively trained memory of it with wide variations in the number of light beats in a foot.*

Poetry has two stresses: the mechanical and the meaningful. When these two stresses fall together too often, the verse becomes soporific. Tennyson once invented a perfect iambic pentameter line to prove that regularity of meter does not make poetry—note that the mechanical accent falls always on the syllable the voice would tend to stress in speaking the line: (the mechanical stress is marked above the line, the meaningful stress is careted below)

$$\breve{\text{u}} \; / \; \breve{\text{u}} \; / \; . \breve{\text{u}} \; / \; \breve{\text{u}} \; / \; \breve{\text{u}} \; /$$
A Mister Wilkinson, a clergyman
$$\land \qquad\quad \land \;\; \land \qquad\quad \land \qquad \land$$

Mechanical stress then is the alternation of light and heavy syllables, and meaningful stress is the fall of accent on those words which demand stress according to the spoken meaning of the line. Meaningful stress, it must be noted, frequently yields fewer accents than mechanical stress.

$$\breve{\text{u}} \; / \; \breve{\text{u}} \; / \; \breve{\text{u}} \; / \; \breve{\text{u}} \; / \; \breve{\text{u}} \; /$$
The flowering and deflowering of intent.
$$\land \qquad\qquad \land \qquad\qquad\quad \land$$

The interplay of these two stresses is the source of all metrical effect.

ELEGY JUST IN CASE

Here lie Ciardi's pearly bones
In their ripe organic mess.
Jungle blown, his chromosomes
Breed to a new address.

Progenies of orchids seek
The fracture's white spilled lymph.
And his heart's red valve will leak
Fountains for a protein nymph.

Was it bullets or a wind
Or a rip-cord fouled on Chance?
Artifacts the natives find
Decorate them when they dance.

Here lies the sgt.'s mortal wreck
Lily spiked and termite kissed,
Spiders pendant from his neck,
Beetles shining on his wrist.

Bring the tic and southern flies
Where the land crabs run unmourning
Through a night of jungle skies
To a climeless morning.

And bring the chalked eraser here
Fresh from rubbing out his name.
Burn the crew-board for a bier.
(Also Colonel what's-his-name.)

Let no dice be stored and still.
Let no poker deck be torn.
But pour the smuggled rye until
The barracks threshold is outworn.

File the papers, pack the clothes,
Send the coded word through air:
"We regret and no one knows
Where the sgt. goes from here."

"Missing as of inst. oblige,
Deepest sorrow and remain . . ."
Shall I grin at persiflage?
Could I have my skin again

Would I choose a business form
Stilted mute as a giraffe,
Or a pinstripe unicorn
On a cashier's epitaph?

Darling, darling, just in case
Rivets fail or engines burn,
I forget the time and place
But your flesh was sweet to learn.

In the grammar of not yet
Let me name one verb for chance,
Scholarly to one regret:
That I leave your mood and tense.

Swift and single as a shark
I have seen you churn my sleep.
Now if beetles hunt my dark
What will beetles find to keep?

Fractured meat and open bone—
Nothing single or surprised.
Fragments of a written stone
Undeciphered but surmised.

TO JUDITH ASLEEP

My dear, darkened in sleep, turned from the moon
That riots on curtain-stir with every breeze
Leaping in moths of light across your back . . .
Far off, then soft and sudden as petals shower
Down from wired roses—silently, all at once—
You turn, abandoned and naked, all let down
In ferny streams of sleep and petaled thighs
Rippling into my flesh's buzzing garden.

Far and familiar your body's myth-map lights,
Traveled by moon and dapple. Sagas were curved
Like scimitars to your hips. The raiders' ships
All sailed to your one port. And watchfires burned
Your image on the hills. Sweetly you drown
Male centuries in your chiaroscuro tide
Of breast and breath. And all my memory's shores
You frighten perfectly, washed familiar and far.

Ritual wars have climbed your shadowed flank
Where bravos dreaming of fair women tore
Rock out of rock to have your cities down
In loot of hearths and trophies of desire.
And desert monks have fought your image back
In a hysteria of mad skeletons.
Bravo and monk (the heads and tails of love)
I stand, a spinning coin of wish and dread,

Counting our life, our chairs, our books and walls,
Our clock whose radium eye and insect voice
Owns all our light and shade, and your white shell
Spiraled in moonlight on the bed's white beach;
Thinking, I might press you to my ear
And all your coils fall out in sounds of surf
Washing away our chairs, our books and walls,
Our bed and wish, our ticking light and dark.

Child, child, and making legend of my wish
Fastened alive into your naked sprawl—
Stir once to stop my fear and miser's panic
That time shall have you last and legendry
Undress to old bones from its moon brocade.
Yet sleep and keep our prime of time alive
Before that death of legend. My dear of all

Saga and century, sleep in familiar-far.
Time still must tick *this is, I am, we are.*

V - J D A Y

On the tallest day in time, the dead came back.
Clouds met us in the pastures past a world.
By short wave the releases of a rack
Exploded on the interphone's new word.

Half way past Iwo we jettisoned to sea
Our cherished bombs like tears and tears like bombs
To spring a frolic fountain daintily
Out of the blue metallic seas of doom.

No fire-shot cloud pursued us going home.
No cities cringed and wallowed in our flame.
Far out to sea a blank millennium
Changed us alive, and left us still the same.

Lightened, we banked like jays, antennae squawking.
The four wild metal halos of our props
Blurred into time. The interphone was talking
Abracadabra to the cumulus tops:

Dreamboat three-one to Yearsend—loud and clear,
Angels one-two, on course at one-six-nine.
Magellan to Balboa. Propwash to Century.
How do your read me? Bombay to Valentine.

Fading and out. And all the dead were homing.
(*Wisecrack to Halfmast. Doom to Memory.*)
On the tallest day in time we saw them coming,
Wheels down and flaming on a metal sea.

ON A PHOTO OF SGT. CIARDI
A YEAR LATER

The sgt. stands so fluently in leather,
So poster-holstered and so newsreel-jawed
As death's costumed and fashionable brother,
My civil memory is overawed.

Behind him see the circuses of doom
Dance a finale chorus on the sun.
He leans on gun sights, doesn't give a damn
For dice or stripes, and waits to see the fun.

The cameraman whose ornate public eye
Invented that fine bravura look of calm
At murderous clocks hung ticking in the sky
Palmed the deception off without a qualm.

Even the camera, focused and exact
To a two dimensional conclusion,
Uttered its formula of physical fact
Only to lend data to illusion.

The camera always lies. By a law of perception
The obvious surface is always an optical ruse.
The leather was living tissue in its own dimension,
The holsters held benzedrine tablets, the guns were no use.

The careful slouch and dangling cigarette
Were always superstitious as Amen.
The shadow under the shadow is never caught:
The camera photographs the cameraman.

ODE FOR THE BURIAL OF A CITIZEN

Recorder, tax collector, landlord, friends,
This man is past his obligation.
Salesman, he is no market to be won:
The index of his power to pay descends
On graphs of strata, closes on a stone.
Like all of us he was a business risk,
Sustained a level after starting brisk,
Finally failed to displace his own depreciation.

He is marketable nowhere, auctioneer:
His liabilities zero, his assets zero.
His card has been removed from the credit bureau.
He is off the mailing list of the fiscal year.
His final real investment was to borrow
Courage from courage on the day's receipts
And so by petty cash and small deceits
To contrive one more contrivance for tomorrow.

His ballot is not collectible, public saints:
His politics are simplified and sound.
He has his ear forever to the ground
To hear the perfect congress of his silence.
Weep for him, learned men. I pass around
The hat of sentiment, drop him your tears,
For you are in the contract of his years:
All that he did not find, you have not found.

THE PILOT IN THE JUNGLE

I

Machine stitched rivets ravel on a tree
Whose name he does not know. Left in the sky,
He dangles from a silken cumulus
(Stork's bundle upside down

On the delivering wind) and sees unborn
Incredible jungles of the lizard's eye:
Dark fern, dark river, a shale coliseum
Mountained above one smudgepot in the trees
That was his surreal rug on metered skies
And slid afire into this fourth dimension
Whose infinite point of meeting parallels
He marks in ultra-space, suspended from
The chords of fifty centuries
Descending to their past—a ripping sound
That snags him limb by limb. He tears and falls
Louder than any fruit dropped from the trees,
And finds himself in mud on hands and knees.

II

The opened buckle frees him from his times.
He walks three paces dressed in dripping fleece
And tears it off. The great bird of his chute
Flaps in the trees: he salvages its hide
And starts a civilization. He has a blade,
Seventeen matches, his sheepskin, and his wits.
Spaceman Crusoe at the wreck of time,
He ponders unseen footprints of his fear.
No-eyes watch his nothing deep in nowhere.

III

He finds the wreck (the embers of himself)
Salvages bits of metal, bakelite, glass—
Dials twisted from himself, his poverty.
Three hours from time still ticking on his wrist
The spinning bobbins of the time machine
Jam on an afternoon of Genesis
And flights of birds blow by like calendars
From void to void. Did worlds die or did he?
He studies twisted props of disbelief
Wondering what ruin to touch. He counts his change
("Steady now, steady . . . ") flips heads or tails and sees

The coin fall into roots. An omen? ("Steady . . .")
He laughs (a nerve's slow tangling like a vine)
Speaks to himself, shouts, listens, hears a surf
Of echo rolling back to strand him there
In tide pools of dead time by caves of fear,
And enters to himself, denned in his loss,
Tick-tick, a bloodbeat building on his wrist.
Racheting down the dead teeth of a skull
(The fossil of himself) sucked out of sight
Past heads and tails, past vertebrae and gill
To bedrocks out of time, with time to kill.

POEM FOR MY THIRTY-SECOND
BIRTHDAY

I

I have driven North after midnight, machined
Past the mandarin festival of shore lights,
Red-eyed radio towers, amber overpasses.
The unreal sea licks at the feet of piers
Conquered as any spaniel. Froths of love
Surf from its jaws, faithful to our lit shore.

On vegetable beds of towels, lovers
Sprawl on the popular sand and dream themselves
Borne on surfs to a delirium
Of rapturous potency and annihilation,
A wish to be magnified under the lens of night
Then rock on sea drift, cradles of dalliance.

I have driven North to a silence of myself
Where, from a headland of the sea-risen moon,
Distance frames an image of the shore—
All ceremonial bowing and jeweled meeting
Of surf and man. A print for silks or screens
Or to be folded inward on a fan.

When once a year surf eats its way inland
Through rock and road, howling Northeast from time
Into the shattering garden of the lights
And the fan splits to ribs of ivory
Glued to a tattered fabric, reckless lovers
Laugh in the wind, but do not save themselves.

Only this eye on headlands saves itself
When it becomes the camera of the scene
Conforming all into its focal length,
Where no line runs from any shore of time
But runs dead center to the self-
Sealed ego: eye, mind, manner of speaking.

I have driven North past midnight, machined
To be that separate engine functioning
On shutters and on sound tracks of myself.
Let in the light, let in the dark, let in
The sound of voices reeled on the intricacies
Of the compassionate ego lingering

The whole length of its life to give away
The legend of itself, and, self-compelled,
Turn from the headland of its isolation
To reappear on screens of public halls
With newsreels of us all, pity and fear
Preambling FINIS on a light-drowned screen.

II

Because there is no experience but myself
I have driven North to gather by the sea
The ceremony of my own ritual night
And mark in anniversaries of dawn
The morning when the breathing world began
Surfs of my birth onto a beach of flesh.

I am thirty-two and have not saved the world
From evils I have known—fears more for you

Than any I have need to dread inside
The armor of myself—too little giving,
Cretin conformity, spastic ignorance,
Migraine intellect, hysterical cash.

I have lived this year on platforms, found my voice
Through amplifiers, gaveled the public air
To call for order in the ruins of state
Where man's foreseeable decline to war
Stamps the pure ego with its political veto
Or smudges it with fingerprints of guilt.

Now at this edge of birth, there is no dilemma:
Elaborately as a soldier between battles
Picking the marvelous lice of his own body
Before the bath and ceremonious touch
Of hands upon himself—an ecstasy
Of pure release in torpors of himself—

I ritualize my interim and survival.
What was to do is done or simply lost;
What is to do arrives. My surf and shore
Meet in a placid marvel giving back
An unacquisitive distance from this night
I issue from myself in years that keep

An album of myself—a skeleton
X-rayed by hope of love—seen year by year
Posed in the changing fashions of its skin
To match at last the medical negative
Anonymous as catacombs of you,
Your unknown twin in the debris of time.

VALE

(*to Irwin Swerdlow*)

Cambridge, an outdoor library stack of bricks,
Files one more year into the catalogue.
It's the end of a season, trains leaving, sailings,
Visits to airports, tail lights fading away.
Goodbye to psychoanalysis by bourbon
And to all gathering of literary drunks
From every specialized professional century
Thronging in quotes around the seltzer and ice
While empties file like footnotes from the sink—
Goodbye. To janitors, to staff, to proctors,
To all doctors and nearly doctors,
To bumpkins, to lumpkins, to fidgets, to flubs,
To freshmen in the Wursthaus, to seniors in the clubs,
To the solvent, to the arty, to the clerical,
To the materio-revivalist-hysterical,
To the high and low and middle-high inane,
To the eccentric, to the sane and the insane—Goodbye.
And goodbye, Widener and the clever apartments,
And to all heads and assistant heads of departments.
Goodbye. Goodbye. To all the year goodbye.

Iubet vicissum, and now all tickets read
The Sphere of Man. God and the Liberal Arts
Far-fling the seed pearls to the jowls of time,
And all neurosis must go home alone,
Trailing the breath and spirits that awake
(Come the next Fall from grace) in Ashtabula.
Sodding the loamy young with moss from Cambridge
For an outdoor ceremony of the arts.

Goodbye, Goodbye. To time by institution,
To the flowering and deflowering of intent.
Goodbye to all ourselves that were and went,
Sending back penny posts of sentiment.
For we were visited if not quite blessed.

Longinus in pin-stripes, Plato in harris-tweed
Left seals on various gates and various walls,
While bibliogs in pince-nez and French-cuffs
Pumped the divine afflatus leisurely
In suburbs of the Beautiful and True.
And there were some, untidy but nearly beautiful,
Who stood by blackboards doodled with good data
And diagrammed civilization's eccentric charm
In smiles of admirable uncertainty.
Their vistas were always real—and parenthetical.
Then, too, there came the specialist from the sea:
Culture's ambassador to all assistant professors
Presented a British glottal to the press
And swapped a charming competence of manner
For God-knows-what-he-knew and never said,
But went away well honored and well paid.

To all of them on every clock, goodbye.
On every door, goodbye. In clubs, in pubs,
In rooms, in restaurants, in offices,
In taxis, in convertibles, in the subway—
Goodbye in tweed, goodbye in whiskey and beer,
Goodbye in books. And year by year by year
Goodbye. Goodbye. We'll see you in the Fall
In Paris, in Kansas City, or not at all.
All we are sure of is goodbye, goodbye.

MORNING IN THE PARK

A green morning of indolence one hedge beyond
The rags-to-riches nonsense of traffic
Suns all my mind. A vegetable with eyes,
I fit my coat to greengoods and give back
The drift of cumulus over my head. My sight
Dizzies through heights of light. Higher than all towers
I soar like bubbles into iris air:

Veils of it gather on my shining. An hour
Of this bemusement crazes the practical sense:
A week of it and I would be unemployable
Forever, a character beyond the hedge,
Sky-socketed in a ringing skull and cracked
With queer illuminations, secrets I'd know
Of local zeniths where devout pigeons
Flattered me for crumbs with wings, wings,
Loud beating storms of love to my St. Francis
In a multi-million stirring of affluent air,
Adorations of my rich escape.

IN THE YEAR OF MANY CONVERSIONS
AND THE PRIVATE SOUL

A sun gas coughed. A million miles of flame
Leaped half an inch across an instrument
For lens-eyed men to give the trick a name,
And papers Sunday-featured the event
In tabloid metaphors, as: a sidewalk brick
Heated to such a temperature in Peru
Would boil the Caribbean dry, half the Atlantic
And Pacific, and char the Americas through
To whatever continents char to when they char:
Be comforted that things are as they are.

We were not comforted. The belching stars
Kept a sky's distance from us. No seas boiled dry.
Converts were converted. Many wars
Were fought and lost. And temperatures ran high—
Still there was always something left. And still
We were not comforted, and the mind's clay
Baked hotter, flaked, turned powder in the skull,
Blew like volcanic ash, sifted and gray.

And on whatever Sabbath senses had
We looked upon our work, that it was bad.

There wild in space, the sun; here lost in space,
The displaced persons of a dying time,
While the star-hurlers, athletes of grace,
Compete for Gothic mountains souls may climb
To be received by sun-belch on a throne
Of saints and zodiacs in eternal heat
Above the earth-belch in iced meat and bone
Shivering our last image on the street:
The world-offended child, the surplus man,
Picking the horn of plenty's garbage can.

COMPOSITION FOR A NATIVITY

iste perfecit opus

There are three central figures preoccupied by toplighting,
A marginalia of angels and new arrivals,
And myself in this corner.

All other eyes are turned to the center,
But I have placed myself so—
My head turned foolishly as if in secret understanding—
To catch your eye and invite your question
Where adorations of my yokel finger (I work here)
Poke the warm flank of air
Dimpling the swollen wonderful cow of—
Birth is it? A time for awe? Or simply rubberneck?

This is a stylized vision we compose here:
The center, the margin, and the surd.
Still there are marvels in all stables:
Mows like firmament spill
Fodder, tinder, and country mattress.
What is not eaten must be guarded

From spontaneous combustion. Between times
We bounced the milkmaids here in dusts of pollen
Sneezing amid our passions.
Now under the cloud of one lantern
They are letting the child down.

In dumb show
The lady's hands make two white ferns for her lord's table
And he is laid in them. The man,
Understanding less than he sees, leans on his staff.
But the angels burn, and even the new arrivals reflect
The trembling night-turn of a vast compulsion.

I am no hand at marvels, but knowing I must return here
Night after night when there are no visitors,
I have placed myself radically among these dimensions
As a gesture of recognition between us,
A private significance you too have needed
To rescue identity from all assemblage
Of night wonders, a way of wishing well.

Elizabeth Bishop

ELIZABETH BISHOP *was born and brought up in Maine. She is at present Consultant in Poetry to the Library of Congress. Her first volume of poems,* NORTH AND SOUTH, *won a Houghton Mifflin Poetry Award.*

IT ALL DEPENDS

To ALL BUT two of the questions raised here my answer is *it all depends*. It all depends on the particular poem one happens to be trying to write, and the range of possibilities is, one trusts, infinite. After all, the poet's concern is not consistency.

I do not understand the question about the function of overtone, and to the question on subject matter (any predilections? any restrictions?) I shall reply that there are no restrictions. There *are*, of course, but they are not consciously restrictions.

Physique, temperament, religion, politics, and immediate circumstances all play their parts in formulating one's theories on verse. And then they play them again and differently when one is writing it. No matter what theories one may have, I doubt very much that they are in one's mind at the moment of writing a poem or that there is even a physical possibility that they could be. Theories can only be based on interpretations of other poet's poems, or one's own in retrospect, or wishful thinking.

The analysis of poetry is growing more and more pretentious and deadly. After a session with a few of the highbrow magazines one doesn't want to look at a poem for weeks, much less start writing one. The situation is reminiscent of those places along the coast where warnings are posted telling one not to walk too near the edge of the cliffs because they have been undermined by the sea and may collapse at any minute.

This does not mean that I am opposed to all close analysis and criticism. But I am opposed to making poetry monstrous or boring and proceeding to talk the very life out of it.

THE COLDER THE AIR

We must admire her perfect aim,
this huntress of the winter air
whose level weapon needs no sight,
if it were not that everywhere
her game is sure, her shot is right.
The least of us could do the same.

The chalky birds or boats stand still,
reducing her conditions of chance;
air's gallery marks identically
the narrow gallery of her glance.
The target-center in her eye
is equally her aim and will.

Time's in her pocket, ticking loud
on one stalled second. She'll consult
not time nor circumstance. She calls
on atmosphere for her result.
(It is this clock that later falls
in wheels and chimes of leaf and cloud).

LARGE BAD PICTURE

Remembering the Strait of Belle Isle or
some northerly harbor of Labrador,
before he became a school-teacher
a great uncle painted a big picture.

Receding for miles on either side
into a flushed, still sky
are overhanging pale blue cliffs
hundreds of feet high,

their bases fretted by little arches,
the entrances to caves

running in along the level of a bay
masked by perfect waves.

On the middle of that quiet floor
sits a fleet of small black ships,
square-rigged, sails furled, motionless,
their spars like burnt match-sticks.

And high above them, over the tall cliffs'
semi-translucent ranks,
are scribbled hundreds of fine black birds
hanging in n's, in banks.

One can hear their crying, crying,
the only sound there is
except for occasional sighing
as a large aquatic animal breathes.

In the pink light
the small red sun goes rolling, rolling,
round and round and round at the same height
in perpetual sunset, comprehensive, consoling,

while the ships consider it.
Apparently they have reached their destination.
It would be hard to say what brought them there,
commerce or contemplation.

THE MAN-MOTH*

Here, above,
cracks in the buildings are filled with battered moonlight.
The whole shadow of Man is only as big as his hat.
It lies at his feet like a circle for a doll to stand on,
and he makes an inverted pin, the point magnetized to the moon.

---

*Newspaper misprint for "mammoth."

He does not see the moon; he observes only her vast properties,
Feeling the queer light on his hands, neither warm nor cold,
of a temperature impossible to record in thermometers.

But when the Man-Moth
pays his rare, although occasional, visits to the surface,
the moon looks rather different to him. He emerges
from an opening under the edge of one of the sidewalks
and nervously begins to scale the faces of the buildings.
He thinks the moon is a small hole at the top of the sky,
proving the sky quite useless for protection.
He trembles, but must investigate as high as he can climb.

Up the facades,
his shadow dragging like a photographer's cloth behind him,
he climbs fearfully, thinking that this time he will manage
to push his small head through that round clean opening
and be forced through, as from a tube, in black scrolls on the
    light.
(Man, standing below him, has no such illusions).
But what the Man-Moth fears most he must do, although
he fails, of course, and falls back scared but quite unhurt.

Then he returns
to the pale subways of cement he calls his home. He flits,
he flutters, and cannot get aboard the silent trains
fast enough to suit him. The doors close swiftly.
The Man-Moth always seats himself facing the wrong way
and the train starts at once at its full, terrible speed,
without a shift in gears or a gradation of any sort.
He cannot tell the rate at which he travels backwards.

Each night he must
be carried through artificial tunnels and dream recurrent dreams.
Just as the ties recur beneath his train, these underlie
his rushing brain. He does not dare look out the window,
for the third rail, the unbroken draught of poison,
runs there beside him. He regards it as a disease

he has inherited susceptibility to. He has to keep
his hands in pockets, as others must wear mufflers.

           If you catch him,
hold up a flashlight to his eye. It's all dark pupil,
an entire night itself, whose haired horizon tightens
as he stares back, and closes up the eye. Then from the
one tear, his only possession, like the bee's sting, slips.
Slyly he palms it, and if you're not paying attention
he'll swallow it. However, if you watch, he'll hand it over,
cool as from underground springs and pure enough to drink.

SLEEPING ON THE CEILING

It is so peaceful on the ceiling!
It is the Place de la Concorde.
The little crystal chandelier
is off, the fountain is in the dark.
Not a soul is in the park.

Below, where the wall-paper is peeling,
the Jardin des Plantes has locked its gates.
Those photographs are animals.
The mighty flowers and foliage rustle;
under the leaves the insects tunnel.

We must go under the wall-paper
to meet the insect-gladiator,
to battle with a net and trident,
and leave the fountain and the square.
But oh, that we could sleep up there. . . .

A MIRACLE FOR BREAKFAST

At six o'clock we were waiting for coffee,
waiting for coffee and the charitable crumb
that was going to be served from a certain balcony,
—like kings of old, or like a miracle.
It was still dark. One foot of the sun
steadied itself on a long ripple in the river.

The first ferry of the day had just crossed the river.
It was so cold we hoped that the coffee
would be very hot, seeing that the sun
was not going to warm us; and that the crumb
would be a loaf each, buttered, by a miracle.
At seven a man stepped out on the balcony.

He stood for a minute alone on the balcony
looking over our heads toward the river.
A servant handed him the makings of a miracle,
consisting of one lone cup of coffee
and one roll, which he proceeded to crumb,
his head, so to speak, in the clouds—along with the sun.

Was the man crazy? What under the sun
was he trying to do, up there on his balcony!
Each man received one rather hard crumb,
which some flicked scornfully into the river,
and, in a cup, one drop of the coffee.
Some of us stood around, waiting for the miracle.

I can tell what I saw next; it was not a miracle.
A beautiful villa stood in the sun
and from its doors came the smell of hot coffee.
In front, a baroque white plaster balcony
added by birds, who nest along the river,
—I saw it with one eye close to the crumb—

and galleries and marble chambers. My crumb
my mansion, made for me by a miracle,
through ages, by insects, birds, and the river
working the stone. Every day, in the sun,
at breakfast time I sit on my balcony
with my feet up, and drink gallons of coffee.

We licked up the crumb and swallowed the coffee.
A window across the river caught the sun
as if the miracle were working, on the wrong balcony.

CIRQUE D'HIVER

Across the floor flits the mechanical toy,
fit for a king of several centuries back.
A little circus horse with real white hair.
His eyes are glossy black.
He bears a little dancer on his back.

She stands upon her toes and turns and turns.
A slanting spray of artificial roses
is stitched across her skirt and tinsel bodice.
Above her head she poses
another spray of artificial roses.

His mane and tail are straight from Chirico.
He has a formal, melancholy soul.
He feels her pink toes dangle toward his back
along the little pole
that pierces both her body and her soul

and goes through his, and reappears below,
under his belly, as a big tin key.
He canters three steps, then he makes a bow,
canters again, bows on one knee,
canters, then clicks and stops, and looks at me.

The dancer, by this time, has turned her back.
He is the more intelligent by far.
Facing each other rather desperately—
his eye is like a star—
we stare and say, "Well, we have come this far."

JERONIMO'S HOUSE

My house, my fairy
    palace, is
of perishable
    clapboards with
three rooms in all,
    my gray wasps' nest
of chewed-up paper
    glued with spit.

My home, my love-nest,
    is endowed
with a veranda
    of wooden lace,
adorned with ferns
    planted in sponges,
and the front room
    with red and green

left-over Christmas
    decorations
looped from the corners
    to the middle
above my little
    center table
of woven wicker
    painted blue,

and four blue chairs
    and an affair
for the smallest baby
    with a tray
with ten big beads.
    Then on the walls
two palm-leaf fans
    and a calendar

and on the table
    one fried fish
spattered with burning
    scarlet sauce,
a little dish
    of hominy grits
and four pink tissue-
    paper roses.

Also I have
    hung on a hook,
an old French horn
    repainted with
aluminum paint.
    I play each year
in the parade
    for José Marti.*

At night you'd think
    my house abandoned.
Come closer. You
    can see and hear
the writing-paper
    lines of light
and the voices of
    my radio

*The Cuban patriot.

singing flamencos
   in between
the lottery numbers.
   When I move
I take these things,
   not much more, from
my shelter from
   the hurricane.

THE FISH

I caught a tremendous fish
and held him beside the boat
half out of water, with my hook
fast in a corner of his mouth.
He didn't fight.
He hadn't fought at all.
He hung a grunting weight,
battered and venerable
and homely. Here and there
his brown skin hung in strips
like ancient wall-paper,
and its pattern of darker brown
was like wall-paper:
shapes like full-blown roses
stained and lost through age.
He was speckled with barnacles,
fine rosettes of lime,
and infested
with tiny white sea-lice,
and underneath two or three
rags of green weed hung down.
While his gills were breathing in
the terrible oxygen
—the frightening gills,
fresh and crisp with blood,

that can cut so badly—
I thought of the coarse white flesh
packed in like feathers,
the big bones and the little bones,
the dramatic reds and blacks
of his shiny entrails,
and the pink swim-bladder
like a big peony.
I looked into his eyes
which were far larger than mine
but shallower, and yellowed,
the irises backed and packed
with tarnished tinfoil
seen through lenses
of old scratched isinglass.
They shifted a little, but not
to return my stare.
—It was more like the tipping
of an object toward the light.
I admired his sullen face,
the mechanism of his jaw,
and then I saw
that from his lower lip
—if you could call it a lip—
grim, wet, and weapon-like,
hung five old pieces of fish-line,
or four and a wire leader
with the swivel still attached,
with all their five big hooks
grown firmly in his mouth.
A green line, frayed at the end
where he broke it, two heavier lines,
and a fine black thread
still crimped from the strain and snap
when it broke and he got away.
Like medals with their ribbons
frayed and wavering,
a five-haired beard of wisdom

trailing from his aching jaw.
I stared and stared
and victory filled up
the little rented boat,
from the pool of bilge
where oil had spread a rainbow
around the rusted engine
to the bailer rusted orange,
the sun-cracked thwarts,
the oarlocks on their strings,
the gunnels—until everything
was rainbow, rainbow, rainbow!
And I let the fish go.

SONGS FOR A COLORED SINGER

I

A washing hangs upon the line,
  but it's not mine.
None of the things that I can see
  belong to me.
The neighbors got a radio with an aerial;
  we got a little portable.
They got a lot of closet space;
  we got a suitcase.

I say, "Le Roy, just how much are we owing?
Something I can't comprehend,
the more we got the more we spend. . . ."
He only answers, "Let's get going."
Le Roy, you're earning too much money now.

I sit and look at our back yard
  and find it very hard
that all we got for all his dollars and cents
  's a pile of bottles by the fence.
He's faithful and he's kind
  but he sure has an inquiring mind.
He's seen a lot; he's bound to see the rest,
  and if I protest

Le Roy will answer with a frown,
"Darling, when I earns I spends.
The world is wide; it still extends. . . .
I'm going to get a job in the next town."
Le Roy, you're earning too much money now.

II

The time has come to call a halt;
  and so it ends.
    He's gone off with his other friends.

He needn't try to make amends,
'cause this occasion's all his fault.
  Through rain and dark I see his face
  across the street at Flossie's place.
  He's drinking in the warm pink glow
  to th' accompaniment of the piccolo.

The time has come to call a halt.
I met him walking with Varella
and hit him twice with my umbrella.
Perhaps that occasion was my fault,
but the time has come to call a halt.

Go drink your wine and go get tight.
  Let the piccolo play.
  I'm sick of all your fussing anyway.
  Now I'm pursuing my own way.
I'm leaving on the bus tonight.
  Far down the highway wet and black
  I'll ride and ride and not come back.
  I'm going to go and take the bus
  and find someone monogamous.
The time has come to call a halt.
I've borrowed fifteen dollars fare
and it will take me anywhere.
For this occasion's all his fault.
The time has come to call a halt.

Delmore Schwartz

DELMORE SCHWARTZ *was born in Brooklyn in* 1913. *He attended the University of Wisconsin, New York University, and Harvard, where he later taught English Composition. He is at present an editor of Partisan Review. His publications include* IN DREAMS BEGIN RESPONSIBILITIES (*poetry and prose*), SHENANDOAH, *a verse play, and* THE IMITATION OF LIFE, *a critical study.*

TWO PROBLEMS IN WRITING
OF POETRY

QUESTIONS ABOUT the practice of writing poetry make me very nervous because my answers look very strange after a newspaper reporter has rendered them. For instance, one time I replied to a question about meter by saying that there was no such thing as free verse, but only different kinds of rhythm. By the time this careless remark reached the printed page, it turned out that I had denied the existence of poems which were called free verse. This inexactitude may not seem important, but I feel that there is too much misunderstanding in the world as it is, and if that is the best that can be done by way of accurate repetition, I would rather shut up. However, it is necessary that one be polite, no matter what or how great the provocation. This requirement of politeness nearly ruined me once, however, when I was questioned as to whether the most important element in modern poetry was the intellectual factor or emotional factor. Naturally I was stupefied. But politeness made me reply that it was just like the weather, sometimes it was too hot, sometimes it was too cold, sometimes it was just plain boring, and the less attention one paid to it, the better. My questioner, a very kind lady, who was just trying to make conversation, looked so alarmed at my answer that I hastened to assure her that Plato and Dryden were wrong when they declared that poets were practically insane. The next questioner was the feature writer, whatever that is, for a fashion magazine which printed literary prattle and the like to break the flow of gorgeous garment prose. Needless to say, I was on guard. The first question was about how I had decided to become a poet, so I explained that as an infant in the cradle I had cried loudly and received immediate and unanimous attention; consequently, putting two and two together, I had tried crying out loudly in public and in blank verse, and the results had on the whole been most gratifying. My questioner seemed to like this answer very much, for she wrote it down quickly in short-hand and then inquired as to the greatest influence upon me. I was about to say Shakespeare and the depression of 1929-1937, but this was all too true, and since the truth had been distorted so often in all previous exchanges, I answered pre-natal experiences, for this was the first thing that came into my head. She took it as a *double entendre,* I think, for she left in a rage.

Since then, feeling badly about how all these well-meant in-quisitions have turned out, I've given the whole subject cool and careful thought. The chief dangers, I've decided, are as follows: one may be too technical; or fleeing from technical observations and shop-talk, one may become oracular and thus very pretentious about poets as unacknowledged legislators and similar braggadocio, and from this extreme, one swings to facetiousness and receives a sickly, uneasy grin because poets are supposed to be very serious; and then, worst of all, one becomes too personal, thus infuriating other poets, although other readers just love these intimate dis-closures.

Conscious of these dangers, and others I have not troubled to mention. I've often resorted to or been reduced to silence. But I feel now that no amount of circumspection will protect me, so I might as well speak freely. I chose two professional problems which have long occupied me.

One of these problems concerns itself with how much poetry one ought to write and how much one ought to publish. After much reflection, I've decided that one ought to write as much as possible and publish as little as possible. The latter conclusion follows from the glum fact that most poetry is likely to be bad, if judged by any standards which would justify the assertion that some poetry is good. On the other hand, one ought to write as much as possible banking on the law of averages because, among other reasons, there is no way of telling in advance whether the poem one writes is going to be good. Moreover, the writing of bad poems is for many poets a way of arriving at the writing of good poems. By publishing only work which one is reasonably comfortable about, or work which is in an idiom one no longer cultivates, one avoids the remorse of looking at one's bad poems in print and the paralyzing effects which may ensue. Horace advises one to wait for nine years before publishing a poem, and a very gifted modern poet told me that it is best to publish as much as possible, for one can always write more poems. Both pieces of advice may be good for some poets or good under certain conditions, but for most poets to wait, to be patient, to re-write and to keep looking at one's poems is the best possible method of procedure, if one is interested in writing good poems rather than in being regarded as a poet. There is nothing wrong in wanting to be known as a poet, but the desire to write good poems is more fruitful in the long run. Many good poets have been spoiled by the belief that they had to rush into print with a new book every year, and only a few have been weakened by revision, patience, and privacy.

This question is important in itself now, since the example of Auden has intensified the natural desire to appear in print very often; and it is a significant problem also because in trying to face it, one has to face the whole problem of the nature of poetry.

So too with the second problem, the relationship of any modern poet to his audience and to the well-known difficulty of modern poetry, a difficulty which obviously involves the audience. Anyone who wants to understand modern poetry can do so by working about half as hard as he must to learn a language or to acquire any new skill or to learn to play bridge well. The real problem is the effect upon the poet himself of the reader's feeling that modern poetry is difficult. His frequent response of late has been one of panic, a panic which leads to false moves and desperate oversimplifications. One fashion tendency has been to try to write poetry which would be intelligible to any audience. And meanwhile the extent of the difficulty has somehow increased in the public's mind, perhaps because the public has been preoccupied with matters other than literature. For a long time, "The Waste Land" seemed the perfect example of modern poetry's obscurity, but nowadays even the beautifully lucid poems of Robert Frost are said to be obscure. Perhaps this development is all to the good, since it may prevent poets from forcing themselves to try to be popular. But the fundamental problem presents itself falsely as long as it is supposed that the kind of poetry one produces is solely a matter of choice or will. Choice and will are involved, of course, but there is also present a large and inescapable relationship, a relationship which may well be prior because it has had a great deal to do with making the poet interested in writing poetry from the very start. Any modern poet exists in an inescapable relationship to all modern *and* modernist poetry which has been written since Baudelaire. He can choose to disregard or forget about this complicated relationship, but if he does, he is depriving himself of what is an important part of his inheritance as a poet, and also a powerful presence in the minds of everyone who is capable of reading poetry.

Consequently the modern poet is bound to be drawn in two apparently opposed directions. On the one hand, it is natural that he should want to write as directly and clearly as Yeats and Frost at their best (which is not to forget that their directness and clarity was accomplished only by means of a great deal of intellectual toil and obscure delvings). On the other hand, he is bound to be drawn toward an emulation of the marvelous refinements in the uses and powers of language which have occurred since the symbolists first appeared.

The best convenient example of this cultivation of language is this little poem which appears in James Joyce's *Ulysses*:

> White thy fambles, red thy gan,
> And thy quarrons dainty is.
> Couch a hogshead with me then.
> In the darkmans clip and kiss.

(I choose this example not only for its convenient brevity, but also because it is an omen or beginning of *Finnegan's Wake,* an overwhelming work which, if it concludes an epoch, also initiates a new one.) The obscurity of the little poem in *Ulysses* is not reduced very much by its context in the novel. And even when the reader finds out, (as he may not unless he reads Stuart Gilbert's commentary on *Ulysses,*) that the words he does not understand, or only imperfectly understands, are gypsy slang, he may be disturbed by the poem or resent the author's use of unfamiliar and special words. Indeed, it can be argued (in a misleading way or in an illuminating one) that the beauty of this poem and the powerful emotion it communicates come through best of all when the reader does not know exactly what the exact gypsy meanings of the words are. For example, "couch a hogshead" means "lie down and sleep," and if one knows this in advance, some of the richness of connotation may be blocked off.

Every modern poet would like to be direct, lucid, and immediately intelligible, at least most of the time. In fact, one of the most fantastic misconceptions of modern literature and modern art in general is the widespread delusion that the modern artist does not want and would not like a vast popular audience, if this were possible without the sacrifice of some necessary quality in his work. But it is often not possible. And every modern poet would also like to be successful, popular, famous, rich, cheered on Broadway, sought by Hollywood, recited on the radio, and admired by Mr. J. Donald Adams. The lack of popularity does not arise from any poet's desire to punish himself and deprive himself of these glorious prizes and delectable rewards. The basic cause is a consciousness of the powers and possibilities of language, a consciousness which cannot be discarded with any more ease than one can regain one's innocence.

Some will doubtless continue to be irritated by the cultivation of language of which Joyce's poem is a somewhat extreme instance. And they will waste time, mind, and energy in defensive attitudes, denouncing or denying the virtues of this kind of writing.

And some will try to imitate and extend literally and mechanically the direction which Joyce represents.

And some will try to find a point at which the clarity of Yeats can be sought at the same time as one seeks the richness which Joyce possessed.

This last effort or ambition may be as quixotic and contradictory as an attempt to square the circle. But given the consciousness of literature likely in any one who wants to write good poetry, anything less than the reconciliation of these extremes is far from enough. As some Indian chief once said on a visit to the White House after he had had two portions of everything but remained hungry: "A little too much of everything is just enough for me."

• • •

Orpheus once visited a colleague. His name was Agathon and he was a famous poet and critic of the time. Indeed he was much better known than Orpheus then, for the latter had not yet attracted to himself the widespread publicity which followed upon his sensational adventures in trying to get his wife to return to him.

Orpheus showed Agathon his most recent work, hoping for praise and admiration, but requesting a critical opinion.

"Frankly," said Agathon, "these poems are worthless. Even a fellow-poet like myself has a hard time understanding them. You can imagine what the common reader will and will not make of them. Why don't you write the way the old boys did? *This is not what the public wants.*"

"I do my best," said Orpheus meekly (he was very disappointed but grateful for his friend's candor), "I write whatever I can."

This story is endless. I hope to discuss it at greater length in the future. One must not be deceived by Orpheus' subsequent career which was largely in the nature of an escapade and *tour de force*. Every genuine poet is now in the same boat as Orpheus was then. Agathon was also right to say what he did say. What would have been the point of being other than sincere, if that was the way he felt?

"Amor omnia vincit," muttered Orpheus under his breath as he left, "love always wins out. Poetry is its own reward. Maybe Agathon is right. Maybe he is wrong."

Obviously the preceding interview may be interpreted in several different ways.

IN THE NAKED BED, IN PLATO'S CAVE

In the naked bed, in Plato's cave,
Reflected headlights slowly slid the wall,
Carpenters hammered under the shaded window,
Wind troubled the window curtains all night long,
A fleet of trucks strained uphill, grinding,
Their freights covered, as usual.
The ceiling lightened again, the slanting diagram
Slid slowly forth.
                              Hearing the milkman's chop,
His striving up the stair, the bottle's chink,
I rose from bed, lit a cigarette,
And walked to the window. The stony street
Displayed the stillness in which buildings stand,
The street-lamp's vigil and the horse's patience.
The winter sky's pure capital
Turned me back to bed with exhausted eyes.

Strangeness grew in the motionless air. The loose
Film grayed. Shaking wagons, hooves' waterfalls,
Sounded far off, increasing, louder and nearer.
A car coughed, starting. Morning, softly
Melting the air, lifted the half-covered chair
From underseas, kindled the looking-glass,
Distinguished the dresser and the white wall.
The bird called tentatively, whistled, called,
Bubbled and whistled, so! Perplexed, still wet
With sleep, affectionate, hungry and cold. So, so,
O son of man, the ignorant night, the travail
Of early morning, the mystery of beginning
Again and again,
                              while Time is unforgiven.

FOR THE ONE WHO WOULD TAKE
MAN'S LIFE IN HIS HANDS

Tiger Christ unsheathed his sword,
Threw it down, became a lamb.
Swift spat upon the species, but
Took two women to his heart.
Samson who was strong as death
Paid his strength to kiss a slut.
Othello that stiff warrior
Was broken by a woman's heart.
Troy burned for a sea-tax, also for
Possession of a charming whore.
What do all examples show?
What must the finished murderer know?

You cannot sit on bayonets,
Nor can you eat among the dead.
When all are killed, you are alone,
A vacuum comes where hate has fed.
Murder's fruit is silent stone,
The gun increases poverty.
With what do these examples shine?
The soldier turned to girls and wine.
Love is the tact of every good,
The only warmth, the only peace.

"What have I said?" asked Socrates,
"Affirmed extremes, cried yes and no,
Taken all parts, denied myself,
Praised the caress, extolled the blow,
Soldier and lover quite deranged
Until their motions are exchanged
—What do all examples show?
What can any actor know?
The contradiction in every act,
The infinite task of the human heart."

A DOG NAMED EGO, THE
SNOWFLAKES AS KISSES

A dog named Ego, the snowflakes as kisses
Fluttered, ran, came with me in December,
Snuffing the chill air, changing, and halting,
There where I walked toward seven o'clock,
Sniffed at some interests hidden and open,
Whirled, descending, and stood still, attentive,
Seeking their peace, the stranger, unknown,
With me, near me, kissed me, touched my wound,
My simple face, obsessed and pleasure bound.

"Not free, no liberty, rock that you carry,"
So spoke Ego in his cracked and harsh voice,
While snowflakes kissed me and satisfied minutes,
Falling from some place half believed and unknown,
"You will not be free, nor ever alone,"
So spoke Ego. "Mine is the kingdom,
Dynasty's bone: you will not be free,
Go, choose, run, you will not be alone."

"Come, come, come," sang the whirling snowflakes,
Evading the dog who barked at their smallness,
"Come!" sang the snowflakes, "Come here! and here!"
How soon at the sidewalk, melted, and done,
One kissed me, two kissed me! So many died!
While Ego barked at them, swallowed their touch,
Ran this way! And that way! While they slipped to the ground,
Leading him further and farther away,
While night collapsed amid the falling,
And left me no recourse, far from my home,
And left me no recourse, far from my home.

THE HEAVY BEAR WHO GOES WITH ME

"the withness of the body"

—WHITEHEAD

The heavy bear who goes with me,
A manifold honey to smear his face,
Clumsy and lumbering here and there,
The central ton of every place,
The hungry beating brutish one
In love with candy, anger, and sleep,
Crazy factotum, dishevelling all,
Climbs the building, kicks the football,
Boxes his brother in the hate-ridden city.

Breathing at my side, that heavy animal,
That heavy bear who sleeps with me,
Howls in his sleep for a world of sugar,
A sweetness intimate as the water's clasp,
Howls in his sleep because the tight-rope
Trembles and shows the darkness beneath.
—The strutting show-off is terrified,
Dressed in his dress-suit, bulging his pants,
Trembles to think that his quivering meat
Must finally wince to nothing at all.

That inescapable animal walks with me,
Has followed me since the black womb held,
Moves where I move, distorting my gesture,
A caricature, a swollen shadow,
A stupid clown of the spirit's motive,
Perplexes and affronts with his own darkness,
The secret life of belly and bone,
Opaque, too near, my private, yet unknown,
Stretches to embrace the very dear
With whom I would talk without him near,
Touches her grossly, although a word
Would bare my heart and make me clear,

Stumbles, flounders, and strives to be fed
Dragging me with him in his mouthing care,
Amid the hundred million of his kind,
The scrimmage of appetite everywhere.

THE TRUE, THE GOOD AND THE
BEAUTIFUL*

HE HEARD THE NEWSBOYS SHOUTING
"EUROPE! EUROPE!"

Dear Citizens,
I heard the newsboys shouting "Europe! Europe!"
It was late afternoon, a winter's day
Long as a prairie, wool and ashen gray,
And then I heard the silence, drop by drop,
And knew I must afain confront myself:
"What shall I cry from my window?" I asked myself,
"What shall I say to the citizens below?
Since I have been a *privileged character*
These four years past. Since I have been excused
From the war for the lesser evil, merciless
As the years to girls who once were beautiful.
What have I done which is a little good?
What apples have I grasped, for all my years?
What starlight have I glimpsed for all my guilt?"

Then to the dead silence I said, in hope:
"I am a student of the morning light,
And of the evil native to the heart.
I am a pupil of emotion's wrongs
Performed upon the glory of this world.
Myself I dedicated long ago
—Or prostituted, shall I say?—to poetry,
The true, the good, and the beautiful,

*This is a passage from a longer poem.

Infinite fountains inexhaustible,
Full as the sea, old as the rocks,

                              new as the breaking surf—"

THE SILENCE ANSWERED HIM ACCUSINGLY

"Don't fool yourself," the silence said to me,
"Don't tell yourself a noble lie once more!"

Then to the silence, being accused, I said:
"I teach the boys and girls in my ageing youth,
I try to tell them the little I know of truth,
Saying, In the beginning is the word,
And in the end and everywhere in love,

In all love's places and in the mind of God.
Three words I speak, though they are bare and far,

                              untouchable as a star,
The true, the good, and the beautiful,
Shifting my tones as if I said to them
Candy, soda, fruits and flowers,
And if they hear what thunderclap uproars,

                              unanimous applause,
(Extremely gratifying signs of pleasure).

'Behold the unspeakable beauty,' I say to them,
'Arise and lift your eyes and raise your hearts
In celebration and in praise because
Plato's starlight glitters amid the shocking wars.' "

SUCH ANSWERS ARE COLD COMFORT TO THE DEAD

"What empty rhetoric," the silence said,
"You teach the boys and girls that you may gain
The bread and wine which sensuality
Sues like a premier or a president.
These are illusions of your sense of guilt
Which shames you like a vain lie when revealed.
The other boys slumped like sacks on desperate shores."

"But well you know the life which I have lived,
Cut off, in truth, by all that I have been
From the normal pleasures of the citizen.
How often in the midnight street I passed
The party where the tin horns blew contempt
And the rich laughter rose as midnight struck,
The party where the New Year popped and foamed
Opening like champagne or love's wet crush,
The while I studied long the art which in
America gains silence like a wall
—I am a student of the lies of light,
I am a poet of the sleepless night
In new and yet unknown America,
—I am a reader in love's long defeat.
I gave the boys and girls my mind and art:
May I not cite this as a little good?"

THE SILENCE IN EMPTINESS ACCUSED HIM THUS
"A PRIVILEGED CHARACTER"

Am I indeed guilty in privilege?
And am I stained in the commonweal's guilt?
What did I do? and how did I assent?
What good and gold will I gain, which they defend?
When did I lie and say this age is good?
I am a twice-torn critic from way back!

America! Tarawa! in the Pacific seas—
I went to Tarawa with the seaborne boys
At the silver screen: how far I was,
Seated in the soft dark, nervous or sick,
(O to be in 4F, now that war is here,
Sang the ground-glass cynics with a jocose jeer).
I saw the marked Marines gaze at the Petty girl
(Nude as a peeled banana, comely as pears),
(Lust never again will rise in some of them),
I saw them pray at sunset in the strength
Young manhood shows in sunburnt summer's health:
(Many of them were dead in the next dusk)

What can I say to down my privilege?
What but the roulette reason, like gold hair?
The grace, the luck, the accidents which tear
The heart and head, formless as fallen rags.
The spinning ball which stops at here, not there,
Made you serene as steeplejacks on high,
Full of the joy of life and the juice and the sleep,
Left me a twice-told critic, whipped by fear,
Shocked by the memory of every year.
—This is no answer to the hopeless dead,
I cannot justify myself or judge
My privilege, my lush largesse, my life.
Description is my only strength and grace,
Merely to love the truth and as I gaze
(Student and paid admission who
Wades forth to Tarawa at the silver screen),
Let John who was as much estranged as I
Now in the last estrangement judge the truth!

THE BALLAD OF THE CHILDREN OF THE CZAR

1

The children of the Czar
Played with a bouncing ball,

In the May morning, in the Czar's garden,
Tossing it back and forth;

It fell among the flowerbeds,
Or fled to the north gate.

A daylight moon hung up
In the western sky, bald white.

Like Papa's face, said Sister,
Hurling the white ball forth.

2

While I ate a baked potato,
Three thousand miles apart,

In Brooklyn, in 1916,
Aged two, irrational.

When Franklin D. Roosevelt
Was an Arrow Collar Ad.

O Nicholas! Alas! Alas!
My grandfather coughed in your army.

Hid in a wine-stinking barrel
For three days in Bucharest,

Then left for America
To become a king himself.

3

I am my father's father,
You are your children's guilt,

In history's pity and terror
The child is Aeneas again,

Troy is in the nursery,
The rocking horse is on fire,

Child labor! The child must carry
His fathers on his back!

But seeing that so much is past,
And that history has no ruth

For the individual
Who drinks tea, who catches cold,

Let anger be general:
I hate an abstract thing.

4

Brother and sister bounced
The bounding, unbroken ball,

The shattering sun fell down
Like swords upon their play,

Moving eastward among the stars
Toward February and October.

But the May wind brushed their cheeks
Like a mother watching sleep,

And if for a moment they fight
Over the bouncing ball,

And sister pinches brother,
And brother kicks her shins,

Well! The heart of man is known:
It is a cactus bloom.

5

The ground on which the ball bounces
Is another bouncing ball,

The wheeling, whirling globe
Makes no will glad.

Turning in its clouded darkness,
It is too big for their hands.

O pitiless purposeless Thing,
Arbitrary and unspent,

Made for no play, for no children,
But seeking only itself.

The innocent are overtaken,
They are not innocent,

They are their father's fathers,
The past is inevitable.

6

Now, in another October
Of this tragic star,

I see my second year,
I eat my baked potato,

It is my buttered world,
But poked by my unlearned hand,

It falls from the highchair down,
And I begin to howl,

And I see the ball roll under
The iron gate which is locked.

Sister is screaming, Brother is howling,
The ball has evaded their will.

Even a bouncing ball
Is uncontrollable,

And is under the garden wall.
I am overtaken by terror

Thinking of my father's fathers
And of my own will.

STARLIGHT LIKE INTUITION PIERCED THE TWELVE

Like intuition, starlight pierced the twelve,
The brittle night sky sparkled like a tune
Tapped and tinkled upon the xylophone:
Empty and vain, a glittering dune, the moon
Arose too big, and, in the mood which ruled,
Looked like a useless beauty in a pit:
And then one said, after he carefully spat:
"No matter what we do, he looks at it!"

"I cannot see a child or find a girl
Beyond his smile which glows like that spring moon."
"—Nothing no more the same," the second said,
"Though all may be forgiven, never quite healed

The wound I bear as witness, standing by;
No ceremony surely appropriate,
Nor secret love, escape or sleep because
No matter what I do, he looks at it—"

"Now," said the third, "no thing will be the same:
I am as one who never shuts his eyes,
The sea and sky no more are marvellous,
And I no longer understand surprise!"
"Now," said the fourth, "nothing will be enough,
—I heard his word accomplishing all wit:
No word can be unsaid, no deed withdrawn;
No matter what is said, he measures it!"
"Vision, imagination, hope, or dream
Believed, denied, the scene we wished to see?
It does not matter in the least: for what
Is altered if it is not true? That we
Saw goodness as it is—*this* is the awe
And the abyss which we will not forget,
His story now the skull which holds all thought:
No matter what I think, I think of it!"

"And I will never be what once I was,"
Said one for long as single as a knife,
"And we will never be as once we were;
We have died once, this is a second life."
"My mind is spilled in moral chaos," one
Righteous as Job exclaimed, "now infinite
Suspicion of my heart rots what I will,
—No matter what I choose, he stares at it!"

"I am as one native in summer places,
—Ten weeks' excitement paid for by the rich;
Debauched by that, and then all winter bored,"
The sixth declared, "his peak left us a ditch."
"He came to make this life more difficult,"
The seventh said, "No one will ever fit
His measures' heights, all is inadequate:
No matter what we have, what good is it?"

"He gave forgiveness to us: what a gift!"
The eighth chimed in, "But now we know *how much*
Must be forgiven. But if forgiven, what?
The crime which was will be, and the least touch
Revives the memory: what is forgiveness worth?"
The ninth spoke thus: "Who now will ever sit
At ease in Zion at the Easter feast?
No matter what the place he touches it!"

"And I will always stammer, since he spoke,"
One who had been most eloquent said, stammering.
"I looked too long at the sun: like too much light,
Too much of goodness is a boomerang,"
Laughed the eleventh of the troop. "I must
Try what he tried: I saw the infinite
Who walked the lake and raised the hopeless dead:
No matter what the feat, he has accomplished it!"

So spoke the twelfth; and then the twelve in chorus:
"Unspeakable unnatural goodness is

Risen and shines and never will ignore us;
He glows forever in all consciousness;
Forgiveness, love, and hope possess the pit
And bring our endless guilt, like shadow's bars:
No matter what we do, he stares at it!
What pity then deny? what debt defer?
We know he looks at us like all the stars,
And we shall never be what once we were,
This life will never be what once it was!"